AF663489

Spiti

A Study in Socio-Cultural Traditions

Spiti

A Study in Socio-Cultural Traditions

Tobdan

Kaveri Books
New Delhi-110002

© Author

First Published in 2015
ISBN 978-81-7479-172-6

All rights reserved including the right to translate or to reproduce this book or parts thereof except brief passages for quotations in articles or critical reviews.

Published by
Kaveri Books
4832/24, Ansari Road
New Delhi - 110 002 (India)
Tel.: 011-4707 2321
E-mail: info@kaveribooks.com
kaveribooks@gmail.com
Website: www.kaveribooks.com

Laser Typesetting by : Deep Graphics, Delhi

PRINTED IN INDIA

Preface

Spiti, a small tract, has been known always as a poor country. Yet, even though living under the most difficult conditions of environment, it has been able to maintain a society with high standard of cultural traditions. It has several monuments, besides the world famous Tabo, worth inclusion in the list of monuments of world heritage. Today Spiti is a popular destination for the serious art connoisseurs, scholars of religious history, and the adventurers, hailing from the world over.

Among the earlier visitors to the area, going with the objective of studying the area, were scientists, administrators, explorers, scholars, like A. Gerard, Alexander Cunningham, Major Hay, P.H. Egerton, James B. Lyall, G. Tucci, A.H. Francke, O.C.Handa, Deborah E. Klimburg-Salter, Roberto Vitali, Kurt Tropper, SC Bajpai, Krishan Nath. Deepak Sanan, and many others. Each one has made contribution in his specialized field. The old Gazetteer gives the most comprehensive coverage of the subjects.

The present study, besides touching the common topics, endeavours to cover some other aspects which are not found described in the works of the earlier scholars.

The harsh living conditions and economic hardship have compelled the society of Spiti to evolve or borrow some typical social systems in order to continue the existence of life in the area. For the maintenance of the household as a permanent institution and giving it strength, each member of the household had to make a sacrifice of portions of his rights. Household is an institution which provides refuge to every member of the family as a last resort even though separated temporarily and he can also be called back in the case of need to join the family and resume the appropriate role in the maintenance of the household. Therefore some of the subjects like the structure and function of the family and the interdependent relationship between the society and the religious institutions are very peculiar. We observe that the conditions of environmental stress was similar in Lahul. There the measures adopted for the sustenance of the household is slightly different. In Spiti the society takes the support of the religious institution, the monastery, while in Lahul it is the economic diversification adopted in the family.

During the course of my study I have received valuable help and guidance from Lama Drimed Lodoe, Chhewang Dorje and numerous others. C. Dorje of Archeaological Survey of India, as always, had been guiding and helping me in many ways. I express my deep gratitude to them all. I am greatly thankful to Shri Rakesh Goel of M/s Kaveri Books for accepting the work for publication and bringing it out in an excellent form.

Tobdan
Kullu

Contents

List of Plates

Chapter I

Introduction

Spiti is bounded on the north by Rubsho (Ladak), west by Lahul and Kullu, south by Kinnaur and east by the Chinese Tibet. It comprises the valleys of Spiti and Pin rivers. Cunningham (1854: 23-24) gives its area as 4865 sq. km. and the length of the Spiti river from its source to its junction with Para as 102 km. The mean elevation of the inhabited parts is 3958 m. The lofty mountain ranges average in elevation measuring 5485 m or more above sea level and one of the peaks measures around 7010 m. The monsoon clouds are blocked much earlier in the mid region of Kinnaur which renders Spiti generally dry weather.

Spiti constitutes a sub-division in the district of Lahul and Spiti in the state of Himachal Pradesh. Administratively before Independence Spiti alongwith Lahul comprised part of Tehsil Kullu, in district Kangra, in the state of Punjab. The same set up continued unchanged for sometime after the Independence. Recognising the region as a remote and backward, Lahul and Spiti were declared as scheduled area and the inhabitants as scheduled tribes. The Government constituted a high powered committee called Tribal Advisory Council under the chairmanship of the Chief Minister with members chosen from among the public of the area and representatives from the various government departments in order to quicken the pace of development in the area.

Spiti and Lahul are two distinct geographical regions separated by a wide uninhabited tract and each possessing its own distinguishing geographical features: one being a typical desertland in the high plateau and the other one located in a narrow valley which remains covered under thick sheet of snow for three to four months in a year continuously. Between Kaza, the headquarters of Spiti, and Kyelang, the headquarters of the district, in Lahul, there is a distance of one whole day's journey by bus. Geographically the area of Spiti is contiguous with Bashahar and the inhabited parts of each other meet at the border. Historically the two regions had not been parts of a single administrative unit except for a short time during the British period. Thus although geographically situated quite inconveniently, the administrative relationship of Spiti with Lahul, originated under the conditions of some necessity on the occasion of the acquisition of the area by the British which later on matured into a permanent bond. When the British government obtained Spiti from Ladak, it firstly entrusted the charge of supervision to Bashahar state, which lasted for about three years. Thereafter Spiti was joined with Lahul and the administration of the area was brought directly under the Assistant Commissioner, Kullu. One reason that could have been for this action is that Bashahar was a princely state and Spiti was a directly administered territory. The Nono of Kyuling was granted recognition as chief of the division. In 1941 Lahul and Spiti were combined to form a sub-tehsil, with headquarters at Kyelang.

In 1947, on the occasion of Independence of the country, Spiti, as a part of district Kangra, was annexed to the Punjab state. In 1960, Lahul and Spiti was converted into a district and Spiti became a sub-division of it. Soon the office of the Sub-divisional Officer was raised to that of Additional District Commissioner. He was granted greater freedom in the matters of administration and his relationship with the Deputy Commissioner was much lightened. He was delegated greater financial powers so as to enable him to implement the developmental programmes more speedily. It was essential keeping in view the short working season and greater geographical difficulties in obtaining sanctions from the higher authorities. On November 1, 1966 the hill regions of Punjab as a result of reorganization of the states were merged with the hilly state of Himachal Pradesh, including Lahul-Spiti, bringing the inhabitants in their natural ambience.

Nomenclature: To the natives of Spiti themselves the country is known as Piti and its residents as Pitipa. In the written form it is spelt as sPiti or sPyiti, however, to be pronounced only as Pi-ti. Early European scholars used both the forms, the spoken form as Piti and literary form of sPyi-ti and sPi-ti, but finally 'Spiti' became the officially accepted name, both as spoken and written. Trebeck (1822) was perhaps the first European to employ the term in writing. He wrote 'Pitti', from the local pronunciation, although he was aware of its literary form. The biography of Rinchhen Zangpo, although the great scholar crossed Spiti and went through Lahul to Kashmir, does not refer to Spiti. rGod-tshangpa (thirteenth century) and sTag-tshang Ras-pa (first half of the seventeenth century), the two great siddhas, have referred it in their *namthar* as Pi-ti. In literary tradition there are found some other variants of the name, viz. Pyi-ti, Be-ti, Bi-ti, etc. Lobzang Shastri discusses various sources of different forms of the name Spiti as found in Tibetan literature (Lobzang Shastri, 2006).

Some scholars have attempted to analyse the term sPyi-ti by breaking it up as *spyi* and *ti* and taking the meaning of each part separately perhaps with the assumption that it belongs to Bhoti language. While sPyi means 'ordinary or common', the second part *ti* cannot be explained in this manner and it does not belong to this language. The word *ti* is found in some dialects of Kinnaur and Lahul which means 'water'. Linguists place this language under the family of Tibeto-Burman languages of the pronominalised class. Rahul Sankrityayan names it as 'Shu'. It belongs to an earlier phase of development of the settlements in these areas. Alexander Cunningham has explained many terms in the Western Himalaya, specially names of rivers, compounded with *ti* with this significance. But even presuming the meaning of the two parts separately as explained above as correct, we do not get any sensible meaning by combining the two. Nothing is said about the terms sPiti and Piti.

In fact the term *ti* is found in use in Spiti itself exhibiting the same meaning as water. In irrigation operations it takes place of *chhu* at several places, the word of modern usage for water. In Spiti owing to scant precipitation the *dogpos* (streams) flowing down from the mountain tops carry less amount of water in the summer and the fields are more thirsty. The villagers carry water from the *dogpos* through *yu-ra* (channels) to their fields for irrigation. It is only in such extreme conditions that instead of one *yu-ra* at places they have two, one below the other, each going parallel: named as *ma-yur* (original channel) owned by the original rightholders of the village and *sa-yur*, the second channel, constructed to catch the water percolating from the upper line. Effort of the owners of the higher line will be not to allow water to ooze out (*dsag-che*). But in the gravelly earth there is seepage and it cannot be prevented completely. As water is valuable, it should not be allowed to be wasted. Therefore the water caught in the lower line is called '*dsag-ti*', the oozed out water.

In the process of irrigation of crops there are three stages and the later two stages are called as *phyir-ti* or *srak-ti* and *gsum-ti* i.e. the later or burning and the third watering. Meaning of the words *phyir* and *gsum* in the above terms as 'later' and 'third' are plainly understandable. '*srak*' means 'burning' which indicates that during the time of second watering the crops are in much greater need of watering. The word '*ti*' has been used here whereas in the modern usage it could have been '*chhu*', like *phyir-chhu, srak-chhu,* etc. In this manner the use of the word *'ti'* in the culture of Spiti is significant. The word *'ti'* perhaps is a remnant of an earlier phase of cultural development in Spiti.

Some scholars explain the meaning of the term Spiti as 'middle country', but as already stated above it is difficult to discern any meaning of the term Spiti literally or intrinsically. Similar problem is met with the names of important places of the region like Kaza, Pin, Dankhar, etc. This perhaps points to some abrupt and extensive cultural change in the region.

sPi-ti and lchogs: In the local literature the term Spiti is inscribed at times with a special epithet like sPiti Phi-lchogs, sPi-ti spi-lchogs or sPiti la-lchog. This epithet for Spiti is found in three important ancient documents, i.e. Ladags Gyalrabs (History of Ladak), *namthar* of *Siddha* rGod-tshangpa and that of local *lama* Rang- rig Ras-chhen of 17th century. Some scholars have taken this term as a name for a different region. Francke, when he enumerates certain names in this context, assumes sPi-lchog for Lahul. Tucci has identified this term with Lipak, that is Lipa in Bashahar or the present Kinnaur district of Himachal Pradesh. Vitali explains it differently (Vitali, 1996: 167). The following illustrations reveal that the term relates to Spiti.

Chog-la: In the local tradition the term chog-la is found used indicating to be a name of a territory, a smaller tract within Spiti. As one enters the territory of Spiti from the southern direction one meets three villages of Lari, Tabo and Poh which are locally known collectively as Chog-la yul-gsum, i.e. the 'the three villages' of Chog-la or by their initials as La-ta-pa. Guge mKhan-chhen describes the name of the monastery of Tabo as Ta-po chog-la-brgyan i.e. Ta-po the ornament of Chog-la (Guge mKhan chen, 1996: 54), showing that Tabo belongs to Chogla. There is a saying in the tradition of Spiti about this group of the three villages as:

Gong mtsho rdol song na,
chog-la yul gsum lhag.

It may be translated that if the lake above bursts out, the three villages of *chog-la* will be destroyed (flooded). The lake indicated here is situated above the village Mane, near Tabo. Here the expression *chog* can be understood as comprising the area of the group of three villages as shown above.

The following example illustrates the fact further. Siddha rGod-tshhang-pa writes *zhang-zhung gi yul rgal nas pi ti bi lchogs gi stod na,* which mean: 'crossing the country of Zhang-zhung, in the north of bi-lchog' in Pi-ti'. *Chog* or *lchog* literally means 'heap' or collection, such as heap of cow-manure, etc., or summit. The inscription at Lha-lung monastery also records the birth of a king in lChog-la, who probably was connected with the said monastery, perhaps in founding it. Thus it may be assumed that once the lower part of Spiti was known as Pi-lchog and the term Piti Pi-lcogs may be construed as Piti including Pichog.

Geology: Spiti preserves some undisturbed geological features of the time of its birth and has been a subject of attraction for the scientists of varied interests. The Gazetteer summarises the features in the manner that, 'The geological importance of Spiti lies in the fact that here is an almost unbroken series of marine deposits, dating from the earliest era in which animal life is known to have occurred on the earth to one of the latest geological periods. These deposits are no less than twenty thousand feet in thickness, and have been sub-divided into a number of systems, corresponding more or less with those of the European scale. Originally formed in horizontal layers one above the other at the bottom of the sea, the marine rocks of Spiti are now seen at altitudes ranging from twelve to over twenty thousand feet above sea-level. In the displacements caused by the rise of the Himalaya Mountains, the oldest deposits, which were at one time twenty thousand feet below the bottom of the sea, were carried up till they appear in places at higher altitudes than the most recent marine system. Details regarding the geology of Spiti, with a map and diagrams showing the different formations, are very clearly shown in a Sketch of the Geography and Geology of the Himalaya Mountains and Tibet, published in 1908 by the Indian Government and in Volume XXXVI of the Memoirs of the Geological Survey of India, which also contains an extensive bibliography of the subject. There is told the story of the great primeval sea, called the Tethys, which stretched over Spiti in days when that country lay on the northern shore of India, one of the oldest continents of the world. We read there how this water was at first not connected with the Palaeozoic Sea of Europe, but later spread westwards to the continent; how the floor of the sea in Spiti rose and fell, the changes between shallow and deep water deposits being clearly traceable; how at one era the dry land appeared for so long a time that, by the action of weather and of rivers, there occurred denudation of beds some thousands of feet in thickness. Finally came the great upheaval which laid bare this wonderful chapter of earth-history from beginning to end.'

Snow avalanche: Spiti receives a very thin layer of snow not enough to be cause of any avalanche, nor there is to be seen any thick and large glacier. But one such incident that occurred in the valley of Chandra that flows opposite to the direction of Spiti river, on the other side of Kunzom, took form of a legend. It is noted that, 'In 1836 the Shigri glacier burst its bounds and dammed the Chandra river so high that (as the story runs) guards were posted on the Kunzom pass to watch lest the water should flow over into Spiti! There are at any rate traces of a large lake formed at the time, and the glacier has ever since lain athwart the old trade route, and is the most formidable and convincing obstacle to trade between Spiti and Kulu.' This incident has been a subject of discussion in the descriptions of almost every traveler. But from the point of view of the inhabitants of Spiti there appears the least cause to fear from any such incident occurring in this part of their country.

Passes and Passages: The mountain ranges surrounding Spiti have many passes opening to different directions. Kunzom is situated between the Upper Chandra valley and Losar in Spiti. It links Spiti with Lahul and also Kullu. Visitors taking round of the part of Himachal pass through this pass and exit or enter through lower Spiti. Hamta pass between Spiti and Kullu lay on the way which once formed one of the busiest routes. The road from Kullu to Spiti left at Jagatsukh, on the left bank of the Beas, and passing through the villages of Prini and Hamta and up the Ruin torrent in Kullu crossed the Hamta pass. Entering into the Chandra Valley it passed through the camping grounds of Chhatru, Futirunhi (Chhota Dara) and Karche (Bathal) following each in succession. From the last place the road crosses the Kunzom La and leads to Losar, the first village in Spiti. This route is used mostly by the shepherds and trekkers.

Between Kullu and Spiti there was another pass named Pin-Parvati. The path originates in the Manikaran valley in Kullu and reaches at the head of the Pin valley in Spiti and must have been very useful in the past between Kullu on the one end and Spiti, Bashahar and Guge on the other. Ruins of two forts named Nyungti Khar, Kullu fort, are said to be located on the side of Pin valley, which could have been installed by Kullu to guard against invaders from Bashahar and Guge. Parang La, between Spiti and Ladak, was commonly used by the traders from Spiti, Bashahar and Jangthang. Starting from Kyibber, one reaches in Rubsho in Ladak on the other side. Cunningham gives its height at 5640m. It is considered as the loftiest and the most difficult; and is said to have been always dangerous, liable to severe snow storms even in the summer. It remained open from June till October.

Spiti is connected with Bashahar through Manirang or Ropak La, the pass known by the name of the village on either side. The ascent from the side of Bashahar is said to be steep and laborious. It was used by the traders between Spiti and Bashahar and travellers from Shimla. Regarding the routes towards the Chinese Tibet, Rose states that traders passing though Spiti used Shangrang Pass for trade or they went through Shipki. Egerton names another pass through which the traders from Spiti crossed over to Guge.

Rivers: The principal river named Spiti flows through the whole length of the valley. Among its numerous tributaries, Pin is the largest which joins Spiti on its right bank around middle of the valley. It rises from near the sources of Chandra and Bhaga near Baralacha Pass at an elevation of about 5029m. Pursuing for quite some length a south-easterly course, leaves the region at a height of about 3353m through Kinnaur to join the Satluj. The river flows smoothly and has a level and broad bed. It has little signs of recent disturbances and the large boulders are not to be seen on its way. The banks rise straight from the river beds and support the inhabited plateaus in the rear. Large green patches of bushes like that of seabuckthorn and other perennial plants mark along the river beds occasionally.

The river gains in size greatly after it is joined by its strong tributaries of Pin and Para. Then its character changes abruptly as can be known from its rugged course. The river has to force its way among the clusters of large boulders and through the narrow rocky gulleys, splashing and roaring. It gains immense strength and momentum equating with the mighty Satluj before joining finally with it. During the winter season, as far as Dankhar, where it receives the Pin river, it is usually fordable and below this it was crossed in olden days by several suspension-bridges.

The rivulets coming from the side valleys have deeper beds, steep falls and are generally powerful and forceful. They are turbulent for short time in the summer. But they don't have much impact in changing the features of the main river except widening its own mouth near the bed of the main river. It is general in the cultures of the trans-Himalayan regions that the main river has no local name and are generally known by *gtsang-po*, river. At the same time the inhabitants are familiar very intimately with the wavering characteristics and erratic behaviours of all the small rivulets passing nearby their villages. They have distinguishing names for them all and some even possess more than one name.

1. Pin: Pin originates between the watersheds of Parvati and Spiti and forms a separate valley.

2. Parang Chhu or Para Ti: The river originates from the mountain on the other side of the Parang La towards Rubsho from which it receives its name and flowing through barren land, taking round through the Chinese Tibet joins Spiti. In around here it is said to have been known usually by the name Zungsam. Some others assign this name to Satluj. Zang, although means copper in Bhoti, in the language of the lower Kinnaur and that of lower Lahul it means 'gold.' Zangsum thus may be interpreted as confluence of three golden or good (rivers).

The river Chandra originates near the Baralacha pass and passes touching the boundary of Spiti externally. Near Chhatru there was a village named Yari Khoksar or Old Khoksar where fields were tilled till quite late by the farmers from Khoksar in Lahul.

Climate: The valley of Spiti is located at a high altitude. Thin monsoon clouds reach here after they have been lightened almost fully of their burdens on their way much before. Annual rainfall is low at about 177mm and in winter also there is very low snowfall. As such Spiti is considered as a typical mountain desert. Cunningham has recorded month-wise data on rainfall and temperature for a full year.

Vegetation of all kinds is very scanty in Spiti. A keen observer describes the situation existing more than half a century ago in the words that 'throughout nearly the whole of the upper half of the valley, no tree is visible. From Kyi village, which is situated half way down the valley, at an elevation of 3780m, downwards a few willows and poplars have been planted in each village, and these supply a very little quantity of fuel and fodder. Lower down a stunted pencil cedar may be seen occasionally on mountain side. It is only in the last three villages, Poh, Tabo, and Lari situated at an elevation of about 3505m that willows and poplars thrive. Thus great difficulty is experienced by the people both regarding timber and fuel wood'.

The government is making huge expenditure in its effort to generate vegetative wealth in the valley. But the outcome of the efforts is visibly too low in proportion to the investments. Perhaps it is mainly due to the lack of proper supervision over the utilization of the valuable funds.

Environment and Dwellings: Spiti was so deeply adapted to its extreme environmental conditions that even though the area is almost wholly treeless, it is said that rain was unwelcome to the people, even to the extent that they would object to the plantation of trees. The position has now changed and it has been observed that, 'the local inhabitants who oppose plantations for fear of rains are now realizing the importance of such plantations.'

As a consequence of the characteristic weather conditions in Spiti, nature appears to have been generally dormant and inactive during the long past ages. River beds, which are empty of big boulders, is witness to this fact. Stones have been quarried scantily for the construction of houses. It is also not an essential material for construction under the prevailing environmental conditions of dry weather here. People used sun-dried earthen bricks for construction of their houses. Yet as Egerton describes the houses in Spiti are comfortably built. They have flat roofs made of earth laid on rafters and twigs. The usual form of building is an oblong square, the lower storey is used for cattle pens, and the upper storey is built on three sides only with parapet walls on the fourth side, so that the centre forms a kind of open court. There has not been much change in the use of the kind of materials for construction and the style of structures after Egerton. But in Kaza and other market places the houses are now generally built with cement and concrete.

The Inhabitants: Alexander Cunningham calls the residents of Spiti as Kanet and in his view they formed the purer of the race among those living in the hills of the Punjab and Shimla. Trebeck considers them as Tartar. Harcourt remarks that, 'The people of Spiti bear unmistakable evidences on their faces of their Mongolian descent. The men are stout, well-built fellows, and the women are also very strongly framed. Many of the men resemble veritable Calmucks.' Bachitter Singh, Settelment Officer, says that they were entered as Kanets in the record of the previous Settlement but they got their caste changed from Kanet to Rajput during the last Settlement. Indeed they were the last community in whole of the Punjab and Shimla Hill territories to follow the trend.

Egerton names the chief four villages of Spiti as Kyibber, Dankhar, Mane and Rareng. Rareng is intended for Rangrig. Csoma de Koros had identified perhaps Kyi monastery as Rareng and then this with the famous historical monastery of Rwadeng which proposition later on had to be discarded. Trebeck writes Rareg for Rangrig.

Literacy: The remotely situated society of Spiti traditionally had been a comparatively better literate society than any other situated in its neighbourhood. In this respect the monasteries played an important role. Substantial number of the population constituted the ecclesiastic section, which was a literate class. The history of literacy here may be directly related with the introduction and evolution of Lamaism in the area. The society here had evolved a mechanism which made recruitment into the priestly class effortless. Besides, a good number of laymen were also literate. In the British period, it is noted, many landowners could read their own revenue entries.

Spiti dialect: The dialect of Spiti in the Linguistic Survey of India has been identified as a form of Central Tibetan. It is further said that in several forms it agrees with Ladakhi and the connected forms of speech. In the survey, analysis of the dialect was done on the basis of the material submitted by some representatives of the Moravian Mission, and the samples from the dictionary of Jaescke. The missionaries were familiar generally with the literary form of the language. The folk dialect exhibits a number of exclusive features and is rich in folk literature like songs, stories, sayings, etc.

Economy: Nature has endowed Spiti with extremely scarce resources. Scant precipitation, both in the summer and the winter, the basic changing factor, is the highlight of the geographical features of Spiti. Though there are abundant wastelands but cultivation is impossible due to lack of water supply. There are no forests. Some grasslands are situated at higher reaches for grazing the cattle. As such people cannot rear sheep and goats in large numbers. Yet agriculture is the main occupation of the inhabitants. Other forms of economy viz. trading, manufacture, service and the activities allied to agriculture are incidental and are followed only to the extent essential to fulfill some immediate necessities.

Agriculture: There grows only one crop in a year, of only a few kinds of grains, and none without irrigation. *Ne* (huskless barley) was the chief cereal. It was staple food. A comparative data of the kind of commodities produced and prices prevailing about a century ago in Lahul and Spiti is given as under:

Name of Crop/ Grain	**Amount of commodity in standard *sers* available per rupee**	
	Lahul	**Spiti**
Barley (*Ne*)	25	18
Wheat	20	18
Peas	15	20
Mustard seed	12	10
Buckwheat	50	18
Cheena	-	24
Potatoes	32	-
Tobacco	8	-
(Diack, 1898:18).		

It may be observed from the above table that except the last three crops in the list, the crops grown in the two divisions are the same. With respect to price except peas, all kinds of commodities are dearer in Spiti in comparison to Lahul, and that too in considerable degree. Two reasons could be assigned for the situation: presumably one is low scale of production in Spiti, and secondly, a more probable reason, the presence of wider market, having great demand for *Ne* from Bashahar, Jangthang in Ladak and Tibet. *Ne* was also sent in substantial quantity to Ladak in revenue collection. Spiti still produces *Ne* and conventional peas and sells at premium price in Lahul, Kullu and Kinnaur. It demands potato from Lahul. Spiti now exports green peas of excellent quality and in good quantity as cash crop. Apple is grown in the lower areas below Kaza and produces perhaps of the best quality in whole of the country.

Animal husbandry: Animal husbandry is the second mode of economy. But natural conditions, a powerful limiting factor, are less favourable for the activity. It was nearly impossible for a household to think of rearing more than one milch cattle.

Sheep: The Gazetteer of 1897 notes that in 1890 there were only six flocks in Spiti, which can be estimated at around two thousand. These perhaps represented mostly the annual migratory flocks from Kullu, etc. who still maintain their flocks near the lake Chandertal. These also do not include those kept in the villages. *Pashmina* goats were also reared but in limited number. Trebeck records that sheep are almost all imported from Jangthang, as well as the goats

Yak: People preferred rearing *yak*, for it had multifarious uses. Observers write that he is extremely sure footed, and climbs the most precipitous places in search of food and was used in carrying loads, chiefly in bringing fuel and fodder from the mountains to store up for winter. *Yak* is the strongest and sturdiest animal to endure and survive even under the toughest and the severest climatic conditions of the high Himalayas. Herds of *yaks* were popular with the parties going on trading voyages. It is not often ridden, the pace being slow, but in crossing rivers he was highly appreciated. His tail, *chowri*, and hide are valuable. A good many half bred were sent to Tibet for sale in the fairs.

Ponies: The Spiti breed of ponies is well known. They were bred in all villages. Egerton says, the ponies of Spiti have attained a great reputation at Shimla and among the Himalayan chiefs. They are extremely sure-footed, but undersized and slow. The animal was reared in Pin in more numbers. Those from Chumurti, a few marches into Tibet, were considered finer. The situation is noted a century ago as: 'Nearly every landowner has two or three ponies and mules and he generally has one for sale every third year. The price realized locally is Rs. 50 to Rs. 100. The purchasers are Bashaharis and Tibetans and the traders and dealers who meet at Patseo in Lahul, a great market for the exchange of the commodities of importance for those of Kulu. Very few Spiti men engage in trade and the ponies are merely bred for the market.'

Commerce and trade: Some observers have remarked that the inhabitants of Spiti had less preference for trade. Sherring found that the wants of the Spiti *zamindar* are few, and he does not greatly care about leaving his valley. Hay records that the Spiti people are not essentially traders, their country affords but little pasturage, and they have seldom more sheep than to supply their own wants.

It may be observed that the particular system of social formation adopted in Spiti was much responsible for the type of the economy. Following the custom it sent much of the surplus able bodied manpower to the monasteries. They had small family within which they did not have the necessity and possibility of division of labour. Therefore there was no member in the family attending exclusively to the profession of trade like in Lahul and Kinnaur where the type of social structure was different. However, in the summer, after the sowing season and before the harvesting period, when the load of works in the fields is light, the people moved out on trading excursions to purchase the goods of their urgent demand. During the harvest time traders from Bashahar, Tibet and Jangthang came themselves to Spiti to purchase their much prized produce of *Ne*, *ghoont* (pony) and others, and then they disposed of their surplus produce. They also took their articles to the seasonal fairs.

Gerard, in 1818, writes that the inhabitants of Spiti trade with their neighbours. The exports to the southern neighbours were wool, borax, salt, and blankets; and the imports from the plains were a number of commodities and a great deal of iron. He also informs that on his way to Kaza he met with a large party of people from Pin proceeding towards Lara, on the road to Jangthang, and forming the third Kafila, caravan, that had gone there within a few days, for tea, wool, salt, etc.

Imports: The people of Spiti bought from the Jangpas their sheep, of a very fine breed, salt, wool, tea, turquoises, and goats and they paid for it grain, woollen cloth, and a few horses. From Lhasa came tobacco, tea, sheep's wool, turquoises, amber, water pots and other wooden vessels. From Bushahar and Kullu came iron, cooking utensils, brass, coarse cloth, copper, tobacco, rice, dried fruits, tea-cups, timber, amber, glass beads, etc.

Spiti also purchased sheep from the shepherds from Malana and Manikaran valley of Kullu who used to graze the herds of their sheep along the mountain ridge bordering Spiti. As the men of both the sides did not know language of each other they had developed a sign language. The sellers from Kullu firstly placed certain number of pebbles before the purchaser which represented the cost of the sheep. The Spiti man understood the symbolic language and he paid the demanded price and then took the sheep away.

Exports: The Jangpas from the north came to Spiti in November, and took about 1000 lacs of grain, and a few *ghoonts*. For grain Spitians received equal weight of salt, and for three lacs of barley they received eight '*kiris*' of wool; the *kiri* in weight differed from 12 to 16 seers. In the time of Egerton the amount of grain thus exported was estimated by the Nono at more than 2000 *bhars* or sheep loads. Grain, both wheat and *Ne*, was sold at uniform price of two *khals* to the rupee and mustard seed at one *khal* a rupee. Besides cereals, Spiti also exported manufactured cloth, half-bred yaks, yak's tails, and a few *ghoonts*, manufactured blankets, and pieces of cloth.

Intermediatry: The Spitians also functioned as intermediary in trade. *Ne*, their own valuable produce, was a powerful medium of exchange. They purchased iron and other goods for *Ne* from one side and sold the surplus and exchanged for salt, wool and other goods with the other.

Trade Fairs: The people of Spiti participated in many trade fairs held in their own area and at places near their borders in the states around it viz. Lavi fair in Rampur Bashahar, Dozam (Patseo) in Lahul, Rubsho in Ladak, Guge (Tibet), etc. and exchanged their produce for the goods of their demand.

Bachittar Singh in his report of Settlement explaining the causes of the drastic downfall in the figures of population of Spiti from 3869 in 1941 to 2422 in 1952 states that at the time of enumeration in August 1950 most of the people had gone out of Spiti for trade towards Rampur Bashahar and Patseo. It may be clarified here that the *mela* at Rampur in the south is traditionally held in the month of November. August was the right season for the northward march for a population intimately acclimatized to a particular type of environment.

Assuming that the population of Spiti remained constant and there was no increase during the decade 1942 to 1951, the number of persons emigrating at the moment of census enumeration counted 1447, more than 37% of the inhabitants. Admitting the author's argument fully, yet discounting the figure, we presume that only fifty percent of the mobile population was on visit for trade. Still the figure works out substantial and is not less impressive. Pilgrimage is done mostly in the winter and such places lie mostly towards the south.

La-Darcha: A trade route lead from Kyibbar through Parang La to Rubsho and Ladak. La-Darcha is situated below Parang La on the side of Spiti, though there is no regular settlement here. Earlier a fair used to be held here annually for 2-3 months. Presently a fair named La-Darcha is held to maintain the old tradition.

Phalong Baldag: Trebeck while coming to Spiti passed through a place which he calls Pha-lung Palrak, before he crossed Parang La. The term Phalung Palrak may be expressed as Phalong Baldak (pha-long bal-sbreg), 'the boulder near where wool is clipped'.

He writes,'The people of Piti and Rupshu annually meet here to barter, the former grain and provisions, for the wool of the latter.' There was also a place near Mud in Pin where a fair was held and the traders from Spiti and Kinnaur exchanged their goods.

Manufactures: Spiti produced wool and also imported from Jangthang. Wool produced in Spiti was found to be of better quality as compared to those produced in Kullu and Kangra. Trebeck observed that every woman knows how to weave in which half of the women population may be said to be employed. He estimated that annually they fabricated two thousand seven hundred and fifty two pieces of cloth, each of seven and half yards long. Of this, one thousand and six hundred pieces were consumed in Piti and the remainder was exported. He notes that three kinds of cloths were woven in Spiti: *therma,* a fine thin stuff dyed red; *puruk*, thick rough woolen cloth; and *shama,* a thick smooth stuff. Some of these entered the Lavi fair at Rampur and some were sent to Gartok. There were workers on iron and wood. Paper was manufactured from grass. The art of pottery is stated to have been in practice with a family in Langza village. The art remained alive till around the time of Independence. At one time it must have been a flourishing industry. The earthen articles manufactured were pitchers of various sizes, pots, trays, cups, bowls, kettles, prayer lamps (*skyong-me*), etc. Also in Spiti there was used a locally designed tobacco pipe. It was made of iron in the shape of a long spoon.

Minerals: It is said that there were lead mines at Lara, Leedang, Pokso, and some other places which were mined on the account of the Raja. They were very productive, but was reckoned inferior to that of Sirmour and Jaunsar. It sold at two or two and a half pounds per rupee.

Ring-go bTang-che: Sometimes, particularly during the harvest season, some people carried on their back small articles of use of women and household like bangles, buttons, clips, hair pins, safety pins, looking glass, locks, etc. and roamed in Kullu, Lahul, Kinnaur and Spiti from village to village and house to house to sell their wares and in exchange they received grains. This kind of trade gave better margins and was more profitable than by selling for cash. This was known as r*ing-go btang-che* and was more popular among the women.

Chapter II

Social Classes and Partition of Household

Spiti is known as a casteless society. Harcourt remarks, 'In Spiti there are no castes in the usual acceptation of that term, for all eat and drink together.' But this trait of caste is not absent totally, as Harcourt himself adds further that Kanets do not marry with Lohars nor the latter with Bedas.

In this regard an example may be quoted from a recent incident. Some boys of the manial and artisan class were sent to Karnatak, in the south, and had taken admission in the Tibetan Buddhist Schools as lama students. However, soon they were expelled and sent back to home on the complaint from some quarters reflecting on their social background. The parents of the novices brought the case before the Dalai Lama. They obtained the blessings and also received the desired fruit. The element of untouchability is, however, undoubtedly absent.

Social Classes: Scholars and visitors to the area have left some valuable notes on the composition of the society. H. A. Rose, on the authority of A.H. Diack, Settlement Officer, names certain classes of the society and gives their descriptions as under:

i) *Jo* or *Tso*: This is a title enjoyed for his life time by one who marries the daughter of any high class family, such as that of the Nono of Spiti or the Thakur of Lahul, or any family of equal importance in Ladakh or Tibet.

ii) Lonpo: This term is applied to the class not so high as the *Jo* or as low as the *chha-zang*. Lonpo means 'minister' and is a hereditary title and office. *Lohrag* and *Da-tong-karpo* (*Dhongrukaru*) are said to be synonyms for *Lonpo*.

iii) *Chhazang*: The word means, middle class, (good position), as opposed on the one hand to 'Tarap' or high class, such as members of the family of the Nono of Spiti, and on the other to 'Marap' or low class which includes the blacksmiths, hesis, etc.

iv) *Lobon*: The word means 'teacher' and is probably the description given of himself by some wandering Tibetan pilgrim (Rose, 1883-II: 164).

From the above description the two terms Lohrag and Da-tong-karpo (Dhongrukaru) cannot be comprehended. Of the four classes mentioned here Jo and Chhazang are two social classes about whom we will learn here in detail. Lobon (*slob-dpon*), Acharya, signifies a teacher of high rank, and does not denote a social class. Lonpo, Minister, is an official designation and the title cannot be inherited. *Tarap* or *ta-rab* or more properly *lta-rab*, literally means good looking, but use of the term in the context of social class is not known. The usual antonym for *ma-rab*, bad mannered or low cultured, is *ya-rab*.

In a rare instance the society is classified on the ground of martial status into two sections of *Mag:* i. *dmag,* military and ii. *miser,* the general public. It is difficult to say if there ever existed this kind of arrangement in Spiti.

Traditionally the society is classified on some other grounds as follows:

1. **Economy:** On the economic ground it is divided into two classes of *Thalpa,* the tax-paying households, and *Zurpa* (*gzur-pa*), those having no such liability.
2. **Religion:** On the religious ground the whole society is divided into two classes of *da-ba* (*grva-ba*) and *ke-bo* (*skye-bo*). All the persons belonging to the ecclesiastical class

of every status come under the first category. The remainder, the un-ordained population, is reckoned under *ke-bo,* the common people. On another ground the society is classified as *Nangpa* and *Phyipa*. Under the notion of caste the two terms mean: insider, the main society and the outsider, the others. This again can be understood as Buddhists and Non-Buddhists.

The traditional society as it existed till around middle of the twentieth century may be broadly classified as under:

I. No-no: Nono is the highest ranking class. Besides the families living at Kyuling and Guling, there are some living in other villages. They belong to the highest ranking *rus-ba,* bone i.e clan. Usually in a village there is not more than one family of the class.

II. The Manial and Artisan Class: The non-agriculturist class of other rank include the *gar-ra* (mGar-ra=smith) and *beda* (musician). Some distances are maintained in the social interactions with the two classes.

a. ***Ga-ra (mGar-ra):*** The smith works on all kinds of metals, viz. iron, gold, silver and copper. He also owns a small patch of land, an average of one acre a family. Harcourt informs that there were one hundred persons of the class under the census of 1868. There were 12 families of this class during the Settlement of 1887-92 who owned total of eight acres of land. Rose holds that four families of blacksmiths also hold a rather small allotment a piece, and pay only a hearth-tax, not full revenue. The above are said to be all independent estates of the same grade as those of the revenue-paying landholders, and inherited in the same way by the eldest son.

b. ***Beda:*** Beda ordinarily earned their livelihood by the profession of playing music and dancing and entertaining the people in the weddings and fairs. Older women play *da-ba* (tambourine), men play the pair of *daman,* kettledrum and *surna,* pipe. They possessed no land and kept on roaming. Their area of work spread through Spiti, Lahul, Kullu and Kinnaur. In Kullu they were known as Hessi or Hensi. Under the census of 1868 they numbered 46 and owned no land. It is said that the *bedas* in addition to their common profession lived by making whips for the men and bracelets of shell for the women. Bracelets of conch shell, usually white, was the common wrist-ornament of Spiti women. They sometimes engaged in trade, but only in a small way by barter.

These classes appear to keep a distance between themselves in the social behaviours, for it is said, 'Blacksmiths do not eat with Beda or take their women as wives.' However they could share a drink in the same bowl and hookah, tobacco, was common to all.

III. Chhazang: The remaining large middle section between Nono and the manial class is known as *Chhazang*. The following types of families are distinguished in the class.

a. ***Jhoba:*** *Jhoba* is a specialised professional family. There were two families of this class and one of them lived at Gungri in Pin. He ranked below Nono and above *chhazang*. He had two important functions. It is said, 'Spiti have next to nothing to do with the burial or burning of the dead, since those functions are in the hands of a certain class of people called Jhoba. They had been allotted land free of revenue demand at Tashigang by the Raja of Ladak'. Sometimes his task is reduced to initiating the process and the lamas do the rest. The major function of *Jhoba* is the practice of astrology which lends him the high social status. This institution of *Jhoba*, excluding the function of astrologer, is unique to Spiti and is unknown in Kinnaur, Lahul and Ladak.

b. ***Amchi:*** Amchi are by profession doctors practicing from generation to generation. They are trained on the Tibetan system of medicine. They prepare the medicines themselves. Bulk of the herbs are gathered locally from the high mountain slopes. Certain families of the class were supported by the state by granting land which was exempted from tax, and by the communities by offering presents and various kinds of services.

Chhazang, The Middle Class

The old Gazetteer notes that in the census of 1891 'the great mass of peasantry returned themselves as 'chha-zhang' or middle class, i.e. midway between noble families, of which there are two in Spiti and the manial, artisan class', (Gazetteer, 1898, Part IV: 92-93). The Gazetteer explains '*chha-zhang*' to mean as the middle. In the local usage the term is also found written as *chha-byang*. Literally the term in both these forms are insignificant. Therefore we may modify the term based on the conception envisaged in it and its pronunciation to *chha-bzang* which means good-mannered or good-cultured. This class is very large and is organized into a very complex structure. The structure of the *chha-bzang* class or a village society may be explained in the following manner.

Village Settlement and Khangpa

A village constitutes a cluster of *khangpa*, households, of various statuses. Some of them are recognized as the original settlers, who had been residing in the village since unknown time.

They are organized into an institution, a decision making body, which has the responsibility to consider all the matters concerning the village. *Khangpa* ordinarily means a residential structure. But in a village settlement a *khangpa* denotes a dwelling unit and a family living therein. The unit can be counted as a full member of the village community only when it also owns a landed property. A new *khangpa* to be able to receive recognition as a full member of the elite group is required to possess all these qualifications, and a bit more.

Even if one possesses all these qualifications, there is another great hurdle which deters any *khangpa* to aspire to enter the elite organization. This is the future liability of payment of numerous kinds of contributions to the village organization, which is quite heavy and it is the main deterring factor. Such instances, as a new family entering into the village community as a full member, are perhaps rare, for it is nearly impossible for a new member to get entry nor the new family itself will aspire to. There are ordinarily found in a village three categories of *khangpa*. The first kind are those who are original settlers and are full members of the village community. The conception of originality lends the household a high status. The continuity of this household must be saved; individual members have to adopt changing roles and have to forsake their natural rights substantially. The other kind of houses are those who have been separated from the main household. They have to abdicate certain rights and are inferior to the former in status. The third category consists of the families of the manial class and the migrant labourer families who have settled in the village with the consent of the inhabitants of the village. The last two classes are dependent on the first one.

Name of Household and Clan: Each *khangpa* has normally a name by which it is distinguished in the village. This name can be changed and there may be others with the same name but may be totally unrelated to each other. Each family inherits a *ru-ba'* (rus-*pha*= bone), clan name, from which it traces its origin from the long past. Such clans may be existing in other villages and they honour the relationship. 'Nono the last offices for each other are called *phuspun* (father-brotherhoods), as well as *phaibat'* (*pha'i-bu,* lit. son of father i.e. cousin brother)'. These two terms are equivalents of *ru-ba*. *Ru-ba* is an exogamous group and in marriage, bone must be avoided. In the matter of inheritance the clan members sometimes receive preference in relation to some other claimants.

Rose notes names of certain clans stating to be tribal divisions. 'In Spiti there are tribal divisions or clans, a few of the more important of which are: (1) Nandu, (2) Gyazhingpa, (3) khyungpo (4) Lonchhenpo (5) Henir and (6) Nyekpas. Marriage is forbidden within the tribe, but one tribe intermarries freely with another. A woman on marrying is considered to belong to her husband's tribe, and the children of both sexes are of the tribe of the father. The tribe's *ru-wa* are not local: members of each may be found in any village. The members (*phaibat*) of the tribe, wherever they may live, inherit in preference to the people of the village in default of the natural heirs.' Principally all the children inherit father's *ru-ba*. The status of a woman will not change on the event of her marriage, and she must retain her father's *ru-ba* till her death, even though she cannot pass on her *ru-ba* to her offsprings. Theoretically also it would be wrong that both husband and wife belonged to the same *ru-ba*.

***Khangpa, Basis of the village Society*:** A *khangpa* apparently consists of two parts: firstly the material part, the estate constituting residential structure and the landed property; and secondly the living part, the family, which provides labour and entrepreneurship. It may be assumed that there may be general apprehension among all the families that under the given conditions, on the one hand the first part of it is static and is unlikely to expand by itself as need changes; but on the other hand the number of right-holders is likely to multiply continuously with each generation unless some appropriate measure is applied to control it. Thus if the things were left to themselves, the result would have been partitioning of the property which in turn would have jeopardized the existence of all in the family. Therefore if all including those of the future generations are to be provided with some kind of security from meeting with such an extreme situation, some effective and permanent measure must be improvised. The solution would be that every member of the family must be ready to part himself with some of his basic necessities or rights.

Apparently the single objective adopted appears to control the division of the property. Agriculture is the main occupation of people in the valley. Under the environmental conditions of the area, the natural resources available are not congenial enough for shifting to the occupations in other sectors. In order to avoid the division of the asset, the division of the family has to be managed. In one generation, only one marriage is possible and that right is assigned to the eldest brother. In the event of failure to get the right successor other options may be tried. Ordinarily a kind of division in a family is compulsory on the occurrence of certain event. At the same time composition of the property does not get affected. The size of the entrepreneur family should be lean and efficient and therefore its size should be kept fixed.

Certain norms that the society endeavours to follow in order to achieve the above objective may be enumerated as under:

1. The property is inherited by the eldest son from the eldest son and is further passed on, on the same principle.
2. On the marriage of his eldest son, his family is separated and a different establishment called *khangchung* is created whose status is inferior.
3. The younger brothers are sent to the monastery to live a life of spinster. The unmarried sisters and aunts may live either with the brother or the parents.
4. The harsh rules of the village community discourage establishment or rising up of any new household in the village as a full member. In fact keeping in view the heavy

burden of liability of the households towards the village community, no small family would venture to acquire the high status.

However, it is essential that the continuity of the managing-family is maintained as far as possible.

Division of household: Division of a household, practically that of the family, occurs essentially once during the period of each generation.

i) Khang-chhen: The eldest brother in the household, if there are more than one, on attaining the age of marriage brings in a wife and upon this the living father, the head of the household, alongwith the mother and the unmarried aunts, has to separate himself and establish a separate unit. This house, which the eldest son succeeds, is known as *khang-chhen*, big or the original house. All the younger brothers move to the monasteries. On the division of the family the estate is not partitioned. Smaller residential units and patches of land are usually kept aside for the separating units including those living in the monastery, as this is a regular feature with each *khangchhen*.

Regarding the responsibilities of the *khangchhen*, Lyall states that the *khang-chhenpa* is primarily responsible for the revenue, the begaar or forced labour, and the share of common expenses of the village community, demandable on the whole holding which includes those of all the separating units of the family. Burdens of the *khangchhen* are heavy. The obligations of the eldest brother are to support the sub-units of the family and pass on the estate to his eldest son. The village society gives recognition to the *khangchhen* as its member and not to its sub-divisions which are virtually considered part of the main stock.

Primogeniture: The system of succession as is followed in Spiti has been termed as primogeniture. However the primogeniture of Spiti has some provisions different from that existing under the

Civil Law. Under the laws of Spiti the provisions become effective from the time the eldest son brings in wife in marriage. It is not dependent on the life of his father, his predecessor. The right of the incumbent over the property is not absolute. The owner has no alienable or transferable right. The existing owner cannot dispose of the property. In case of his failure to have a valid progeny all the rights of *khangpa* including that of the property devolves on the next younger brother who may be recalled from the monastery. There are further provisions to appoint the manager in case this step too fails. The ultimate aim is to perpetuate the existence of the estate in whole as a single unit in order to ensure support for all the members of the existing generation and those of future.

ii) Khangchung: On the succession of the household by the eldest son, the father retires to a *khang-chung* (small house) whence he is called *khang-chung -pa*. He has nothing more to do with the family estate and its burdens. He is given a residence, usually attached to the main house, and a small plot of field known as *dri-oo*, small field, for subsistence. Lyall says that the amount of land attached to the small houses differs on different estates; where it is big, the *khanchungpa* pays a sum of cash or cash and grain, about equal to its rateable assessment as revenue. But where it is small as is usually the case, he pays a small cash fee only, which is really rather a hearth tax than a share of the land revenue. The *khangchungpa* is not liable for any share of common expenses (a heavy charge in Spiti) nor for performance of begaar. On occasions of a great demand for men to do some work near the village he may be impressed, but the principle is that he is free. Sometimes in the absence of a living father, the widowed mother, or the grandfather or an uncle, aunt or unmarried sister, occupies the small house and land on the same terms.

iii) Yang-chung: The structure of the household may extend another step down which is called *Yang-chung* (smaller than the small) and this is the last stage seen in the process of succession. Diack says that in addition to these two kinds of estates the large holdings which descend intact from eldest son to eldest son and the smaller plots which similarly descend from ousted father to ousted father, there are still smaller (*yang-chung*) plots held either by the grandfather if he survives the ousting of his eldest son by his eldest grandson or by female or illegitimate relatives of the family, or by the tenants.

In respect to this kind of dependent families Lyall writes that, a small plot of land is generally attached to the house, and a few annas of revenue paid, but rather as a hearth-tax on account of grass, wood, water, etc., than as the share of the land tax on the plot held. Some *yangchungpas* have no land attached to the house, but pay like the others. Most of these people would be entitled to some maintenance from the head of the family, if he did not give them a plot of land. They are not liable to be impressed for ordinary begaar, but must help on occasions of great demand near home. They often do distant begaar, however, in place of the head of the family by mutual agreement. Existence of these subunits are temporary. On the disappearance of a family a new incumbent may take over the estate or else it will revert to the *Khangchhen*.

Continuity of the Line of the successors and succession: Rose writes that, "once a monk always a monk" is not the law in Spiti. Supposing the head of a family to die and leave a young widow, with no son or a son of tender age only, then the younger brother, if there is one, always acts to leave the monastery, and thereupon he is at once considered as his brother's widow's husband. She cannot object, nor is any marriage ceremony necessary. If there was a son by the elder brother, he of course, succeeds when of full age, and his mother and uncle retire to the small house, and the other sons, if any go into the monasteries in the usual way. So, again, if the head of the family has only daughters, and having given up hope of getting a son, wishes to marry one of the daughters and take her husband into the house as a son and heir, it generally happens that the younger brother in the monastery objects, and says that he will leave the priesthood and beget a son. In such case his right to do so is generally allowed: sometimes he will marry a wife to himself, and put his elder brother in the small house: sometimes, by agreement, he will cohabit with his sister-in-law in hope of getting a son by her. A monk who throws off the frock in this way has to pay a fine to his monastery. Many decline to become laymen; this is a rule in the case of those who have attained to the grade of *gelong*. Where the lama brother declines, then it is agreed that in the lower part of the valley (i.e. Pin and Sham), the father or widow mother can take a son-in-law to live in the house and succeed as son and heir, and no kinsmen (if there are any) can object. In the upper part of the valley this right does not appear to be so clearly established: the objections of near kinsmen are sometimes attended to, or a field or two given to them by way of compromise. Kinsmen, however, are, of course, very few, as the only way in which younger brother can found a separate family is by becoming son-in-law, and adopted son to another landholder. Such a man might claim on behalf of his younger son, but not on his own behalf or that of his eldest son, as it is a rule that for each holding or allotment there must be a separate resident head of the house to do service for it, as well as pay the revenue. Sometimes an illegitimate descendant of the family who has been living on the estate as a *yang-chung pa*, will claim as a kinsman and succeed, but he cannot be said to have any absolute right or title, (Rose,1883- III: 27).

In case the eldest brother fails to have a progeny, his younger brother may be called. In case there is no such suitable male living, the wife can bring in *magpa,* male bride, for herself. Exhausting all the measures, if there is a sister, she can bring in a *magpa,* or otherwise for a daughter.

iv) Dudthulpa: At the extreme edge of the structure there lives another category of families called *dudthulpa* attached to a *khangchen*. *Dudthulpa* is one who has only a house, being literally a smoke- maker (*dud* = smoke; '*thul-ba*=emit), smoke symbolizing a separate living house. He is a man who works for food or wages.

These families appear to have been some migrant individuals and were generally dependencies of a particular large household who were in need of more labourers, as it is said that 'they were found living in a dependent position towards the *khangchenpa* or head of the family'. Such a person slowly established family and also raised property. Sometimes they own a small field attached which they have reclaimed from the waste with the consent of the household with which he is attached. They all pay a small fee towards the revenue of the village by way of hearth tax.

In respect of payment of house tax and with regard to liability of begaar, *dudthulpa* are much on the same footing as the *yangchungpa*, the fundamental difference is that they are not related to the head of the family and have got their house, or house and land, not with reference to any claim to maintenance but out of favour, or for the mutual benefit of both parties. They are therefore expected to do a great deal of fieldwork for their master. To mark the fact, the hold of one particular landholder, the word *ranki (rang-ki)*, meaning private or particular, is added. Such families were settled by a *khangchhen* for its own benefit. All the land held by the *khangchungpa* and by *yangchungpas* and *ranki dudthulpa*, pertain to the primary holding or allotment and cannot be alienated, and lapses to the khangchhen. Lyall says that the latter could not of course evict a *khangchungpa*, and the general feeling is that when he has once given a plot to a *khangchungpa*, he could not resume it, except with consent, but he could resume from a '*ranki dudthulpa*', and would be considered quite justified in so doing on the grounds of customary service not having been properly performed.

There existed in some villages another system known as *thong-ba* (ploughman), collateral to *dudthulpa*. The households adopted a man who would remain with his master to work as ploughman for a few years. He was given a piece of land, about a *bigha* or two, for his subsistence. At the time of his parting away the land reverted to the landlord. Such arrangements with agricultural operations became necessary because the task begins simultaneously with all the farmers which has to be finished within the limited time catching with the fleeting summer crop season, and there is none at this time to whom look for assistance.

The following data shows the size of the different sections of the society and the share they owned in the national asset:

(area in acres)

	Name of Class	No. of Proprietors	No. of Holding	Area total	Of which Cultivated (%)	Average size per holding (Cultivation)
1.	Chhazang Khangchhen	333	330 (77)	992	988	3
2.	Chhazang Khangchung & yangchhung	196	196 (17)	217	215	1
3.	Blacksmiths	12	12 (0.5)	8	8	1
4.	Temples & Monasteries	23	27 (3.50)	48	48	2
5.	Shamlat (common village land)	–	29 (2)	24	23	1
	Total	564	594 (100)	1289	1282	2

(Diack, 1891, statement No. 1). Figures in brackets represent percentage to the total. It may be observed that ninety-four percent of the cultivated land is owned by the chha-zang, the middle class.

Shares among Brothers: Rewaz-i-am, the Tribal Customary Law, a set of rules which was collated from the social customs was codified during the British period. The Law was applied in the legal procedures and still holds good. It clarifies certain typical points from some live instances related to succession. It is said, that "In Waziri-Spiti, the eldest son inherits while the younger ones become lamas." It further lays that the next "three younger brothers are entitled to maintenance only while the remaining get nothing." Regarding the shares of the sons of different mothers, it holds, "In Waziri Spiti the inheritance goes to the eldest son." And quotes an instance: "Tashi Durje son of Cho of village Mane, Kothi Sham had two wives. Both of the wives had children but inheritance of Tashi Durje deceased went to the eldest son of the First wife and all others became Lama," (Riwaz-i-Am, 1954: Section IV, Succession – Sons, answers to question numbers 40 and 41). Among the daughters the eldest among all the daughters received the full set of ornaments from her parents on the occasion of her marriage.

Custom of Inheritance in the other classes: It is observed that the same kind of law of inheritance was followed in the families of the other two classes also: viz. the Nono and the smiths. When Egerton visited the Nono at Kyuling he found that: "Here the Nono has a very nice compact little estate, with two good houses and plenty of out-buildings on it. The Nono himself lives in the smaller of the two houses, the larger one, together with the management of the estate, having been made over to the eldest son, in accordance with the Spiti custom," (Egerton, 1863: 57). Regarding the other class the Gazetteer notes that the four families of blacksmiths also hold a rather small allotment a piece, and pay only a hearth tax and not full revenue. The above are all independent estates of the same grade as those of the revenue paying landholders, and inherited in the same way by the eldest son.

Founding of a New household in the village: It is noteworthy that even though the khangchhen is heavily burdened with responsibilities, yet it will accept them all without any grudge. All the sub rules of the society automatically tend to support the ideal family structure of *khangchen*. In the decision-making body of the village only khangchhen are members. They decide all the issues concerning the village viz. construction of paths, irrigation channels, their repairs; celebration of fairs and festivals; management of the village monastery; appointment of village functionaries; attending to the important visitors to the village; attending to royal orders, etc. The *khangchen* are responsible for arranging the funds required for completing the above works besides the usual payment of the revenue to the king or the state, begaar and *bun* to the big monasteries. These expenses are quite heavy. These factors are responsible to discourage any small household to aspire to become a full household, *khangchen*.

Also the above factors will discourage any full household from partitioning the establishment into two or more of equal status. No member in a *khangchen* will be able to gather courage enough to issue a threat to get himself separated and establish a new household. The reason is that on the division of a household, while the two dividing parties each receives half of the estate, from which they will derive their income, they receive the liabilities equal to the same as that of the original household, because each will now be member of the village society equal in status to all the others. Thus there is rare instance of increase in the number of the households with full status to be formed in a village by this process.

Woman: Under the prevailing social conditions women too had limited opportunity to opt for a married life and many of them remained spinsters for life. There were not many nuns also. They could live either with their parents or the eldest brother and were valuable assets as additional working hands. Sisters in rare cases were required to own burden of arranging for the manager of the household by bringing in a *magpa* for herself and have the chain of existence of the managers of the household unbroken.

On the status of woman the Gazetteer notes that, 'They are entitled to maintenance from their father, brother, or nephew, that is, from the head of the family, for the time being; he must either let them live in his house on equal terms with his own family, or must give them a separate house and plot of land; they forfeit their claim if they go away to live in any other man's house, but no other act of theirs will entitle their father or his successor to cast them off, or resume the house and plot of land once given during their life time. Many women live and die as spinsters in their father's or brother's houses: their chance of marriage is small, as all younger sons become monks, and the monks are bound to celibacy (except in Pin kothi) and bigamy is only allowed in the case of the head of a family who has no son or expectation of getting one by the wife he first marries. In case the brothers in law of a widow does not come out of the monastery to take his deceased brother's place, or in case there are no brothers in law, the widow can marry again, and does not forfeit her interest in the estate by so doing so long as she continues to reside on it: on the contrary, in default of issue by the first husband, the children by the second will succeed to the estate. She can marry any person of the same class as herself: if there happens to be a near kinsman available, she would be expected to select him. A marriage feast is given to celebrate the event.'

Marriage Customs: It is noted that, a marriage not being a common event in a family a good deal is spent on the occasion. The bridegroom's father presents the bride's with two or three ponies and 30 *khals* of grain, and also gives the bride's mother a present of Rs. 6 in cash. On the other hand, the bride is provided by her parents with a dowry clothes and ornaments of the value of Rs.100 or more including the *perak* that distinguishes the married women. It is usual to spend about Rs. 50 on the marriage feast. In Spiti if a man wishes to divorce his wife without her consent, he must give her all she brought with her, and a field or two besides by way of maintenance. On the other hand, if a wife insists on leaving her husband, as she cannot be prevented from so doing, but if no fault on the husband's side is proved, he can retain her jewels; he can do so also if she elopes with another man, and in addition can recover something from the co-respondent by way of fine and damages. There is a recognized ceremony of divorce which is sometimes used when both parties consent; husband and wife hold the ends of a thread, repeating meanwhile: one father and mother gave, another father and mother took away: as it was not our fate to agree, we separate with mutual good will: the thread is then severed by applying a light to the middle. After a divorce a woman is at liberty to marry whom she pleases; if her parents are wealthy, they celebrate the second marriage much like the first, but with less expenses; if they are poor, a very slight ceremony is used.

Regarding the forms of marriage it is said that monogamy is the rule in Spiti, and that a husband takes a second wife during the life time of his first only under exceptional circumstances. On the other hand, polyandry is not practiced, except among the *dudthulpas* and among the *buchhen.* However both the systems aim at the same objective, 'to keep down the number as much as possible'.

Chapter III

Religious Traditions

Spiti is predominantly Buddhist. Accroding to Major Hay, during his time, about thirty-three percent of male population constituted lamas. But besides Buddhism the people also follow the ancient pre-Buddhist religious practices which constitute worship of natural objects and forces. They are related to their social and economic life. The custom has survived for long under all kinds of adverse conditions. But now the position appears to have changed much and the practice is on the declining trend.

I. Lha-Chhos, the Pre-Buddhist Indeginous Religion

In many villages, besides the dominating monasteries, there are seen small primitive structures of one room, named *Lha-khang*, dedicated to a lha, a local deity. Among other kinds of representations, a small stone structure of about three or four feet high called *lha-tho* (pillar of deity) are constructed at places. Horns of rams and ibex, and branches of *shugpa* (juniper) are placed over it and small strips of cloths are tied. In some villages a stack of branches of *shugpa* of about five-six feet high, unique and not seen elsewhere, may be seen raised over the roofs of some houses dedicated to yul-sa, a deity. They may also be represented by some natural structure like a tree or rock. Lyall tells, 'Even less pretentious things are to be found on the summits of small eminences, or sometimes in the fields in the shape of niches cut in rocks, or left open in the sides of large masonary pillars.'

Usually these *lha-khang* have no symbol inside to be worshipped. Presently some of them house statues of Buddhist deities. At Sagnam the deity is named Zambala, resembling the Buddhist god Jambhala. There the idols of the Buddha (in the centre), Jambhala and Guru Rinpochhe are placed, although all the practices and celebrations are non-Buddhist.

Traditionally the deities are attended by *labdag (lha-bdag),* a priest, who offers the periodical worship in the *lha-khang* and does other services to the deity. Presently lamas seem to have taken over the charge at some places and they light there lamps regularly. There are but few *lha-pha,* a priest who receives the spirit of the deity and speaks on its behalf.

The temples are allotted some fields in the villages, income from which is employed to meet the expenses for burning lamps, remuneration for the attendant, repairs, annual feasts, maintenance, etc. During the period of Lyall there were 23 land owning temples and monasteries, owning on an average 2 acres by each establishment. But the holdings of *lha-khang* are very small in comparison to those of the monasteries.

The Settlement Report of 1887-92 notes that in many villages there are one or two fields known as *lha-zhing* or god's land attached to the village *lha-khang* or temple. These were considered as common property of the village and revenue on them was not exempted like those on the lands owned by the monasteries. One of the landholders or other residents cultivated them, and paid a fixed rent to the temple. Such a tenant could be evicted by a vote of community; sometimes all the landholders united to cultivate these fields, and the whole produce went for the temple expenses.

Yul-sa: *Yul-sa* is an ancient deity propitiated in Spiti and upper Kinnaur. This is not a name of an individual deity, but is a generic name, which literally means god of the village. Many of them have individual name. *Yul-sa* perhaps is actually a corrupt form of Yul-sad (*yul*=country; *sad*= god), equivalent to *yul-lha*. *Sad* is a usual term for god used in some parts of Lahul and Kinnaur.

Da-lha of Hansa: The folk deities are at places addressed as Da-lha. At Hansa there is a deity named *dgra-lha rta-thugs dkar-po*, also known as *Sa-bdag Shag-tse*. This deity is famous for its identification with the great god Jamlu of Malana in Kullu. It is attended by a lama and the traditional *lha-bdag* has been overlooked. The temples including the statues have been reconstructed, hardly distinguishable from a monastery.

Sa-dag in Guling: There used to be a *yul-sa* in the house of *mKhar* named *Dongba Dong-dun* (Seven faced). The deity was propitiated at two places under the name of sTod-chha Gyalba Godtshangpa at Guling and sMad Dong-ba dong dun in Lidang. Gradually one of them was neglected. Guling mkhar used to have *lha-tho* of *shugpa* dedicated to *yul-sa* on the roof of their house, also identified as *sa-dag*.

Gergan writes that *Shag-tse* is propitiated every year in the sixth month at Kyodo, Kyomo and Hansa. He enumerates the *yul-sa* deities of Spiti, propitiated in other villages as follows: Ro-mgo-log and gDung-pa-chan at Kyibbar; rDor-lha at Chijim; gDong-ba-chan at Kyi; Shel-rkyong dkar-mo at Lara; rGod-tshang at Lithang; Jo-dar and Seb-lha at Dankhar; Seb-lha is reckoned as the deity of whole of Spiti; Yul-sa chhen-mo sKu-la khyung, Yul-lo-ring, Chu-li-murti, kLu-ma, sRung-ma, Khyu-dbang-ma the six at Pog, they also hold under them eighty small godlings; rDo-sku-lha at Lhalung; dMan-'grong gnyan-po at Tabo; Jo-dar and Jo-pe-dar at the wild place called nying-du-pur; Ga men-rgyal-mo and Ko-wang-nab Tul-mo at Lari; and Tshering bcho-lnga at Rangrig, (Gergan, 1976: 325-326).

The Gazetteer names some deities and says that local deities are worshipped, such as Cho-tar at Dankhar, Cho-brang at Mane, Kula Kyeng at Pog, Dangbachan at Kyibbar, Angbo Gyabjin at

Losar and Gakbo Lha at Sangnam in Pin. On New Year day lamps are lit, but there is no festival.

Yulsa of village Khar: At the village of Khar in Pin there is a temple built on the top of a hillock dedicated to the *Yul-sa* named *rTse-lha* (god of summit). He is supposed to be the chief among all the local deities of Pin Valley. Near the temple there are ruins of old structures. It is said that the deity does not allow anyone to lift stones from here. There are *sKu-dung* (relics of the body) of Karma Jnyana, Meme Ngabang, Lama Chhosbzang and Lama Chhering, and a thanka of Dabla. They are said to have been *labdag* of the deity. On the day of new moon a festival, covering the whole Pin valley, is held here before the harvest of the crops.

Yulsa of Gungri: Village god of Gungri village is named as *sGe-nyen sKu-lha kha-ri*. People call it *Chho-dabla*. It has no *labdag* and is not propitiated separately but is worshipped alongwith the other deities in the nearby Buddhist monastery.

The time of worship of the dieties coincides with the important occasions of agricultural operations, such as sowing, harvesting, thrashing, etc. On these occasions people pray from them good crop, abundance of wealth; timely rain and abundant water; and absence of diseases, pestilence and war, etc. Many of them are propitiated as srung-ma, personal protective deity, and some were recognized as the gods of individual household and of the village. On the advent of Buddhism most of them were initiated into the Doctrine and became *chhos-skyong* and *srungma* (guardian gods of the Doctrine).

We observe that the ancient tradition of lha-chhos is weakening gradually and yielding to Lamaism. Their temples are changing their forms to monasteries, the priesthood is being taken over by the lamas and the deities are seen changing their ancient names.The three powerful deities of the past, viz. *da-lha*, *sa-bdag* and *yul-sa* are losing their individual identity and the three names are becoming synonyms of a single diety.

II. Buddhism

Buddhism as is practiced in Spiti is the form of Lamaism or Tibetan Buddhism. No evidence of existence of pre-lamaistic Indian Buddhism is reported to have been discovered in Spiti. Religion occupies very important role in the life of a Spitian. The form of Buddhism practiced here has assumed greater importance in view of the fact that the society and the Order are interdependent and have been supporting each other and growing together.

Religious organization in Spiti is next, in power, to the state. The proportion of the religious practitioners to the total population had been much larger than anywhere else. The Nono of Kyuling and Guling, supported a monastery each in his respective area. One of their brothers held the position of the head of the monastery.

Spiti lay on the pilgrimage route of the devotees and *siddhas*, coming from Tibet and going to the important Buddhist centres of pilgrimage like Jalandhar and Uddyan, in the north-western India. Reaching in the Satluj valley at the lower end of Spiti or upper part of Kinnaur, they either went through short route through Suket and then to Jalandhar (Kangra), or mostly took the longer route through Spiti, Lahul and Chamba, to get themselves better acclimatised. They passed on the way through the famous places like Kailash, Mansarovar, Guge, Spiti, Garzha Phagpa (Triloknath), Jawalamukhi, Nagarkot in Kangra, etc. Rinchhen Zangpo, rGod-tshangpa, Urgyanpa and sTag-tshang Ras-pa are known scholar pilgrims who passed through this route. Many unknown pilgrims lost their lives on the way due to unsuitable climatic conditions and other reasons.

Besides being quite large in size, the religious community here is highly organised. The five big monasteries of Tangyut, Dankhar, Kyi, Tabo and Gungri in Pin were considered as the institutions of provincial level and it was the collective responsibility of the whole Spiti to maintain them. The Settlement report notes, 'The monasteries, they are five in number. The monks or lamas of the Ki, Dhankhar and Tabo monasteries belong to the celebate sect called Gelugpa. Those of Tangyut monastery are also celebate Gelugpas but are distinguished by the name Sakya, it is to this monastery that the younger members of the family of the hereditary Nono or chief of Spiti are sent, and one of them is its abbot at present.' Among these some like that of Pin were able to retain their original form to great extent, but others could not resist the strong forces of change. It is told that earlier the monasteries of Kyi and Tangyut were both situated at village of Rongtong from where they were shifted to the present locations. It is also told that earlier Dankhar and Tabo also belonged to the Sakya sect.

Advent of the Doctrine: The main sects of the Doctine existing presently in Spiti are: Nyingma, Sakya, and Gelug. It is possible that earlier there existed some other sects like Kagyud, etc. which were later on gave way to the successive incoming stronger waves of other sects. Rinchhen Zangpo's campaign had great influence in strengthening the base of the Docrtince in the valley. Gelug spread fast replacing other sects except the Sakya at Tangyut and Nyingma in the Pin valley.

Tucci observes that the state of Buddhism as it exists in the present time is the same as it existed at the time of rGod-tshangpa (1189-1259 CE). He writes commenting upon the travelogue of the *siddha* that, 'Spiti was already a centre of Lamaism. In its mountains rGod-tshangpa finds many famous ascetics'.

Vitali divides the history of evolution and development of Buddhism in Spiti in three phases. He writes, the earliest known phase in Spiti goes back to the Second Diffusion of Buddhhism in the Himalayan territories, which took place in the late 10th and 11th centuries. The intermediate phase was engendered by the Kagyupa sect and occurred in the 13th century. This phase is especially renowned for its hermit and meditational practices. Later, after the Sakyapa period, from the second half of the 13th century to the second half of the 14th, during which Sakya ruled, the Gelugpa phase, beginning in the 15th century led to a new renaissance in these lands, which protracted for successive centuries (Vitali, 2000: 77-78).

Advent of Buddhism and the Prominent Monasteries: Study of the big monasteries of the region is helpful in understanding the evolution and development of Buddhism in the area. The following are the six chief monasteries of the area:

1. Gungri gonpa is adherent to Nyingma sect, probably belonging to the earliest phase of propagation of the doctrine in Spiti.
2. Tangyut is Sakya.

3 & 4. Tabo and Lhalung belong to the period of Revival of Buddhism and Renaissance movement of Rinchhen Zangpo which were later on taken over by the Gelugpa Order.

5. Kyi gonpa was founded during the period of the expansion of the Reformed sect, Gelug, in the region.
6. Dankhar, possesses a complex history.

1. Gungri - Nyingma Gonpa: In the village of Gungri (=dGu-ri, nine hills), also pronounced as Kungri, in Pin there is an ancient monastery named Gungri gonpa, generally known to the outsiders as Pin gonpa. It is the main monastery of the valley. The residents view it presently in three phases.

i. Thub-bstan spre'u dgon gsang sngags chhos-gling is considered to be the oldest about 600 years old. People consider the first part of its name Thub-stan spre-'u dgon' as uncertain and unreliable.

ii. Thugs-rje chhen-po mun-sel gron-me'i lha-khang is a monastery said to be the place of residence of thirteen teachers who donned long hairs. This is said to have been constructed by Thogs-med khrin le dPal bzang and dGos Rigs-'dsin Padma Lingpa and is said to be about 300 years old.

iii. Guru Lhakhang is said to have been founded by the famous guru dGe-long gYo-med Rinpo-chhe. It is told to be about 150 years old.

Of the three names enumerated above, the first can be interpreted as 'The Seat of the Doctrine of Mysticism of the Muni' and the second named as 'The Monkey Monastery of the Great Merciful, the Lamp which removes Darkness'. The epithet 'Thugs rje Chhenpo, Mahakarunika, the Great Merciful', is generally understood for Avalokitesvara. In the name of the third monastery the term Guru is assigned to a local teacher, a rare instance, but ordinarily in such matters Guru is indicative of Guru Padmasambhava. These names indicate to the ancient origin of the monasteries. The dates given by the informers appear to be indicative of those of the renovation or reconstruction.

Recently a new and much larger monastery named Urgyan gSang-snags Chhos-gling has been founded, close to the old one, which was consecrated by the Dalai Lama in 1994.

The history of monastery in Pin appears to be quite old. There are several factors which point to this proposition. They belong to the oldest sect of Nyingma. One of the monasteries is dedicated to Padmasambhava and the main statues are those of Padmasambhava who is flanked by his two consorts Mandarava and Yeshe Tshogyal. Be-dkar 'dra-lha rgyalpo is the guardian deity of the monastery. *Chham* is held at Gungri on the 10th day of the 5th month, celebrating the birthday of Guru Padmasambhava. It has saying, similar to that at Dankhar, that this was the first monastery to have been founded and the last to crumble down. Ancient name of the Pin monastery is gSang-snags chhos-gling. The valley is famous for the important feature of the Bucchens. They are followers of the Nyingma, are dramatists and they deal with the literature belonging to the earliest phase of spread of Buddhism in the area.

The edict of Dechhog Namgyal (Annx. I-A) issued in 1671 from Dankhar in the context of Pin valley mentions that the tradition of the festival of *tchhechu,* the festival of birthday of Padmasambhava, celebrated in Gungri dates from the period of Urgyan Padma i.e. Padmasambhava himself. This gives an indication that the tradition of the Doctrine here goes anterior to that of Rinchhen Zangpo, although Francke comments that, none of the monasteries in Spiti is attributed to the period older than that of Rinchhen Zangpo. The third wave of the Sakya could not have been much less strength as we know since some of its establishments were later on converted to Gelug.

Pin was successful in evading two powerful waves of reformation, one that of Rinchhen Zangpo and the other of Sherab Zangpo. Politically also although it was under overall dominion of Dankhar, at times this control from Dankhar was loose. Like the Nono of Kyuling, the family of Nono at Guling patronized the monastery of Gungri. He sent a brother of the family to head the monastery. Cunningham says that the lamas of Pin wear a long hat. They kept long hairs.

2. sTeng-rgyud and the Sakya Sect: The region above Kaza comprising the villages of Lang-za, Hikkim, Kaumik and Yul-dun is known as sTeng rGyud, upper region. There is a monastery dedicated to the Sakya sect which is known by various names as Sakya Gongmig, Gonmig, or Ten-rgyud gonpa. The monastery was originally located on the tip of a spur, over a ridge protruding out between two gorges below Kaumik and above Kaza. Ruins of the monastery can still be seen there. Trebeck writes that at some distance from Kaj (=Kaza), 'on the platform, to the left, at some distance ahead, were two temples, Tenguit and Gingul, with villages and lands attached'. The name Gingul or Gyungul is presently unknown in the area. As regards its indentification there is variation in the descriptions of various authors. Rose appears to indicate to Ghieu and Trebeck to Lhalung. Reference in the Gazetteer may be a copy from one of the above two sources.

It is noted that the monastery was desecrated during Zorawar Singh's expedition to Tibet in 1841. Egerton writes that the monastery of Tangyud is situated very picturesquely on a point where the uplands jutted out above the valley. It appears that the monastery was renovated soon after it was damaged and in the time of Egerton it stood at its ancient site. Presently the new monastery is situated in the village of Kaumik. The land is said to have been provided by the Nono of Kyuling. The monastery serves the area between the villages of Hansa and Lingti.

The monsastery according to one tradition was founded by Tanzin Chhos-phel Zangpo who was resident of Guge, about eight to nine hundred years before. If this is true then it was not Sakya at the time of its founding. Another school gives credit to Grung-pa rDo-rje, the founder of the Ma-sro gonpa in Ladak, which also belongs to Sakya sect. This fact is more reliable. During the repairs of the monastery some old objects were unearthed.

Liturgical name of the monastery is *steng rgyud lhun sgrub rtse* (Nagarjun peak in the upper region). The name describes unambiguously the chief deity for whom the monastery is dedicated and its geographical location. Its significance has not changed even today. Various segments of the name may be explained as under. It receives the epithet *rtse* from the position of its location, it being situated on a *rtse,* spur. *Lhun-grub,* Nagarjuna, is the central subject of the name. Wadell writes about the philosophy of the Sakya sect that its special gospels are Nagarjuna's *Avatansaka*, Vasubandhu's *Paramartha*, and so on,

(Waddel, 1895: 69). The nomenclature pays honour to the reigning philosopher and confirms the affiliation of the monastery to Sakya sect. Geographical description of the area, Tangyut became proper name of the place.

The name Gongmig: Colloquially the monastery is generally called Sakya Kaumik, Khaumik, Gongmig or Gonmig. Kaumik or Khaumik appear to be transformation from Gonmig or Gongmig. Francke calls it Sakya Gonmig. The two terms Gonmig and Gongmig, which are two forms of a single name in colloquy, are corruption of Gongma, meaning literally the former or the superior. We also hear the names of Sakya monasteries at other places as Sakya Gongma. It is a prominent term of the Sakya literature which signifies the group of the five early and elite teachers of the Sect. They constituted Kun-dga‘ sNyingpo (1111-1158), bSod nams rTsemo (1158-1172), Grags-pa rgyal mtshan (1172-1216), Kun dGa‘ rGyal-tshan (1216-51) and Phags-pa blo-gros rgyal-mthsan (1251-1280). In the lineage of the teachers they rank from third to the seventh. The last teacher of the group lived till 1280 CE. These five teachers are famed as Sakya Gongma (The Five Senior Sakya teachers). Thus it is evident that the monastery is also dedicated to Gongma, the early Sakya teachers. From the term Gongma developed the other forms of Gonmig, Gongmig and Kaumik.

Advent of Sakya sect: The Sakya tradition was founded in Tibet by Khon dkon-mchog rgyal po (1034-1102), who built the first Saskya monastery in 1073 CE in the Tsang region in central Tibet and laid foundation of the Sakya lineage. It grew into a powerful heirarchy, enjoying the temporal soveriegnty over the greater part of Tibet before it was eclipsed by its rival Gelug. The teacher of the founder claimed inspiration from the celestial Bodhisatva of wisdom Manjusri through the Indian sages ranging from Nagarjuna to Vasugupta and he mixed together the old and the new Tantras.

Phagspa Blo-gros rgyal-mtshan was one of the five great masters (Saskya gong ma lnga) of this school, and in 1254 he was authorised by the Mongol emperor Kublai Khan to govern the whole Tibet.

The term Gongma may be assumed to have originated during the lifetime of the last of the five teachers or after him. On the basis of this assumption the faith could have spread towards Spiti in the last quarter of the thirteenth century or in the early fourteenth century. Tucci presumes that its expansion towards the west and particularly to Spiti occurred in c. 12th-13th century and that it might also have received some royal protection.

The Nonos of Spiti had been patronising the monastery till recently. Egerton found one of the younger brothers of Nono as lama in this monastery. Egerton says, 'the abbot of the monastery has the honour of ranking among its monks the Nono's younger brother. His relationship to the great man is, however, by no means forgotten. He was very conspicuous in a long robe of bright yellow satin, with a high conical cap of red cloth and was formally presented to us. The abbot wore a head dress composed of a small copper saucepan, on the top of a large one, with a round knob above all'.

At Tangyut the *Chham* of Jigjed (*Bhairava*) is held in the month of October. After one month from this the celebration of Gutor, dgu-gtor, is held at the other four big monasteries. This fact is interpreted in the way that Gutor cannot be held before Jigjed, thus it is taken as an evidence to prove the superiority of Tangyut over the other big four. Three Panchayats viz. Tangyut, Demul and Langza now are responsible for the maintenance of the monastery.

Sakya monastery of Kaze: There was a small monastery at Kaza belonging to Sakya sect as Francke also confirms. Sometimes Tangyut has been mistaken with Kaza as it is said, 'The Kaze monastery has always been favoured by the Nonos of Spiti.' Kaza appeared on the map of Spiti only recently. Earlier it was an ordinary village. The highway passed through Tangyut and Dankhar, bypassing Kaza. The place has received little notice in the accounts of travelers. Recently a new and large monastic complex has come up at Kaza devoted to Sakya sect in place of the old one which was consecrated by the Dalai Lama in 2006.

The Sakya learning in Spiti was well known outside the area. Around middle of the fifteenth century a Sakya monastery was founded by a great teacher at Mustang in Nepal. A *chhoskhor* (religious council) was also held there. He did the very best to maintain the religion on a pure and high level. He brought Sakya scriptures and other holy objects from Tibet and invited scholars from Tibet and other areas. On this occasion a teacher from Spiti named mKhanpo Rinchhen Sonam was also invited in the year 1446 CE, on the advice of Khri Namkha Bangpo, the king of Guge (Tucci, 1956: 19).

3. Tabo: Tabo is a widely renowned monastery and has been studied and restudied. Tabo is a monastery situated on a level land close to the village and does not follow the usual norms of a gonpa, a solitary place. It was perhaps Francke, who first brought the importance of the monument to the notice of the scholarly world. The monastery was built by the great translator Rinchhen Zangpo (958-1055) and his patron king Yeshe 'Od, and renovated after 46 years during the reign of the Jangchhub 'Od, as is learned from an inscription found in its premises. The biography of the great Translator names it among the several monasteries attributed to him.

The family of Rinchhen Zangpo originally belonged to Khva-rtse, a village in Guge and was born at Radnis. Initially some writers had attempted to identify Khva-rtse with Kaze of Spiti. The present 19th incarnation of the Translator,bsTan-'dzin-skalbzang Rin-chhen (b.1961) was born at Shalkhar, Kinnaur and lives at Kyi monastery.

Nomenclature: Today the place, after which the monastery takes its name, is formally known in all respects as Tabo, a word not found in the lexicons. Various traditional documentary sources write the name in several ways, of course, although following nearly similar pronunciation as Ta-bo. The inscription from the Vihar does not mention its name. Guge mKhan chhen Ngag dbang Gragspa in the expression, in Spiti (Pi-ti) Ta-po cog-la-brgyan was constructed by Rinchen Zangpo, records the name of the monastery as Ta-po. A document from Pin names it as T'a-so (horse tooth). The Blue Annals writes it as Ta-bo. Other forms of the name found are rTa-po, rTa-bo, lTa-pho, Ta-po, sTa-po, rTa-pho and rTa-so. Some local people explain it as rTa-sgo.

It is notable that the biography of the Great Translator writes the name of the place as rTa-pho (male horse) i.e. 'sPe-ti rTa-pho'. This appears to be the original form of the name as we will learn below.

Tabo Chhoskhor: The name Tabo generally accompanies the epithet of *Chhos-khor* viz. *Ta-pho chhos 'khor or Ta-pho Chhos-sde. Chhoskhor* (Sangiti), religious council, was an important attribute of the practice of the Dectrine. The monasteries with such epithets make a distinct class like those of Tabo and Tholing and hold greater reputation of being the place of religious discourses, where great scholars gathered and held disputations (Sangiti), following the old Indian tradtion. This epithet seems to have been later copied liberally. Kashmirian pandita Jnansri, while going to Tibet, took up his residence at 'Chos-'khor Tabo'. After a three year's stay, this *pandita* learned to speak Tibetan and gNal, a lotsava, studied under him for three years'. This was immediately after the death of Rinchhen Zangpo, i.e. about the last quarter of the 11th century.

Date of Construction: It is now generally accepted that Tabo was founded in 996 CE. Its 1000th year of foundation was celebrated by the Government of Himachal Pradesh in 1996. The inscription upon which this fact is based was first read by Francke in 1909 alongwith some other. Francke found an inscription at Lhari mentioning the name of the monastery and including some other information. He writes, 'At Horling, on the plain towards Lhari, I found a large stone containing an inscription of Tsongkhapa's time. It mentions besides the names of the reformer and one or two of his contemporaries, those of an ancient lama king of Guge, Byang-chub-'Od, of the famous lama Rin-chen-bzang-po of the year 1000 A.D., and also of Tabo monastery.'

Francke says that Tabo escaped the destruction of the Dogra, while all others in Spiti, were ravaged, because Spiti in those times was under the Bashahar and the Dogras did not wish to interfere with the government of that state. Spiti in those days was under Ladak, i.e. the Dogras. It is doubtful if the lower portion of the valley was effectively under Bashahar. No evidence has been discovered to prove this fact, although visitors like Gerard and JD Cunningham, have been stating that Spiti paid a small amount as tribute to Bashahar and Kullu.

4. Lha-lung Monastery: Lha-lung, although artistically and historically in no way different and inferior to any other similar structure in the region, was less known to the world. Lha-lung is also not reckoned among the group of the five great monasteries of Spiti. The monastery has a moderate establishment and there resides only a small group of monks. In 1924 H. Lee Shuttleworth, a British Officer, visited the temple with Yoseb Gergan, a Ladaki scholar of the Moravian mission, and prepared a report on the study. Shuttleworth found "an almost perfectly preserved eleventh century temple, smaller than the famous main hall at Tabo, but no wise inferior to it in artistic merit. "The important document was later on published as a monograph by the Archaeological

Survey of India. Gergan had copied two inscriptions from the premises upon which Francke had made studies but were not published. Recently Kurt Tropper made a fresh study on the historicity of the monastery. He on the basis of the orthography of the inscriptions dates the monastery to between 1025 and 1250 CE (Tropper, 2008: 13). The monastery was perhaps built by a Chief born in the region of Chogla. Gergan says that during the time of Singe Namgyal a *mane dungyur,* mane wheel, was built in the monastery.

Lhalung and Tabo-the Relationship: Scholars generally rule out any relationship of Lhalung monastery with Rinchhen Zangpo. Lhalung does not figure in the list of monasteries founded during the time of Rinchhen Zangpo. The name is also not found in other sources. Yet some others have at their first glance attributed the monastery to Rinchhen Zangpo as it is comparable in many ways with Tabo. The two have common subject and similarity in style. Apart from this, the two places of Lhalung and Tabo exhibit some kind of relationship. We quote here a literary piece which says:

> *Lhalung dpal gi rdo-rje, ri la phyin kyang;*
> *rTa-pho'i zhabs yang dang yang thang la bzhag.*

Literally the couplet explains that although Lhalung Pal-gi-dorje has strong intention to go up the hill, his horse, a strong male horse, is unwilling to follow his master's orders, and is adamant to put his hoofs again and again on the plains. The skillful poet, by means of pun, tells more than what is stated.

The terms Lhalung and rTa-pho, on the one hand indicate the two individuals, the person and his horse, and on the other they indicate the two places of the same name by which we know today. The names might have been given on this occasion. Lhalung is situated at a high place in the hills and rTa-pho or Tabo below in the plains. There is a distance of a few kilometers between the two, and the geographical description given by the composer in his words fits here squarely with the actual geographical situation of the two places.

Lhalung Pal-gi-dorje, we know quite well, is the same hero who eliminated the king gLang darma, the staunch follower of Bon, and villain of Buddhism, in 842 CE. Historically there is no evidence that Lhalung after the event came towards the west. He is said to have fled to the north. The couplet shows to indicate his having come first to the west to mNgaris from where he might have turned towards the north i.e. north-east. This is not the sole incident. Rahul Sankrityayan relates another similar instance. He notes that during the coercive rule of gLang darma, when it was difficult for the Buddhist monks to live in his kingdom, three monks named Rab-gsal, dGe-'byung and Shakya-muni, had escaped to the wild in the hills of dPal-chhu-bo-ri and while they were living there, they saw the monk Kyi-ra-byed-pa coming towards them and from him they learned about the severe atrocities meted out to the Buddhist monks by gLang darma. At this the three monks loaded their 'vinaya' books on the mules and fled to mNgaris and from there they went to Hor (Turkistan), (Rahul Sankrityayan, 1948:27).

rTa-pho, the stallion, which Lhalung Pal-gi rdorje was riding has been given a befitting honour for his heroic task. He enabled his master to fulfil his special aim and then brought him to the far west saving the latter's precious life. Therefore the place, the plain of Tabo might have received the name after the horse as rTa-pho. Lhalung the name of the person can be easily identified with the place of the same name. From the description it may be inferred that Lhalung desired to escape to safer place from the plains to the hills and perhaps further away from there, but the people of Spiti were entreating him to stay here. The north must have been then safer for refuge. The residents then must have named or renamed the two places and might possibly have raised some kind of memorials culminating into the present shape of monasteries. This also reveals the true form of the name of Tabo as rTa-pho.

5. Kyi: Kyi, situated at a conspicuous place, on the top of a spur in the middle of the province near Kaza, is one of the largest and important monasteries. Its full name is 'dKyil dgon norbu dgephel', or Norbu Gephel in short. This name belongs to the Reformed Sect. Kyi is a corrupt form of dKyil which means middle. The name is written in several ways as dKyil, Khyil or Khil. Francke presumed it dKyid, happiness. The monastery is known to have been originally founded as of Gelugpa Order to which it still adheres.

Advent of Gelug Sect: The new sect of Gelug, Gedan or the Reformed Sect was initiated in Tibet by Lozang Dagpa, Tsongkhapa (1356-1419). The Sect assumed a great power and soon expanded beyond the borders of Tibet. Jangsem Sherab Zangpo, distinguishingly known as sTod Sherab Zangpo (1380-1457), to differentiate him from his contemporary and companion of the same name but belonging to a different region, was responsible for bringing the new faith and propagate it in Ladak. He was born in Thigse village in Ladak. He went to Tibet for study and attained the position of being one of the six famed disciples of Tsong-kha-pa. He returned home after completing the education and devoted himself in propagating the faith and founding new monasteries in Ladak and Zanskar. Presently they are considered among the leading monasteries in the areas. He had a few good disciples who carried out further his wishes. In Spiti Kyi monastery is attributed to him which he is said to have founded with the assistance of his companion Sherab Lodoe in c. 1450. Vitali says that Nagpo Kusum is the most ancient extant chapel at Kyi which is attributed to Sherab Zangpo and his disciple Sherab Lodoe (Vitali: 2000: 81). Dankhar, Tabo and Lhalung also belong to Gelug.

According to the *Namthar* of Sherab Zangpo the monastery of dKyil, i.e. Kyi, in Spiti, named as Norbu Gephel was founded by Dagpa Sengge and Sherab Lodoe (Ann. VII). Dagpa Sengge died in 1445 CE from which it may be concluded that the foundation of the monastery had been laid before this date.

From the *Namthar* it may be learned that Sherab Zangpo's activities are limited to the areas in Ladak and Zanskar only and he did not visit Spiti. He died in Zanskar which is confirmed from tradition also. During this period many other new monasteries belonging to the Reformed Sect were also founded and some other ancient temples were converted into the new order. The famous monasteries of Spiti viz.Tabo, Lhalung and Dankhar might have been converted into this sect during this period. In around 1683 dGadan Tshewang, the Tibetan General of the Tibeto-Moghal war, also worked to convert monasteries of mNgaris into Gelug. The monastery is believed in some quarters to be of about 800 years old. Egerton was informed the age of the Kyi monastery as 700 years old.

Here also resides the 19th incarnation of the great translator Lotsava Rinchhen Zangpo.This tradition began from the 17th incarnation onwards. Two scholars from here became Kachhen which degree they obtained from the monastery of Tashi Lhunpo in Tibet. The ceremonial performances here are said to be followed on the lines of Tashi Lhunpo. In the time of Egerton in June there were about 20 monks which number increased to about 80 in the winter. Some others estimated the figure at 200. Presently it is leanred that about 335 monks are attached to the monastery which is the largest in whole of Spiti. The number for others viz.Tangyut, Dankhar and Tabo is estimated at about 170, 100 and 50 respectively. Out of this almost fifty percent remain commonly away in pursuit of studies or other engagements in Dharamsala, Karnataka and elsewhere.

Chham is held on the 29th day of the fifth month. Francke found at Horling four or five stones which, he says, must have been carved in the fifteenth century. They contained the names of the great reformer Tsonkhapa and three of his contemporaries, mKhas grub pa (1384-1437), Lha-dbang blo-gros (1388-1462), and dGe'dan grub (1389-1473). They testify to the enthusiasm with which Tsonkhapa's reformation was welcomed in these tracts.

The monastery had been ravaged and the valuable articles had been looted number of times in the turmoils of history. The Kullu army is said to have taken gold from here and used in the temple at Manikaran. The library was destroyed during the Dogra war.

6. Drang-mkhar: Drang-mkhar was capital of Spiti since ancient times. The headquarters of the province were shifted to Kaza during the British period. The unusual location of the monastery became a subject of attraction for the people. Trebeck sketched the typical scene and included it in his book. A skilfull local poet expresses the experiences of the topography by the residents in the following manner:

> *Nyi-ma shar-she snga la skyod-che phyi-ya. Lug-zi sdug-po'i gnas yin … 1*
>
> *Brang-mkhar chhang-sa ma-ba la do-ya ma-ba. Ra ro-ba sdug-po'i gnas yin … 2*
>
> *Brang-mkhar gyen-yur ma-ba la chhun sna ma-ba. Chhun-pa sdug-po'i gnas yin …3*

It may be translated as: the sun rises here at Dankhar early, but sets late, which makes the day longer, and is a cause of concern for the shepherds who have to graze the cattle and sheep for longer time. In Dankhar there is plenty of *chhang*. But also the place is too much undulated, and there is too much up and down, which is a cause of worry for the drunkards. In Dankhar the irrigation channels are located at the places too high as well as at too low, which is the cause of great difficulty for the women who have to draw water for irrigation from the upper *yura* and also the lower *yura,* and much time is wasted in walking up and down between the two distant places.

The Monastery: At Dankhar there is an old and an important monastery. Francke tells that monastery of Dankhar is called Lha-'Od-pa'i dgon-pa. 'Lha-'Od seems to be the local pronunciation of Zla-'od, the name of a famous lama who was born in 1121 CE, according to Reu-mig. Zla-'od-pa would then mean, "a follower of Zla-'Od". He is apparently the founder or renovator of the monastery which now belongs to the Gelupga order. He further says that the monks assert that it was not only of earlier origin than the Tabo monastery, but also earlier than the time of Srong-btsan-sgampo. Francke also assumed that there used to live the ruler of Spiti at Dankhar of the clan of Lha-'Od gsal gdung rgyud'. Relationship of the teacher Lha-'od with the monastery, besides Francke, is also attested from other sources. However, we cannot comment on the details. In another tradition it is told that the monastery was founded by Rangrig Sangey Hodzer and another source says that it was founded by bLa-blama Jigsjed. We know nothing about the learned teachers.

About the antiquity of the monastery there is a saying current among the lamas, like in Pin, claiming the monastery to have been founded the earliest among the five big monasteries of Spiti:

Chhag-pa'i sngon-ma, zhigs-pa'i rting-ma.

The phrase means to say that it was the first to be constructed and was the last to have crumbled. The liturgical name of the monastery is *Lha-phel bkra-shis chhos gling*. The complex nomenclature indicates to the antiquity of the monastery and as having been founded anterior to the coming of the Gelug faith to which the monastery is presently dedicated. The chief images of the monastery are Byamspa (Maitreya), Tsong-kha-pa and Shakya

Thub-pa, ostensibly representing the Gelug faith, a later arrangement. Its present sectrerian name is "Norbu dGe-'phel", as we learn from a local document (Annx. II-B). Here *Chham* is held on 29th of 9th month every year.

The fourtieth Gadan Thipa, the occupant of the prestigious seat of Gadan in Tibet named Paldan Gyaltshan, is said to have belonged to this monastery, who remained in the position for seven years from 1654-1662 CE.

Jomo Gonpa (Nunneries): There are three old nunneries in Pin valley: (i) Phug-chung (ii) Karma gang, and (iii) Zong-zong. The nuns propitiate the same deity *sku gsum mkha' dro* i.e. *Khro-ma* (Bhrikuti) in *nirmankaya* (bodily existence) in all the three monasteries. The second deity is *lha-mo* in peaceful posture, i.e. *kun-tu bzang-mo (Samantabhadrika)*. The third is *rdo-rje phagmo* (*Vajravarahi*) in *sambhog-kaya* (celestial existence). *Khroma*, wearing a garland of skulls, is seen standing on the left foot and holds a*gri-kug,* sickle, in her right hand and *thod-pa* (*kapal*, skull) in the left. The right leg is lifted upto the height of knee of the left leg. Under the left foot is pressed down a human body. On her head is held a pig's head. *Brag-srin-mo*, fiendess of the rock, is another goddess of the class propitiated by the nuns. New and much larger nunneries have been opened in Losar, Morang and Pangmo.

Siddhas in Spiti

Spiti had been birthplace of a number of renowned scholars and had been visited by celebrated lamas and *siddhas*. It had been sending lamas for services in the monasteries in different places outside the province since long past. In Lahul they held the monastery of Chhoskhor. Presently their lamas hold the Nyingma monasteries at distance places like Manali in Kullu, Padar in Pangi, Chamba and some other places.

i. Siddha rGod-tshangpa: rGod-tshangpa while going from Tibet to Jalandhar passed through Spiti where he appears to have spent fairly good time. He met with several *siddhas* in its mountains sitting in meditation. Tucci observes that, 'Spiti was already a centre of Lamaism. In its mountains rGod tshang pa finds many famous ascetics.' 'Above Bi lcogs he met the great *siddha* Kharag pa who was unrivalled in the meditation of the *rDsogs chhen* system and had been continually sitting in meditation cross legged for thirty years. rGod tshang pa asked him for the explanation of the law, but since he wanted some presents, he replied that being a beggar he had nothing to offer. The other then said that he could not impart any teaching. rGod tshang pa presented him mentally with the seven elements of worship and the *siddha* then said that this was the best offering. He, then, imparted to him the instruction concerning the five meditations.'

Then, going upwards he found in a small monastery a bareheaded monk who continually counted the syllable 'hum'. While counting the 'hum', he had become a *siddha* who had realized that all imaginations are self-contradictory. Proceeding further he met a great *siddha* called Brag smug-pa' or 'Brag-phag-pa'. This master was continually sitting in meditation and did not speak a word to anybody. And he kept his eyes closed continuously. He did not move from the position of cross-legged even upto the age of eighty four years' (Tucci, 1940: 14-17).The journey of rGod-tshangpa towards the west started in the first quarter of XIIIth century. rGod-tshangpa had travelled through whole Spiti.

ii. The Siddha from Ghieu:A few years back a mummy of a youth, a young monk, was unearthed from village Ghieu, in the posture of meditation, testifying to the strong tradition of the *siddhas* in the area as described in the travelogue of the great *siddha* rGod-tshangpa. The body had been lying buried underground for long time. Yet it was found unharmed, intact and fresh. The posture of meditation assumed was unusual. The bust rested on his hips and a strap was tied over the body passing through the neck and under the bends of the legs which were closely stuck with his chest indicating that he was practising a special kind of meditation. Scientists ascertained that it belonged to a healthy young man of around 45 years old who had been sitting in the position without taking food for about three months before his death and he belonged to the period c. 1475 CE.At Ghieu, Francke found, during his visit in connection with the archaeological survey, a *mane* inscription erected by a man of Ghieu-mkhar, the house of the chief of Ghieu.

iii. Rang Rig Raschhen: Rang Rig Raschhen was a great lama from Spiti who was known widely outside the area. His immediate disciple Lung Ngag-dbang rDorje wrote his *namthar*, biography. He was born to father Shakya Tshering, a lama, and mother Tshering Dolma, at Manjusri monastery in village Rangrig. The boy having both the parents educated received education from his childhood and with his constant and hard labour became a learned man. He began his studies at the age of seven and was ordained by Pad-dkar Phrin-le, his teacher, as Kun-dga' rgya-mtsho. He visited Nagarkot, Jawalamukhi, both in Kangra, Margul in Lahul, Nepal, Bodhgaya, Kashmir and Tibet. He stayed in Lahul and at Zongkhul monastery in Zanskar for long time. In Nepal he assisted in repairing the famous monastery of Khashor (at Kathmandu). He was contemporary to king lDe-ldan rNam-rgyal (1645-1675) of Ladak. He belonged to Kagyud sect and lived between 1607-1683 CE (Tobdan, 1989: 95-109).

Local tradition says that Rangrig Raschhen was expelled from his birthplace in his boyhood for his being of birth from the parents by socially unrecognized conjugation. His works go to about five volumes out of which only two or three are available. There is shown a cave near his village where he is said to have meditated. The *Namthar* also tells that Rinchhen Zangpo had built a monastery in Rangrig.

Besides the *siddhas* described above, there were some learned lamas from Spiti who served in high positions in Tibet. Yeshes Tshetan was the thirty third occupant of the Kyilkhang of Tashi Lhunpo in Tibet.

Chapter IV

The Buchhen of Pin Valley

dGu ling mkhar and dGu ri dgon pa: Pin, spelt as sPrin and sPyin, is a side valley situated towards the southern end of the main valley. It is one of the five kothis of the province. Climatically it is slightly better favoured than the main valley and receives more rain. It is linked with Kullu and Bashahar-Kinnaur through high passes and also had been often victim of their frequent incursions and raids. The prominent villages of the valley are Guling, Gungri, Sagnam and Mud. Mud is the last village situated at the high end of the valley. Documentary evidences reveal that during the seventeenth-eighteenth centuries Pin was equal in status to the main valley and formed a separate unit of administration. There were two *kharpons*, one in Pin and the other at Dankhar. Pin has made great contribution in the promotion of culture and religion of Spiti. Nyingma is one of the oldest sects of Lamaism and is practiced in Pin. Bucchen is a special class of educated artists.

1. Gungri: Gungri (dGu-ri) or Kungri is a small village where the ancient monastery of Gungri, more popularly known as Pin monastery, is situated. This is the monastery of the *Buchhens*, renowned for their practice of dramatic performances. It belongs to the ancient sect of Nyingma. The principal part of this monastery is called *tsuglag khang* (vihar). Sangey Hozer perhaps renovated the monastery in the year 1330 (Dorje, 2011: 69), although some faithful ones believe him to be its founder. The principal households here are: Jhoba, Pharma, Yogma and Khyim-tse. Jhoba ranks next after the Nono.

2. Guling: The residents of the place explain the origin of the term Guling from Gur-ling (*gur*=tent; *ling*=place), but an old literary source gives it as dgu-gling (nine-places) and similarly Gungri also should be understood as dGu-ri (nine hills). It is capital of Pin valley and is residence of Nono, the Chhota Nono. There are some caps of the former head lamas of the Gungri monastery kept with the family of Guling mKhar from which came the head lama of the monastery. The caps have resemblance with those found worn by the leading secular persons like the donors seen in the paintings in the walls of Tabo monastery (Klimburg-Salter 2005: 24, 54).

The families residing here are those of *Khar* known as *gya-zhing*, *Ta-ma*, *Gu-ma* and *Pharma* who are all *khangchhen* and there are two more of this class. Two others are of the category of *khangchhung*. The family of Nono besides sending a lama to head the main monastery of Gungri also provided an *amchi,* the chief doctor of the valley. A well-known person Khri-bdag bsTan-'dsin chhos-grub belonged to sPin dgon-pa and came from the family of Nono of Gungri. Thog-med Thille of this family is said to have lived five generations before.

3. Sagnam: Sagnam, written as bSagnam or rTsagnam, is a large village situated on a flat land about three kilometers away from Gungri towards Mud. The original households or *khangchhen* are: *Gongma, Dong Gongma, Pharma, Dong-sham, Dong-stod, Yogma, Yang-zur Ta-ma* and *Larten Gronma*. The *brgyudpa* or lineages are named as *gyurbun-churbun, yag khra-bo*, etc. There are two households of mGar-ra. One of the families works on iron and the other one functions as musician and plays on *daman*. There are two families of Beda who sing and play on instruments.

Gara and Gatuk: Gatuk is a personal name quite common like Gatuk Sonam, Gatuk Dorje, etc. It has an interesting background to tell. It is said that there was a tradition that if in a family the first boy failed to survive after his birth, a ceremony had to be got performed at the birth of the second boy in the family, so that he could survive. The ceremony was performed by a person from the Gara family of the village. After the ceremony he gave the boy his first name as Gatuk (mgar=smith; khrug=son or boy; Garthuk, Gatuk), an essential part of the name. He also gives a full set of the articles of his profession and others like cap and set of bangles, all of iron, for all arms and legs. The custom is said to have been followed all over Spiti.

About 150 years back, a great performer of *Buchhen* named Ga-tug was born in Sagnam. He died while he was in meditation. His mummy is preserved in a *chhod-rten* called *dung-rten* at one corner of the village.

Marriage Customs: Marriage used to be ceremonised in three ways like at other places. Choice of the type depended on the socio-economic status of the family. *Bag-len*, in which the groom's party goes with full preparations to fetch the bride, is an elaborate and expensive custom. In the other type of the marriage, called *Chhang-srad* (Offering *chhang*), the bride is departed by her parents with simple ceremony. The third type of ceremony, called *sKus-de-khyer* (stealing), is a poor man's custom in which bride is brought unceremoniously. A light feast is given, but the penalty for a miss-choice may be sometimes manifold.

Under the *Khangchhen-Khangchhung* system, the eldest brother of *Khangchhen* has to marry from the house of the same status, that is from a *Khangchhen*. The younger brothers, however, can bring brides from *Khangchhung*. *mKhars* should marry from *mKhars*, may be from outside the area like Lahul, Ladakh, etc.

Some important stages of the ceremony are explained as follows:

1. Ras-chhang (Chhang or Request): A party constituting the maternal uncle and three or four others from the side of the groom are sent, to ask for the hands of the girl, carrying with them *chhang*, *chhang* of request, which is presented to the girl's parents. The leader who presents the *chhang* and *khatak* (scarf) is called *maula*.

2. Mi-gyur chhang (Chhang of Confirmation): The second *chhang* is presented after some days in order to get confirmation of the commitment. The parents of the groom of the *khangchhen* present ornaments and cash as *zong* (*gzungs*) (elemental present). *Berag* is the real symbol of prestige which is costly and is essential. Other symbolic presents, called *dagza*, are bow, arrow and clothes of five colours. As is the custom here, and also elsewhere, the groom does not go with the bridal party but a conveyer called *bag-khridpa* (bride-leader) is sent. He is assumed to have acquired the relationship of brother and sister with the bride and the two honour the relationship by regular exchange of gifts all through their life. He should be having both of his parents living (*pha-den ma-den*).

At the bride's house, the groom's party is allowed to enter the house only after a competition of songs is held at the reception. Some pillars are raised, three, five or seven. On each point the bride's party asks questions in songs and the groom's party answers in the same manner and then a pillar is felled and the groom's party is thrashed with green willow branches symbolically. The scene is similarly repeated at each pillar, till they reach at the entrance. It is said that in earlier times the number of pillars raised used to be upto eighty. This is the most attractive and entertaining scene of the marriage performance. This custom exists in Ladak, sTod in Lahul, Spiti, Upper Kinnaur, Zanskar and among the Khampas. *Rin-gchod,* striking the price, the bride gift, is another stage, ceremonised, among others, inside the house. After the marriage the bride returns to her parent's house which is termed as *bag-log* (return of the bride). She is accompanied by her friends, *bag-rog-ma* (companions of bride).

Ceremonies connected with Agriculture: It is well known that there grows only one crop in a year. Therefore the farmers leave no deficiency in their efforts. But in order to prevent all kinds of calamity and ensure successful harvesting of full yield of crops, they have to take some extra measures also. A number of prayers and ceremonies are performed. Fortunately there are no wild animals who can cause any kind of damage to the crops. But the birds are the biggest enemies of grains here, starting from the occasion of scattering the seeds in the fields and sprouting of tender shoots, up to the end of the operation, putting the grains in the barns. They are seen constantly whirling swiftly around the village and the fields in clusters. It is sin to kill a living but they must be prevented from harming the crops in any way. The ceremony of *dbyar bya kha gag-che*, shutting the mouths of the summer birds, is celebrated with the same objective.

After sowing of the crops is complete, a festival is held in the *lha-khang*, temple, of the local deity. The villagers gather. The *Labdag* (priest) comes in trance, as the spirit of the deity enters him. People pray from the god that there should be rain and good crops. It is feared that birds may eat away the tender plants as they shoot up in the fields. Therefore through this ceremony they also pray that the mouths of the birds be shut up. The children sing:

dbyar gi bya kun bya-ka-lag
dgun gi bya kun bya-ka-lag

Birds of the summer, may their mouths be shut.
Birds of the winter, may their mouths be shut.

Thereafter they sing taking the names of all the villages in the valley of Pin and then the names of all the fields in the village. The men prepare models of birds with the flour or soil, about fifty to sixty in number and the children burry them under the soils. Then they all dance.

gSang-snag: Thereafter, after having the first watering done in the fields, a series of prayers called *gsang-snag* begins. It is done everyday in a different household, till the harvesting of crops is over. After the harvests have been brought to home *bru-phud,* offerings of grains, is made to the village deity. Then *chhang* and *arrack* are prepared from the new grains and another ceremony is held. The village deity is taken out.

The deity has a small icon wrapped in white clothes and about 10 to 15 tridents of either iron or silver are tied with it. The *labdag* comes in trance who wears *lha-gos,* a white gown and clothes of five colours of silk. He holds the *rten* in his hand, a bundle of sticks of bamboo about two and half feet long representing the god which is taken from house to house. He is asked, about the omens. In the event of bad omens, he dances frantically, he pierces his cheek with the end of the trident and dances holding a sword in his hand. In the event of good omens he dances peacefully. In the winter, in December, *Gun chhang phud*, the ceremony of winter offering of *chhang*, is held. The deity is thanked for the good rain and good crop. The varied ancient customs of the people have now been mostly replaced by the uniform Lamaistic practice like *bum-khor.* Under this system loads of religious books are taken round the village and the fields, when the crops have grown fully and the grains start setting.

***Chhos silche,* Reciting Scriptures:** During the winter when the work in the fields is over many activities of social and religious nature are held which keep the people engaged. Sacred books are recited in each house by turn which begins with the beginning of the snowfall. During this period every person, specially women, keeps fast, either on the full moon day or on the new moon. Women keep fast on both these days. The village deity is propitiated every month. In the month of March, in the villages of Khar, Bar and Sagnam, before the spring season comes, a great fair called *Chhanka* is held. On this day the people wear ornaments and their best clothes, whatever one owns to please the deity. Otherwise the deity may become displeased. This is the fair of the deity. Competition of reciting of *mane* mantra is held. Traditional dances of *Gar* and *Shon* are held. Competition in the use of absurd languages is also held. As the spring comes, people start spreading earth in the fields, for melting the snow. Here we observe the folk tradition getting mixed up with the Buddhism. It is learnt that earlier Maheshwar, the chief deity of the Bhaba valley in Kinnaur, used to visit Pin valley periodically.

***Soljog*:** If in a family there are three sons, perhaps a lucky sign, the ceremony of *Soljog* has to be performed for every boy, once in his lifetime, to wash away the misfortunes and ill omens. About 100 lamas are called and the ceremony lasts for three days.

Buchhen, the Holy Actors

Buchhen is a well known traditional class of dramatists who live in this valley. They are a settled population, yet they follow usually a wandering life for their profession, which is normally seasonal. They travel from village to village in the areas of Spiti, Kinnaur, Lahul, Zanskar and Ladak generally in the autumn playing dramas and entertaining the people and earning some income. It is told that 'some of the *buchhens* obtain plots for their maintenance from their families but the majority are landless and get a living by plays or by carrying loads and doing other odd jobs'. There is no prohibition to do any kind of manual work for them. They can marry, do all kinds of domestic chores, agricultural activities and other kinds of activities as all laymen do.

The profession has been on the declining trend since long. Even in the nineteen-twenties it is remarked that the "practice is now seldom performed." In the census of 1931 there were nineteen families of *buchhen* in Pin Kothi. Presently also they number the same. Roerich and Lyall took great interest in their activities and have left valuable descriptions of their entertaining performances in record. It is told that there also used to be a family of *buchhen* in Kyibber. In Ladak *buchhen* were known as Manipa. There were two families there, one in Shara village and the other in Leh.

The term Bu-chhen: The term *bu-chhen* is ordinarily heard and written as *Bu-zhen*. The true form of the term is bu-chhen which literally means the eldest or the elder son (*bu* = son; *chhen* = elder or older). In the present context of the religious conduct it means the eldest among one's pupils, as is observed in the practice and tradition of *buchhen*. Thang-stong rGyal-po, who was the progenitor of the tradition, is known as 'Pha grub-chhen thang stong rgyalpo,' thereby meaning the 'Mahasiddha Thang-stong rgyal-po, the father.' Here the teacher has been addressed as the *Fathe*r, the progenitor or initiator or teacher. As such it is understandable that his pupils should be called as '*bu*,' that is spiritual son or sons, the seniormost as 'bu-chhen.'

Founding of the System: Lyall narrating the story of origin of the practice of *buchhen* in Spiti from Thang-tong, says that the famous Lang Darma, a king of Lhasa, converted the people of Tibet from Buddhism to a new religion of his own. He succeeded so well that in the course of fifty years the old faith was quite forgotten, and the *Om mani padme hum,* or sacred ejaculation quite disused. To win back the people, Chan-re-zig, the divinity worshipped at Triloknath, caused an incarnation of himself to be born in the king's house in the person of Thang-tong Gyalpo. The child grew up a saint and a reformer; he saw that it was impossible to reclaim the people by books; and he therefore adopted the dress since worn by the *buchhen*, and spent his life in wandering from village to village, offering to amuse the people by acting miracles plays on condition of their repeating after him the chorus *Om mani padme hum,* wherever, it occurred in the chants or recitation. In this way the people became again accustomed to repeat the sacred sentence, their mouths became purified, and the religion of Buddha revived.

Shangs pa bKa'gyud and Thang stong rgyalpo: Thang-stong gyalpo had adopted the doctrinal lineage of Shangs-pa of the bKa'gyud sect. It originates from the *siddha* Khyungpo who is said to have visited India and Nepal thrice and studied there *sutra* and *mantra* from about 150 teachers. On his return to home he founded many monasteries in Tibet in Shangs-khul of gTsang and Phang-yul of dBus. He preached his teachings for thirty years and founded a line of his teachings as Shangs-pa bK'a-rgyud. He is said to have lived for 150 years somewhere between 900 and 1140 CE. This long span of life appears to be a unique feature of the teachers of this sect. Thang stong rgyalpo, following the tradition is also assigned similarly a long life span of 125 years. According to one tradition he died at the long age of 105 years in 1509 at gChung-ri-bo-che. Thang stong rgyalpo lived from 1385 to 1464 CE. The time of advent of the practice in Spiti is not known.

The act of 'breaking the stone', an important act of the performances, is said to have been first performed by the great *siddha*, Pha grub-chhen thang stong rgyalpo. His real name was Kam Kam brTson 'Grus bZang-po. He was born in the north of gTsang at Hol ka Lha tse. He was contemporary to Tsong Khapa, the founder of the Gelug sect. He traveled in Bu, Tsang and Khams of Tibet and India, China and did many worldly activities. In Tibet he established many iron bridges and monasteries. He is famous as the great builder of the Chu-bo ri bridge on the Yaru Tsang po, south-west of Lhasa. At Chagspori he founded a monastery which came to be known as sMan-rgyal Ri. Chagpo Ri was famous for its medical college. Some good *amchis*, doctors from the regions of Spiti, Ladakh and Lahul were educated and trained there. He researched on new medicines also. He also composed dramas on the basis of the biographies of the Kings of Tibet whose performers became famous as Achi Lhamo. Besides, he composed occupational songs which accompany ploughing, mowing, thrashing, building construction, and other activities, and series of drama for them. He was also a 'text-discoverer'.

It is told that in Tibet the dramatists displayed the Thanka paintings of the stories from Dimed Kundan, Padma 'Od 'bar, sNang-sa, Do-ba Zangmo, etc. and explained them to the spectators. But the system of breaking the stone was not practiced there. Thang-stong gyalpo started this performance in order to educate the laymen to stop sinning and to adopt good work to learn about the cycle of the life.

Recruitment: The Gazetteer of 1917 notes that every son of a lama or monk becomes a *buchhen*. Sometimes the younger son of a landholder becomes a *buchhen* in preference to going into the monastery. Presently any person from any house can enter the order of *buchhen*, but traditionally persons from the households of *khangchhen* did not like to join the order. The performers form a group and then go on the round. A member of one group can join with another with the consent of the leader. Groups have not divided areas. At present there is one group each in Tiling, Khar, Bar and Upper Guling, two in Sagnam and three in Mud, in total there are nine groups, in the entire Pin valley. *Buchhen* belong to *Chha-zang* class.

Training: An entrant into the profession of *buchhen* has initially to join a performing party as a *yog-po* (assistant or helper) and accompany them. He helps the team in every way he can and also avails himself of the opportunity to exhibit his talents by singing, dancing, playing jokes, relating stories in dramatic manner, etc. In this way, in the first stage of his learning, it takes for him about two to three years, depending upon the interest shown by him and his capability. Thus he familiarizes himself with the profession. On attaining sufficient ability to become a *buchhen*, he enters into the actual course of training which may be given as follows.

1. **Phyag-bum:** The novice takes one lakh *phyag* (bowing), before the deity, and recites the *mane mantra* of *om mani padme hum* for one lakh times.
2. **Sems-skyed:** He has to recite one lakh *mantras* of *sems-skyed* (orienting-the-mind).
3. The *mantra* of *yig-brgya* (hundred words); *mandal* and d*ge-va,* combined together; and *lama'i rnal-jor*, consisting of eight words, all have to be recited for one lakh times.

Thereafter he has to sit in *tshams* (meditation), necessarily for one year. In case he wishes to become a member of the performing party it has to be done for two years. For becoming a head *buchhen* or *Lochhen*, one has to perform *lo-gsum chhos-gsum,* i.e. he has to sit in *tshams* for three years. Then he is eligible to become head *buchhen*. Thereafter also he sits in *tshams* every year for at least a week or two. On acquiring the position of *Lochhen*, he is required to initially perform in his own valley.

Literature: The following list enumerates some of the works from which they perform their drama.

1. Spyan-ras gzigs chhos-rgyal nyi-ma kun-ldan. 2. Au-rgyan dri-med kun-ldan. 3. Bram-dse zug gi nyi-ma. 4. mkha'-'dro bo-mo dro-ba bzang-mo. 5. 'das-log sangs-gyas chhon-zom. 6. 'das-log ling-dsa chhos-skyid. 7. 'das-log snag-sa hon-'bum. 8. 'das-log karma dbang-'dsin gyi rnam-par thar-pa'i lcags-kyu. 9. chhos rgyal yun ral ba. 10. khe-'u padma 'od-bar. 11. rje btsun mi-la ras-pa 12. 'brog-pa kun-'dra. 13. do-cha mo-cha, (stod-chha smad-chha). 14. 'byung-po don-yod. 15. ran-ga pa-ta. 16. Nor bzang (Sudhana Jataka).

These are mostly life stories. Those at serial numbers 5 to 8 are imaginative stories and relate to the visit of the hero to the land of death and his return to the real life ('das-log = return from the death). Sudhana had been a popular subject among all kinds of artists like the painters and carvers.

Besides the above, there is another class of literature treated by the *buchhen* which relates to the marriage of the Tibetan king Srong-brtsan sGampo with the Chinese princess Kongjo. One set of the works is named as Kashog (letters), a part of which is given in the annexure. Another one, more elaborate work is named *zang-yig*.

The Stories: Lyall gives gist of a story which he saw being performed. He relates, a certain anchorite who had lived alone for twelve years in an inaccessible forest one day washed his robe in a pond in the hollow of a rock. A doe drank the water in the pool; conceived there from, and gave birth at the door of the anchorite's cell to a creature in the form of a girl. Under the anchorite's care she grew up into a beautiful woman, was called sun-face, and married to the king. The other queens conspired against her and accused her of being a witch and eating human flesh; they murdered her child, and made the king believe she killed it to feast on its baby. Sun-face is driven out, and leads a wandering life in the forests till the king discovers the plot, puts the conspirators to death, and recalls her.

Another famous story tells that there was a prince named Dri-med Kun-ldan who was a great benefactor of the people. Once he gave away a great part of the wealth from the treasury of the kingdom, in donation to the enemy of the kingdom. The king-father was greatly enraged. He ordered to extract both the eyes of the prince and then send him in exile. He was also separated from his wife and his two sons. But with the power he obtained from the almighty he was able to gain his eyesight back and union with his family. The king also was pleased to place him on the throne.

The Drama

The whole group of actors is known as *buchhen*. There are three classes of them in a performing party: *buchhen*, the leader and the main performer, also known as *Lochhen*; *bu-chhung*; and the *mirgod* or *lug-rdsi* (wild man or shepherd).

The Icon: The performers carry a metal icon of the teacher Thang stong rgyal-po and place it at the head of the stage. In one aspect the teacher is seen seated on a cushion of lotus. He has four arms, the first two are joined in prayer, and one of the lower ones holds a glass rosary and a white lotus in the other. Silken dress and precious ornaments adorn his body. Skin of wild animal forms his upper garment. The legs are positioned in *Vajrasana* posture. Stainless moon is seen on his back. Behind this they used to spread a large *thanka*. The artists pray and bow before the statue before beginning their performance.

In another form Thang stong rgyal po is seen as a sage naked and sitting cross legged, his white hair arranged in a kind of knot on the crown of his head like an Indian *sadhu*. In his lap, he holds a *tshe bum* or *amrta* vase. Behind him two painted images or *thanka* are placed one representing the four armed manifestation of the Boddhisattva Avalokitesvara, and the other representing the life story or *namthar* of Dri med kun ldan.

Lochhen: *Lochhen*, the leader of the plays, is a learned and a serious actor. He maintains long hairs which is collected and twisted into a pigtail. He looks attractive as he wears many accessories over the dress of a common monk. His cap raised in the middle is surrounded by about a foot long eight or five silken strips in varied colours hanging all around from the edges. In the ears he wears *pan-thap,* silver ornaments; *g-yu* turquise and *ju-ru,* beads, and *ol-thik,* necklace in the neck. He carries two *gau,* charm box, the smaller one on the chest and the other one on the back. Four square pieces of conch shell are studded on the *ong-*

jug, coat, in the front. Other apparels are *ton-kag*, jacket; *kyerag*, red waist ribbon; *smad-sham*, lower garment; and tò*ad-pa* (boot of cloth and hide with high legs).

Initiating the play the *buchhen* is seen holding a rosary in his left hand and *mane khor-lo*, prayer wheel, in his right hand. He then after blowing the conch recites a prayer. A part of it may be given here.

Gsung dang blama rnams la phyag 'tshal lo,
Rje 'gro- ba mgon- po'i zhabs la 'dud,
Bla-ma mi-'gyur chhos kyi ngang la bzhugs,
Spyan ras gzigs kyang chhos kyi ngang la bzhugs.

Thugs-rje chhen-po chhos kyi ngang la bzhugs,
Thang stong rgyal po chhos kyi ngang la bzhugs,
Lo-chhen gong ma chhos kyi ngang la bzhugs,
Rgya sde khrom-pa yig grug ma-ni drongs.
Auom ma-ni padme hum!

Translation

I bow to the Teachings and the teachers,
I bow at the feet of the Lord of the World,
The great teacher manifests the unchangeable Doctrine,
Avalokiteskvara manifests the Doctrine,
Mahakarunika manifests the Doctrine,
Thang -stong rgyal- po manifests the Doctrine
The former Lochhens all manifested the Doctrine
Oh, the large assembly of the town,
Recite mane, the *mantra* of the six letters,
Aum ma-ni pad-me hum!

Nya-ba: Next come the two second ranking lamas who are called *bu-chhung* (younger sons) and also as *nya-ba* and the one on whose stomach stone is broken, also known as *da-bo*.

Mi-rgod or Lugzi: The third kind of performer is *lugzi* who represents a simple local village worker, the shepherd. His typical dress and unassuming actions and unsophisticated attitudes attract the spectators. In some stories the place is occupied by *mi-rgod* (wild man) or *rngon-pa* (hunter). They also represent the mass, the class which is required to be tamed, civilized, educated, and initiated into the Doctrine. The *lugzi* wears a common man's dress, a cloak of sheepskin, a skin cap, comically reversed, and his face is white by smearing *tsampa* (barley flour). On the back he carries a bag in which there is a ball of *tsampa*, lunch of the shepherd and a *yug-rdo,* sling in his right hand. These are all paraphernalia of a village shepherd. He acts as a joker. He displays as if he is totally ignorant of the principles of the Doctrine. His actions, gestures and statements are satiric and casts jokes on the Doctrine, its followers and the Lochhen.

A Recent Play: Presently the dramatists have shifted their subjects and emphasis from the classical themes to the tastes and likings of the modern spectators. Instead of enacting the stories, as they were doing traditionally, these days they play magical tricks.

The *Lochhen* blows the conch. Then there comes forward the *lugzi*, the jester. Singing and whistling, he swirls the sling as if throwing stone to turn back and retract the leading straying sheep or to round up the herd. He also brandishes the sling to mark stops in his speech, while relating a story or telling an anecdote. His actions fill the intermittent gaps between the scenes of the main play. He raises many questions on the Doctrine and then answers himself, which are mismatching, jesting and mocking at the Doctrine. Everybody laughs. Then he brings out the ball of *tsampa* and placing it on his palm, and playing with it he explains many things. Then the *Lochhen*, in the gesture of vanquishing over the wild man, expels the shepherd from the scene. Sudhan tamed the wildman of the north.

The *Lochhen* wear a piece of red or yellow silk cloth, about a square foot, stitching over the skin on his back with the aid of two needles pinned at the two upper corners of the cloth and piercing through the skin, as if a piece of paper has been stitched over a cloth or another paper. Then he pushes a thick needle through one side of cheek and brings out on the other side. He holds two swords in his hands and displays many tricks. He keeps a pair of swords standing over their handles placed over the earth and then playing and jumping throws full weight of his body over it, resting his stomach over their tips. He shows pricking his stomach, mouth and eyes with the tip of the sword. The spectators pronounce '*Buchhen mkhyen*', 'Oh! *buchhen* you know', and they try to touch the sword. The drama is entertaining and captivating

Question and answer between the Lochhen and the Lugzi: The *Lochhen* asks questions to the *Lugzi* which is just a hint. The *Lugzi* answers them in detail. An instance is given below:

The *Lochhen* asks: *spo-rta rtse ru bzhugs-pa rig-'dsin tshhang-yangs rgya-tsho.*

At the Potala palace resides the Vidyadhar Tshang-yang rGya-mtsho.

The Lugzi answers:

Po-ta de-ru bzhugs-pa rigs-'dsin tshang-dbyangs rgya-mshto

Lhar-rtse'i khrom du bzhugs pa grung mgor pa spro shig-shig

Yi-ge a gchig mi-shes snyug-gu mda' sang ring.

Lhar-rtse'i khrom du bzhugs pa, chhos sems bla-gtsang dbang-mo

Dam-tshig gtsang-ma yin yang dgnos-sgrub yong-rgyu mi-'dug.

Sgom-pa bla-ma'i drung-du sems skyed zhu-ru phyin-pa sgom-pa zhal-re yid-la 'khor-rgyu mi-'dug.

The answer is in detail and is satiric and attempts to highlight the reverse side of the coin. The shepherd says: Rigzin, the learned,

Tshangyang Gyatsho (6th Dalai Lama, b. 1683) lives at Potala. In the market of Lhasa there live many who pretend themselves to be great and take seat at the head of the rows (of men). They don't know even the letter 'a', yet they hold pen as large as an arrow. The religious minded Latsang Wangmo resides in the bazar of Lhasa. Although her vows are pure, she is incapable of getting the perfection. She goes before the teacher for the training of her mind, yet she fails to concentrate on the subject as her mind strays elsewhere.

Lyall describes a performance: Lyall writes that there is something rather impressive about the performances of the *buchhens*. A long screen is first put up formed of pictures illustrative of the legends, and quaintly painted in brilliant colours on cloth edged with silk. An image of the patron saint or founder of the order is enthroned in front of the screen; the leaders of the company then appear in front of it, wearing a head dress formed of a mass of streamers of bright coloured silk. Conch shells are blown to collect the crowd, and barley thrown into the air as an offering to the saint, the proceedings then commence with an introductory chant by the leaders to the accompaniment of a kind of guitar, and every now and then the whole crowd of men and women join in with the chorus of *Om mani padme hom* which they give with much fervour, keeping good time, and blending their voices harmoniously. After a time the rest of the company come forward dressed up and masked and perform a play with interludes of dances to the music of cymbals, the dancing ends in the wildest gyrations; the little stage hemmed in by the quaintly dressed crowd, and with the huge barren mountains lowering behind for background, makes a picture not easily forgotten.

Pho-bar rDo Chog-pa: Breaking the Stone

The show of breaking the stone on stomach is the final, and an important and attractive item of the whole drama. Origin of the act is traced by Michael Aris from Thang sTong rGyalpo and may be given as follows.

It is told that once in Lhasa the demon gZa-bdud (planetary demon, Rahula) caused a great many diseases, especially the disease of the bowls and pains in the intestines. Doctors administered their medicines, magicians their charms, but these were of no avail. Some died while collecting wood in the mountains, others while partaking of food. Some died while dressing, others while enjoying themselves. The Precious Lord of Lhasa (rJe-rin po che Tsong kha pa) pondered over the matter, and said: 'The people of Lhasa are mostly dying out. If the great *mahasiddha* Thang stong rgyal po of the Cung Ribochhe Monastery possesses no means to control the disease, no one else can do anything.' The Precious Lord dispatched messengers to the Cung Ribochhe with the message: 'My people of Lhasa are mostly dying out. You are the only one who can subdue this disease, others can do nothing, Come at once.'

The great *siddha* after reflecting on the matter said: 'This being a command of the Precious Lord, I must go!' Pointing his fore-finger to heaven, he perceived a mighty white tailed eagle flying high in the sky. The *mahasiddha* having assumed the form of an iron Atsara, set out on his journey.

The Precious Lord issued order to his seven door-keepers: 'I am expecting tomorrow an important guest to arrive. Let him come upstairs without hindrance!'

The great *siddha* having arrived, the door keepers did not recognize him, and detained him for a while. The Precious Lord perceived this in his mind, and said to the door keepers: 'My guest did not arrive as yet!' The door-keepers replied: 'There is no other guest, except one Atsara who came riding on a mighty white tailed eagle. Is this the one!' The Precious Lord exclaimed: 'Why did you not let him in at once?" The door keepers opened the gate and led the guest into the presence of the Precious Lord. The Precious Lord said, "Nowadays my people of Lhasa are mostly dying out! If you are unable to help in this, no one else can do anything.'

The *mahasiddha* then requested the Precious Lord: 'Where resides the spirit of the present epidemic?' To this the Precious Lord answered: 'At present he is found under the threshold of my door and has the shape of a stomach.' Then the *mahasiddha* having caused the spirit of the epidemic to enter inside there in brownish stone, which had the shape of stomach, invited the stone to the market place of Lhasa. From the five fingers of the *mahasiddha* five flames sprang up. One assumed the form of Avalokitesvara, and acted as preacher of the Doctrine; another assumed the form of Vajrapani, and acted as his assistant, a third one assumed the form of a goddess possessing a melodious voice.

Having placed the stone in a yard, all the elderly people of Lhasa gathered to see the ceremony, saying, "Today a mahasiddha will perform some crazy things!" And there in the presence of the assembled elderly people of Lhasa, who came to the ceremony, Thang stong rgyal po broke this stone, which was just the size of a stomach, with another stone similar to a magic dagger.

In the present evil *kalpa*, one has to use a bigger stone to break it, for the purpose of subduing demons, ogresses and evil spirits. If one breaks the stone with the first stroke it signifies *dharmakaya*. If one breaks the stone with the second stroke it signifies *sambhogakaya*. If one breaks it with the third stroke it signifies *nirmanakaya*. If one breaks it with the fourth stroke it signifies the Lords of the Four Quarters. If one breaks it with the fifth stroke it signifies the five Dhyani Buddhas. If one breaks it with the sixth stroke it signifies the manifestation of the Buddha in the six states of existence. If one breaks it with the seventh stroke it signifies the seven groups of Buddhas. If one breaks it with the eighth stroke it signifies the eight Sugatas. If one breaks the stone with the ninth stroke it signifies the nine stages of the vehicle of the Doctrine. If one breaks it with the tenth stroke it signifies the ten forms of the Teacher. If one breaks it with the eleventh stroke it signifies the eleven headed Avalokiteshvara. If one breaks the stone with the twelfth stroke it signifies the twelve manifestations of the Earth-goddess. If one breaks it with the thirteenth stroke it signifies the sphere of Vajradhara. If one is unable to break the stone, one should not proceed with the ceremony, this being an evil omen. If the stone is found under the threshold of a monastery a great lama should subdue it, again if it is found under the threshold of a castle, a great king should subdue it. If one is unable to break it in a region where there are no castles or monasteries, one should place it at the meeting place of three highways, and there it should be broken either by a hundred blacksmiths' striking it with the hammers, or by a hundred boy's attacking it with loud cries, or by eight strong young men smashing it.' Each stroke with which the stone is broken corresponds to a divine manifestation.

The final scene: Then the last actor called *da-bo* takes out his upper garments and draws black lines on his forehead. The *Lochhen* pronounces a *mantra* before him and hits thrice with a sword on his stomach saying *phat.* Then the *da-bo* lies on the ground, face upwards. A block of stone, about two feet long, half feet broad and half feet high, called *rdo-chog,* the stone to be broken, is placed on his stomach. One blow from a globular stone about a foot in diameter, called *yar-rdo,* the upper stone, cleaves the block into two portions, which fall on either side of the *da-bo*. The boy then springs up immediately to his feet unharmed.

Sometimes the stone is split in two parts with one hit. At others it has to be hit twice or thrice. As soon as the stone is broken the people shout 'Lha rGyal Lo,' 'Victorious be the god! The stone embodies the enemy and it represents ill omens and obstructions which, therefore, has to be smashed. Then a player collects offerings from the spectators. The *buchhen* then play music, sing melodious songs and dance.

Merits of breaking the stone: With the breaking of the stone it is believed that the the region have been cleansed of evil omens. It is told that at first when the teacher Thang sTong rGyalpo was erecting the monastery of Chung Ribochhe, evil omens made their appearance. Whatever was built by the humans during the day, was destroyed by the demons during the night. After performing the ceremony of breaking the stone for the first time, they were able to resume the work and complete the construction of the monastery.

At the time of building the iron bridge of Chu-bo-ri, the demon dBang-rgyal caused the water in the river to rise, and thus created hindrance in the construction work. After performing the ceremony there for the second time, the work on the bridge could be completed successfully.

Chapater V

Nono: The Native Chief

Nono is title of the hereditary native chief of Spiti. He has his residence at Kyuling, a small isolated village, situated on the right side of the Spiti river, opposite to Kaza. Nothing significant of historical importance is reported to have been discovered from the village. The only significance is that it may be said to be located slightly at more secure place. British government granted recognition to Nono of Kyuling or sKyid-ling, as some scholars knew it, as the right holder of the title.

Nono in common parlance means 'younger brother'. It is a kinship term, a term of address for a boy or a man younger than the speaker, used within the families of the class of 'Jo' or by a member of any other class for a person in similar position of the Jo class in the areas of Spiti, Ladak, Zanskar and Lahul. It is also a polite way of address. Jo is a class of families of the highest ranking clans in the society. The ruling chiefs usually come from this class. The title of 'Nono', as chief of Spiti, however, could be assumed by only one person at one time.

Origin of the term Nono: Atkinson gives an interesting and long drawn account explaining the origin of the term No-no in Spiti. He traces the origin from very ancient times connecting with the countries situated in distant places as far as Greece. He finds that 'it is used throughout India among the prominent rulers of highly honourable origin', and that 'this may have been derived from Greek title 'King of Kings' rendered by Indo-Skythic and equivalent to 'Rao Nono, Rio', or Ra in Gilgit, Nono in Spiti and Nana in Maharashtra.' 'It may be traced latter still in the old

Indo-Skythic Provinces of Gujarat in the title of Junagarh, in Gilgit where the old rulers had the title Ra' and the old name of which is 'Sargin' throughout Rajputana, the Dakhen in the title 'Rao'. In most Rajputana clans in the titles of 'Rao' and 'Rawat' whilst the headman of Spiti is called 'Nono' and the honorific title of NANA is common amongst the Marathas,' (Atkinson, 1882, Vol. 2, Part I: 404). The inhabitants of Malana in Kullu, also knew themselves by a similar term as 'Ra deo'. However, these arguments fail us to equate the term Nono in use in Spiti and the surrounding states with the similar term in use elsewhere.

As far as our knowledge goes the usage of this term is local to the few states of the western trans-Himalaya as stated above. It was in use more commonly in Ladak, particularly in the circle of royal families. Meanwhile it may be presumed that the term spread to other areas from the royal family of Ladak. How the term originated there cannot be known. A. Cunningham notes that in Ladak the highest ranking authority after the Gyalpo was the Kahlon, the Prime Minister. Below him there were again Kahlon but they were all distinguished with certain epithets and some by that of Nono. They all belonged to the ruling family of the respective area. Similar could have been the position of the chief of Spiti as a province of Ladak. Nono was a honourable substitute for 'junior'. It may be that the family had a local origin but the title of Nono might have been bestowed by the Gyalpo (king) of Ladak. This title of Nono is distinct from the same term of kinship relationship.

Nothing is known about the origin of the family of the Nono of Kyuling. The history of Zanskar records that after the upheavals and destructions in the state, Zanskar was resettled. Then a wise counsellor advised to invite Sakya Thubpa from Spiti and they acknowledged him as their king, (Francke, 1972-II: 161). This fact already existed in Zanskar as has been noted by Nawang

Tshering (1657-1731), a famed lama from Zanskar. He writes that, from Spiti one from the line of the ruling families named Sakya Thubpa migrated to Zanskar and settled at Padum and latter on became king of the whole Zanskar,' (Nawang Tshering, 1975- I: 9-10). It indicates that there existed some noble family in Spiti before the resettlement of Padum in Zanskar. This family might have belonged to the line of descendants from the time of the division of mNgaris. But nothing can be said about the relationship of the existing line with the former. Presently, it is difficult to determine any definite date to the incident. Francke is uncertain on the point 'whether they are descended from a native Spyiti family or from certain governors of sPyiti, posted there by the kings of Ladak.' His opinion appears to lean more towards the latter view. Attempting to relate the origin of the Nonos of Spiti from Ladak, he says that a rdZong blon-chen-po, mentioned on a votive tablet, is called sTan-'dzin rnam-rgyal. He may be identical with king Sen-ge-rnam-rgyal's step brother, bsTan-'dzin rnam-rgyal. Mr. Howell had deputed two pundits in 1908 to Spiti and they had collected certain manuscripts and inscriptions. Francke has selected some names from them and presumes to belong to the family of Nono of Kyuling. They are:

1. Ga-ga mKhyen-rab supposed to have been the first No-no of Spyiti.
2. sTan-'dzin rnam-rgyal, mentioned again in an inscription from Rang-rig.
3. The name of a certain Ga-ga rDo-rje is found on a dedication sheet from Kyi-bar. He was a contemporary of Tshe-dpal don-grub rnam-rgyal of Ladak (beginning of the nineteenth century).
4. Name of one Gaga Sod-nams was found written on a *mani* stone at Kaza who 'held the office of Resident at the castle but the name of the king of Leh was missing.'

It may be observed that these names generally bear the prefix Gaga and not Nono. We cannot say with any certainty if any of them belonged to the family of Nono of Kyuling.

Historical traditions in Spiti, however, do not show any kind of familial or clan relationship between those of Leh and Kyuling. Spiti was a directly ruled state of Ladak. There was an office of the Ladaki officials at Dankhar from quite long time whose chief was addressed as Gaga and to which the Nono of Spiti was subordinate. Technically in the social context Gaga is superior to Nono and the two terms have been adopted as official designation maintaining the same difference in official status as in social.

Ga-ga: The chief officer, Kharpon, posted by the Ladaki kings who stayed at Dankhar was always addressed as Gaga. Gaga is a kinship term similar to *nono,* addressed to the brother elder than the speaker, opposite to *nono*. A person may be a *nono* or *gaga* in relation to the speaker according to the situation. Indeed the two terms of Gaga and Nono are not used in the first person. As a designation of an administrative officer or as a title, the term Gaga has never been used for the Nonos of Spiti. Thus the two terms of kinship applied as official designation enable us to distinguish the respective position between the two. It may be that when Ladak brought Spiti under itself, it gave lower rank of Nono to the local chief of Spiti. A Kharpon is Gaga, even as 'Khaga Khan'. In view of all these it may be presumed that the Nonos of Kyuling are of native origin.

Gergan says that the families of the rulers of Ladak, Zanskar, Lahul and Spiti have originated from the common lineage of Lha-nyi-ma (Gergan, 1976:325). It may be clarified that at least in respect of Lahul this statement is not true.

The Other Nonos: Rose writes that the title of Nono is given to any male member of the four noble families of 'Kuiling,

Mane, Pin and Gyungul in Spiti'. The title is retained for life but would be forfeited if its bearer married out of his own rank. The Gazetteer 1897 notes that there are four noble families, the males of which are called Nono and the females She-ma: the hereditary wazir is called Gyalpo. These families reside at Kyuling, at Mane below Dangkar, at Kuling (i.e. Guling) in Pin Kothi, and at Gyungul near the Lingti stream. Rose writes the head of Kyuling family is recognized by Government as the Nono of Spiti, but he is never known in his own territory by any other title than that of Gyalpo or king. It is essential to clarify here that in the history of Spiti the chiefs of Kyuling have always been known as Nono. The official documents issued from Dankhar by the Ladaki authorities, as a few of them are available, appear to avoid to even make mention of the term Nono. They have never been addressed as Gaga, not to speak of as Gyalpo.

The highest class of the society designated as Jo elsewhere is known in Spiti as Nono which status is acquired at the moment of birth of a person and he normally owns it throughout his life. A woman may not be able to transmit one's status to the next generation on the marriage with a spouse of the lower clan. The Nono of Kyuling in addition to the social role as Nono also held the official title of Nono which he enjoyed till the pleasure of the crown. Here Gyungul is indicative of Ghieu. A family of Nono lives there.

Nono of Pin, Guling: The Nono of Guling i.e. dGuling, Pin, has been termed as Chhota Nono, an epithet received during the British period, indicating him as junior to that of Kyuling. Pin being a distinct geographical tract might have enjoyed a limited independence, thus the chief of the area upholding the title of Nono. Pin had occasionally been falling prey to its neighbors like Bashahar. History of Pin is known only in short and in bits, is rich. The present incumbent of the family has a short list of the pedigree to tell as: Sa-rub > Dunba> Chhering Angrub> Chhering Dorje, the existing family member.

When Egerton was at Dhankar, two Nonos, both from Pin valley, presented their claim before him for the privilege and independence from Nono Kalzang (Koolyung) of Kyuling. One of them was called Chhota Nono. His ancestors were professors of medicine and surgery, and in lieu of all fees were granted certain lands in the Pin valley free of revenue. Some fifteen years ago the Nono Kalzang's wife's brother's daughter became widow. The Nono induced the Chhota Nono, then a mere boy to marry the young widow. When he came to man's estate, this youth asserted a separate jurisdiction in the Pin valley, independent of the Nono. The history of Pin valley and its Nonos is much older and quite impressive.

Egerton tells that, the other claimant of independence, named Chiring, called by his friends as Garpon is descended from ancestors who certainly held the office of Garpon in the Pin valley. He produced a 'sanad' (or patent) addressed to one of his ancestors granting the office to the then holder and his descendants. The document produced by the would-be Garpon was signed by the Wazeer of Le' (in Ladak) and sealed with the red Chapa, *lal Chapa* (= seal). It was written in the character now in use for letter writing. The Nono and several of the best readers in Spiti had considerable difficulty in deciphering it. We are not sure whether Egerton means to say here Kharpon or Garpon. There was a Kharpon posted separately in Pin during the time of the Ladaki king Tashi Namgyal (1555-75), (Ann. II.B.). There was also a Garpon from Guling posted in Guge who might have been appointed during the reign of Singe Namgyal or slightly later and might have belonged to the family of the Nono. The monastery of Tashigang was assigned to the lamas of Pin by Singe Namgyal. The document alluded to above by Egerton is purported to have been written in the year of fire ape probably sometime in the seventeenth century.

The family of Nono were patrons of the ancient Gungri monastery of Nyingma sect. The head lama of the monastery, like that of Tangyut from Kyuling, always came from this family. Secondly another brother from the same family was traditionally official *Amchi* (doctor) of the area.

We meet with several stray but important names relating to this family or hailing from Pin. Gaga sDe sKyong Namgyal from Gungri, was a Kharpon. Jigmed Tanzin Dorje Rinpochhe, a great lama, was born in the Nono family. Sangey Hodzer renovated the monastery of Gungri. Grubthob Marpo was a *Siddha*. gYo-med Rinpochhe, a siddha, pupil of Ye-she Paldan of Lhagpa of Chhumurti, built the Guru-lhakhang of Pin monastery. He brought statues of Padmasambhava of gold and silver. Thog-med Thille is said to have lived five generations before. He was educated in Tibet and was a learned man. He collected the works of Padma Lingpa and renovated the monastery in his village. The Settlement of 1900 records that Khri-bdag bsTan-'dsin chhos-grub belonged to sPin dgon-pa and came from the family of Nono of Gungri. Jigmed Tanzin Dorje, incarnate of the siddha gYo-med Rinpochhe, founded the present new and separate monastery.

The Pedigree of Nono of Kyuling: Some of the members of the family of No-no of Kyuling are known as follows:

1. Nono bsKal-bzang (Egerton: Koolyung) was in office during the visit of Egerton in 1863.
2. bsTanzin rNam-rgyal resumed office from his father in 1864 or 1865. He resigned from the office in 1878, due to old age. Harcourt writes that the Nono is a well-meaning but very ignorant man, and has but little influence over the Spiti people. He is also unaquainted with any language but his own.

3. rDorje Tshetan (b. 1833) resumed office in 1878 from his father. He lost his eyes.

   Massy writes that he is the sixteenth among the Vice Regal Darbari of the Kangra District, (Massy, 1890: 411).

4. In 1891 his younger brother bKra-shis Rin-chhen, a monk, was appointed as Nono during the minority of the former's son.

5. Tshe-dbang bsTobs-rgyas held the office in 1955.

It is significant to note that the decree issued by the Ladaki king from Dankhar in 1671 makes no reference to Nono. Among several documents originating from the local families reference to Nono is found only in one. Reference to the Nono of Spiti comes from a local source in the form of a song (Ann. V) which may be assigned to circa 1700 CE in which his position is quite clear.

Powers and functions of Nono: Major Hay is perhaps the first authority to show involvement of Nono, whom he calls Wazir, in the administration of the district. Trebeck does not mention the name Nono or that of any other local authority at all. Major Hay says that the revenue of the district was collected by the hereditary Wazir and in the work he was assisted by the Gatpos or Mukiahs. During the British period the Nono was bestowed certain functions and powers and received the prescribed remuneration. 'The Nono of Spiti exercises jurisdiction as a magistrate under the Spiti Frontier Regulation with power to try all classes of offences except murder, but to punish with fine only. He has to receive the land revenue from the village headmen, and is responsible for its safe delivery in October of each year at the Kulu treasury, together with the amount of the fines levied by him. It is also his duty to make the necessary arrangements for officers visiting Spiti. His emoluments consist of 6/16ths of the cash *khalsa* land revenue which worked to Rs.282 and of the whole or the pachotra cess (5 percent, on the land revenue levied in addition to it). He is owner of land of 5 acres and his revenue is free'. There were some fields at Dankhar attached to the old fort which were like the property of Government. The Nono, in virtue of his office, got the fields cultivated, and took the produce. He in return was bound to keep the fort in repair.

Chapter VI

History: Some Notices

Spiti has been studied little on the aspect of its history. During the British period some officials and travelers expressed academic interest on various subjects besides pursuing their own objective and some of them have left valuable accounts. Focus of the modern scholars lies on monasteries.

Regarding the local sources a reference is widely made by the people throughout the region of a mysterious object called *yig-sgam dmar-po* (red box of letters) which is stated to have contained documents relating to the history of Spiti and was lost some generations back. None is able to tell about any content that might have been conserved in the box.

Availability of written sources on the history of the area begins from circa tenth-eleventh century CE after the advent of Buddhism in the valley. Spiti had been a literate society since quite early time. Monks constitute a sizeable section. *Buchhen* in the Pin valley is another such elite section. There are number of monasteries with long traditions and having indelible bearing on the history of the region. Tabo and Lhalung have yielded inscriptions concerning their foundation. Biographies of certain reputed monks like Rinchhen Zangpo, rGod-tshhangpa and Rangrig Raschhen contain some references to Spiti. Mane stones contain mantras and names of certain important historical persons inscribed on them.

Some references, including a few documents, of historical importance begin to be available with the foundation of the administrative office of the Ladaki king at Dankhar. As some of them relate to the collection of the funds for the big monasteries, they have been found at Dankhar, Kyi and Pin. A few of them are dated or are datable. Another extent source, which has not yet been explored fully, is the sacred books lying in the private households all over Spiti copied to commemorate certain holy occasions. They contain certain valuable incidental remarks in the colophons.

European travelers and explorers started visiting the valley from the beginning of the nineteenth century. Many of them were specialists in different fields like geology, botany, administration, archaeology, etc. Francke (1909) and Tucci (1933) were prominent among them whose main interest lay in history and archaeology. Some other noteworthy visitors were: Trebeck (1822), Gerard, JD Cunningham (1842-43), A Cunnigham (1846), Major Hay (1849), Egerton (1863), Harcourt (1869), George de Roerich, James B Lyall, etc.

Archaeological Survey of India made explorations and conducted surveys of the various sites and objects of archaeological interest in the valley. The kinds of objects surveyed included Lhakhang, chaitya, chhorten, mane walls, paintings, miniatures, stucco images, etc. which mostly concern Buddhism and all have been placed between tenth-eleventh to seventeenth-eighteenth century CE. Of special interest is the stone circles discovered at Chhota Dara, (ASI, Review, 1999-2000: 38-49). It is important that some rock carvings have also been discovered at more than one place.

Spiti, it is noteworthy, failed to attract attention of the *siddha* sTag Tshang Raspa (1574-1651), a great *siddha* and learned scholar, and famed as Urgyanpa. He had been successful in completing pilgrimage to Urgyan (Uddyan). He remained in the area for about three decades and travelled in all the divisions of Guge, Kinnaur, Ladak, Zanskar and Lahul, surrounding Spiti almost wholly. Spiti is not found mentioned in his travelogue except once as 'Pi-ti'on the occasion when the the administration of Ladak was divided among the three successor princes of king Singe Namgyal.

Capital of Spiti: Historically Dankhar had been the capital of Spiti. Presently Kaza is headquarters of the sub-division. The Nono had been the local chief of Spiti who lived in Kyuling. Except this, Kyuling has not yielded any other evidence concerning its contribution towards the formation of the history of Spiti.

i. Kaza: Kaza, as is written officially these days, is pronounced as Kaze locally.

Attempts have been made to trace its origin to the ancient phrase *mkhar-tse* which means a palace or fort on a summit. Kaza does not possess such features. Kaza had been neither seat of the Ladaki ruler nor residence of the local chief. The situation has now changed. The highway passes right through the town. It is situated in the middle of the valley on a vast plain, wasteland in the past. Physical location of the town has now become advantageous and has congenial environment for the growth of the town. It is evident from the two names it has acquired: Old Kaza and New Kaza.

Petech writes that G.Tucci in 1933 found a group of inscriptions at mKhar-rtse (Kaja). A palace of the Ladakhi kings existed there, and Nyima Namgyal (c.1694-1729) caused the Sa-skya-pa monastery of mKhar-rtse to be renovated, (Petech, 1977: 82-83). There is no doubt that there was a Sakya monastery at Kaza as Francke also writes that 'there is a small temple of the Sakya sect at Kaze', but there is no information that there ever existed any *mkhar* (palace) there nor is the town situated on a *rtse* (summit). In Spiti names of two places or monasteries of Tangyut and Dankhar end with the word *rtse,* and they are geographically located so. Therefore the reference, even if the inscriptions were found at Kaza, might be taken for Dankhar, as the inscription itself tells that there existed a palace of the Ladaki kings, which always had been at Dankhar.

ii. Dangkhar: Dankhar has been capital of the state since the earliest time known. There was mKhar, castle, residence of Kharpon, the representatives of the kings of Ladak. The castle also functioned as fort and there was also a monastery. Visitors to the place have been fascinated by its unique location and view. Trebeck, when he visited in 1822, drew a realistic drawing of the whole perspective to incorporate it in his famous work with Moorcroft.

Lyall describes the capital of Spiti stating that it is a large village, 12774 feet above the sea built on a spur or bluff which stands out into the main valley and ends in a precipice, columns of a hard conglomerate. On the top of the hill is a large house known as, the fort, which with some cultivated lands attached belongs to government. Lower down is a large monastery. The aspect of the whole place is very picturesque. It has been the seat of government of the country from time immemorial. Gerard (1841) counted here forty houses. Importance of Dankhar was reduced after the Ladaki officers vacated the capital and during the British it became deserted. They had no official who would stay there. Egerton says that the Nono keeps his record office in the fort here and always comes here when he has a case to try. Presently Dankhar is known for its monastery. Kaza has taken over the place of Dankhar.

Dankhar, commonly written in local literature as Brang-mkhar and Grang-mkhar-rtse, the most important name in the history of Spiti, is found expressed in a number of ways. There is no variation and ambiguity in writing and meaning of the second and third parts of the name, *mkhar* (= castle, fort), and *rtse* (= summit). But the former part is found written in a number ways although following the single voice of *grang*. These are: *grog* = ant, ravine; *sgreng*= straight, upright; *brang*= breast; *brag* =

rock; *grang* = cold, etc. These appellations appear to attempt to describe an outstanding geographical feature of the place. Hugh Whistler interprets it as 'cold fort' and Schlagintweit as 'steep or vertical fort'. A nineteenth century local document associated with the place writes the name as Grang-mkhar (Ann. II-D). But when we take into consideration the writings on the point from two most reliable local documents, all the above explanations seem to loose significance. One of them issued under the seal of the Kharpon, resident at Dankhar, belonging to the medieval period, and the other one from Pin, express it unexptectedly as Yang-mkhar, meaning 'the other castle', (Annx. 2-I-A & 2-II-B). Authenticity of the documents is unquestionable. This may be taken as the original form of the name which might have been given by the Raja of Ladak, the ruler of Spiti, as his other residence or the second to that of Leh.

It appears that Dankhar was founded by the kings of Ladak. They selected the site for a fort and palace, looking at its strategic importance. Taking into consideration the above facts together, it may be assumed that after the place was selected by the Ladaki authorities as proper for founding the capital, the *mkhar,* castle cum fort, might have have been constructed. Thus the place became settled and came to be recognized as *mkhar* which was located on a *rtse*. Thereafter other establishments like the monastery might have come into existence.

Traditional Administrative Divisions

Spiti was under Ladak for long time and before it passed on into the hands of British administration it was under the rule of the Dogras. The representative officers of the Raja of Ladak resided at Dankhar. The Nono of Kyuling was the local chief responsible for collection of revenue and in assisting the Ladaki officials. Trebeck despite his prolonged stay, is completely silent on the subject of Nono.

Gerard observes that there were three divisions of Spiti: Mane, Pin and Losar, and each one was under the charge of an officer called Lafa. It may be construed that the main valley was divided into two parts of Losar and Mane as Pin forms a separate valley. The instance of division of the main valley into two parts of Losar and Mane, which villages, however, had never been of much historical significance, and the fact belonging only to a couple of decades before, seems unfounded. The relevant form of the term Lafa may be rendered as *las-pa* (worker). Las-pa was a village level worker in Pin. JD Cunningham also explains the term similarly saying that 'Lafa is the title of the deputy of the head-man of the village, and he was a very small functionary'. During the British period two offices of a messenger and a policeman in Pin valley were designated as *laspa* (worker).The informations of Gerard do not seem to be based on authentic source.

Major Hay, before he was appointed Assistant Commissioner, Kullu, visited Spiti in 1849 and prepared a report on the status of the district. He says that the area is divided into five kothis. Gazetteer of 1898 gives detail of the kothis and names of the villages comprised in various kothis as follows:

i. **Kothi Chhoezhi:** Pangmo, Tabo, Kyomo, Sumling, Komak, Ki, Khurik, Langza, Lithang, Losar, Morang, Hanse, Hal, and Yikhyim.

ii. **sTod:** Tashigang, Kyikhyim, Rangrik, Sumling, Khurik, Kibar and Kyoto.

iii. **Bar or Barshik:** Tsuprang, Gyungal, Rama, Sanglung, Sumling, Kaze, Gowang, Khurik, Kyuling, Lara and Lhalung.

iv. **Sham:** Dang-khar, Rama, Lari, Lithang, Mane-Gongma and Mane Yogma,

v. **Pin:** Pharpa, Totnam, Tingti, Tiling, Tsut, Siling, Sangnam, Gungri, Guling, Khar and Mut.

There are 49 villages named here. But actually they are 44, since names of some villages are repeated and they find place in more than one kothi. Local tradition divides the five kothis equally, each constituting fifty households, saying *nga-bchu nga,* five fifties, i.e. five divisions of fifty households each.

Waziri and Kothi: Major Hay reports the administrative situation existing in his time saying that, 'The revenue of Spiti has hitherto been collected by a Vazir (hereditary); whatever revenue is required has been levied equally from the five kothis; in the collection, he is assisted by the Gatpos, or Mukhias. The Vazir holds the village of 'Kiuling' in Jaghir' (Hay, 1850: 437-438). Wazir, of course, here refers to Nono of Kyuling. We hear the terms of Wazir, Waziri and Kothi in respect of Spiti for the first time from Major Hay and the Gazetteers later on use them regularly. No European traveler before him has noticed these terms. Trebeck, who stayed here for two months and similarly prepared a comprehensive report on the status of the district, does not make any mention of the above terms. Nor we meet with any of the terms in any local source.

These administrative terms are germane to the state of Kullu. The system of division of the area into Waziri etc. existed in Kullu and not in Ladak. Therefore it could not have originated under Ladaki rule under whom Spiti remained for long time. However, in the history of Kullu or that of Spiti there is no instance to show Kullu ever having had held an independent control over Spiti, not to speak of reasonably long enough time to reorganize the area into divisions of kothis, etc., although Kullu shared in a small measure in the collection of contribution from Spiti regularly and Kullu claimed in proxy Spiti as one of its Waziri.

The highest point of influence of Kullu power in its history over Spiti appears in the time of Raja Man Singh (1688-1719). He was a great warrior and he invaded Spiti with a larger motive. He fixed the boundary of Lahul with Ladak at Phalong Danda on the plain of Lingti. Then he turned to Spiti and, overrunning the whole region and plundering on a considerable scale, returned home but did not annex it, as remarks Hardyal (Tobdan, 2000: 87). Spiti during this time was under Ladak which was in quite strong position. Therefore Kullu could not have interfered further. However, Man Singh must have been able to persuade the Ladaki rulers for a small fixed amount of taxaction from Spiti which amount continued to be paid to Kullu till the time Spiti was taken over by the British. Ostensibly Kullu never had any opportunity to apply its conditions over Spiti. These terms of Wazir, Waziri and kothi for Spiti might have been coined by Major Hay. As these terms were found convenient to use in comparison to the local terms which were hard to pronounce, they were adopted promptly and permanently. The Gazetteers and others thereafter are found using only these terms. The British also did not attempt to reorganize the divisions even though traditionally the fifth kothi, kothi Chhoszhi, was spread over covering the areas of existing three kothis in the main valley and it itself had no separate geographical area of its own.

The boundaries of the administrative divisions, by whatever name they were known, remained the same under all the rulers viz. the Ladaki, Dogra and the British. The local name for a division was 'gZhi' for we find this epithet surviving in use with the names of at least two divisions viz. Chhos-gzhi and Barshik, i.e. 'Bar-gzhi', the divisions of Chhos and Bar.

The division of Spiti into four natural parts as seen above appears to have remained unchanged since its origin since time immemorial. The main valley is divided into three parts of sTod, Bar and Sham, i.e. the upper, middle and lower. The names just indicate the position of the parts of the geographical sections. Pin is a separate valley. No attempt appears to have been made to propose any particular name for them. Thereafter when the necessity of the eccliastic class increased the fifth division,

Chhoszhi, might have been created. Chhoszhi has no compact geographical area and the villages falling in it are spread in three divisions falling in the main valley. Chhoszhi, which literally means 'religious establishment', had special objective of making conbtribution of *bun,* revenue, to the five big monasteries. The households of the division were exempted from the payment of revenue. This must have been done with the full knowledge and consent of the kings of Ladak. The monastery of Pin was mostly supported by the residents of the Pin valley.

Of the five big monasteries of Spiti, Kyi was founded latest upon the advent of the Reformed Sect into the valley in the mid fifteenth century. The division of Chhoszhi may be presumed to have been founded sometime thereafter.

Prehistoric Spiti

Megalithic Sites: It has been reported that a site of megalithic type has been found on the Kunzom pass and that on this wide space of the pass, with almost the dimensions of a plateau are a number of standing stones most of which have collapsed or been displaced by the snow; a considerable number, however, are still *in situ*. This is not merely a *lha-tho,* cairn, which are still regularly erected on the highest points of mountain passes. A considerable number of them are entirely covered with large slabs of stone and boulders. The site was visited by a team from the Archaeological Survey of India in 1999 and re-examined, and perhaps they also found burial sites and potsherds. Similar finding in Chhota Dara has been referred to already. Francke had gathered a blunt old stone axe (7 by 6 and half inches), used for breaking wood, from Spiti (Francke, 1926-I: 113).

Rock Carvings: Tabo, besides the famous Chhoskhor, inherits another important monument. There are a number of ancient drawings on rocks, similar to those found in Ladak and Zanskar, said to have been around a hundred in number but now left only between twenty and thirty. The big red boulders containing the carvings lie close to each other in a cluster and are partly embedded in the earth. The site lies on a plateau, on the right bank of the river Spiti, on which the monastery and the village are located. Similar carvings are reported to exist in Lhari and one or two other villages.The finds of the rock carvings are confined to lower Spiti.

Francke notes that at Tabo there are countless rock carvings. They represent mostly ibex and the svastika and are possibly of pre-Buddhist origin. He also found many similar rock carvings at Lhari, which in particular, he observed are ibex and svastika. One of the carvings, says Francke, appears to represent the 'willow of the world', with its six branches and six roots, one of the symbols of the pre-Buddhist religion of the people. Another symbol appears to represent the sun and the moon (Francke, 1926-I: 37-38). Handa has reproduced a few photographs with long explanations. He divides the whole group into three classes, and writes, 'The Tabo rock-carvings may be grouped in three different categories on thematic and stylistic considerations which may define sequential stages in the evolution of native Bon-pa society from the ritual-ridden primitivism to the nomadic system which till recently had been the mainstay of Spitian livelihood. The earliest and the most primitive ones may be those carvings in which, ibex is depicted either singly or on herds essentially as a cult device'. 'In the second group may be placed those carvings in which stylised anthropomorphic representations have been depicted prominently in the main field. In the carvings of the latest stage may be defined those few carvings in which horses and panthers are depicted' (Handa, 1994: 148-153).

The graffiti found in Zanskar are estimated to be around 2000 years old. There they appear to exhibit specimens of more than one culture following one after the other and continueing to and connecting with the present culture.

The Spiti rock carvings differ somewhat from those found in Zanskar, Ladak and Jangthang. The carvings here appear to belong to one culture and is widely separated by time space from the present culture. As may be observed from the specimens now remaining in Tabo, the subjects relate to the local environment. The carvings are mostly of domestic animals like horse, sheep, goat, dog and wild animals like ibex, deer, etc. but none carnivorous could be observed.

In one of the drawings there is a mare with a colt behind it and a man in front of them. Both the animals have their tails stretched. In another picture there is a dog, with tail curved upwards. The parts of its body are in right proportion. A man is standing in the front, as if touching the sniffing animal at its nose. The two men standing before the mare and the dog, are smaller in size in proportion to the figures of the animals. At the same level on the right side is another animal like a goat or could be an ibex. One is a deer. The existing graffitis of Tabo have secular subjects and none is religious. Among the existing specimens from Tabo, swastika, and some other complex compositions, as observed by Francke, cannot be discerned.

The Early Settlers: About Ladak and Zanskar it is stated that bronze-age hunters penetrated the valley and left their mark on stones near what were probably hunting camps found at several sites in the valley; these might have been summer visitors. The study of the petroglyphs from these areas suggest, it is told, that their creators were steppe peoples of Central Asia who lived between Kazakstan and China from Bronze Age until the fourth century before Christ. Luciano Petech assumes that Dardic peoples lived in the area prior to its Tibetanisation around the seventh century CE and that these people were converted to Buddhism under the influence of the culture of the Kashmir valley. Dainelli on the basis of anthropometric measurements argues that the Dards filtered into Ladakh from the West fusing with or replacing an earlier Indo-European stratum of inhabitants often known as the 'Mon'. He further suggests that the later invasion by Tibetan peoples from the east produced the higher frequency of Mongol characteristics in the east than in the west of this country. In neither case it is supposed that eastward (Dardic) and later westward (Tibetan) movements replaced totally the original stock. The society of Ladak is composed of classes each of which retains its original characteristics of the time of its advent. We cannot say if the same culture extended towards Spiti. It might be that for some aspects of the history of Spiti for this period one may have to look towards the areas in Central Asia. But to a greater extent Spiti in the pre-hisoric period probably shared in its history with those of its neighbours in the high Himalayas like in the upper valleys of Sutlej, Sindhu, Chanderbhaga, etc. It is known that some graves belonging to the pre-historic period have been found in Ladak, Lahul, Kinnaur and Kumaon. But no such discovery is reported from Spiti. However, it is surrounded by these regions from three sides.

Gold country: Hieun Tsiang writes that on the north of Brahmpura, which forms a part of the existing state of Uttrakhand, is situated the country called Su-fa-la-nakiu-ta-lo (Suvarnagotra) and from there comes a superior sort of gold and hence the name. Varahmihira's reference to a country named Suvarnabhu, which the author classes among the countries like Brahmpur, Kuluta, Cheen, Kashmir, etc. falling in the direction of Ishan, north-east of India, is also usually identified with the same area of gold-country. The region is also identified with the Kimpurush or Kimpurushavasha of the ancient Indian literature. This area near the renowned Kailash mountain and Mansarovar lake is usually identified with the area of ancient pre-Tibetan Zhang-zhung, later known as Guge and mNgaris. To the states lying on the Indian side and speaking Indian languages, it was known by various names viz. Hieundesh (Himvata, country of snow), Un-desh (wool country), Hun-desh (country of the Huns) and Goggadesh (the Guge country). Suvarnagotra lay on the neighbourhood of Spiti.

Kinnars: According to the ancient and classical Indian literature of all the three great religious traditions of Brahminism, Buddhism and Jainism the regions of mount Kailash and lake Mansarovar were inhabited by the tribes like *yaksha*, *gandharva* and *kinnars*, who were related to each other. Everything about them is not myth as has been shown in some of the scriptures. Among all of them the habitation of the *Kinnars* was spread more widely which comprised the higher reaches on both sides of the Himalayan slopes in the west and the middle. The parts of the river heads of Sindhu, Satluj, Chandarbhaga, Ganga, Jamuna, and Karnali comprised in the area. Kiratas were their neighbours. All the tribes living along these areas in the border countries recognized as Kinnar and Kirata in the Indian terminology were known in Tibetan tradition as Mon. In the eyes of both these great cultures the Mons or Kinnars were backward and inferior. The area might have included Ladak, Zanskar, Spiti, Lahul and Kinnaur and much beyond extending towards the east to Uttrakhand and Nepal, and to the west to Gilgit and Baltistan. That the *kinnars* have been inhabiting the high Himalaya since ancient times may be best illustrated from an old Jataka story from the Buddhist tradition.

The Kinnar and Canda-Parvata

Chanda-Kinnara Jataka of the Buddhist Jataka stories narrates the Buddha in his one of the previous births as Boddhisattva in the life of Kinnar. While the Lord, Tathagata Buddha, himself was named Kinnar, his spouse Yashodhara was named Chanda, Moon. They were born among the *kinnars* and lived on Chanda-Parvata in the Himalaya. The names of the characters in the story and the geographical setting in which the story was set up gives an indication that in the time when the plot of the story was set, the Kinnars lived there or there was a belief about their having had lived in those areas in the former times.

Chanda-Parvata may be identified to have been located somewhere in Lahul. Although there is no such mountain named in Lahul or in whole of the Himalaya, there are certain geographical marks associated with the name Chanda which testify to the presence of a mountain so named. There is the river Chandra, and the lake named Chandertal from which the river Chandra emanates. Then there is the river Chanderbhaga, the united rivers of Chandra and Bhaga.These landmarks indicate that a mountain named similarly viz. Chanda existed among them. There are also literary evidences of the presence of the Kinnars there. The Chandrabhaga valley has been mentioned in another ancient Buddhist scripture to have been inhabited by the Kinnars. The inhabitants of Kinnaur, who are identified as Kinnars in the Indian history, do not live much far away from Lahul. Spiti is located between Lahul and Kinnaur. The habitation of the Kinnars might have been quite extensive including all these areas and the areas around the mount Kailash and lake Mansarovar (Tobdan, 2010: 239-243).

Canda-parvata, although does not actually exist today, is name of a real mountain. Monier-Williams, quoting the same term Candra-parvata, from a different source, translates it as 'Moon-mountain', and he means by it a 'name of a mountain' (Monier-Williams, 1899: 386-387). Spiti being more exposed, the Kinnars of the Spiti and Guge might have been constrained to yield to the migrating much powerful waves of races from the eastern direction.

The legend of the Lady of Chandertal: An interesting folkstory is related in Spiti connected with the lake Chandertal. It is told that once long ago a shepherd from the village of Rangrig used to take the flock of his sheep for grazing in the meadows near the lake of Chandertal. The shepherd was skilful in playing on flute and he enjoyed playing on the shore of the clear Moon-lake. In the lake there lived a *khadoma* (colloquially *khandoma*), *dakini*, a semi-goddess. The *khadoma* could not resist the attraction of the enchanting melody of the flute echoeing over the calm surface of the ethereal lake. She became a regular visitor to the lake to listen to the music. One day as the shepherd was playing on flute the *khadoma* appeared before him in the earthly appearance. Then they met in this manner regularly. Meanwhile they had a handsome boy out of the union and they became very happy. The *khadoma* had instructed and had obtained vow from the shepherd not to disclose the secrecy to anybody else.

One day the shepherd, who was already a married man, was at his home in the village and had an argument with his wife. In the course of the row he argued that he had a *khadoma* living in the Moon-lake as his spouse and before her she was insignificant. The wife challenged him to bring her home. The shepherd accepting the challenge went to the lake and started playing the flute as usual. The *khadoma* appeared with the child who then was infected with a severe skin disease and was looking very ugly. She handed over the child to the shepherd and she herself disappeared in the lake never to be seen again. The heavenly relationship of love came to an end in this manner. It is told that the descendants of the deseased child still live in Rangrig, above the village (Chhopel Dorje).

Expansion of Tibetan Empire: Srong brtsan sgampo consolidated the numerous small states into one Tibetan Union and around the second quarter of the seventh century expanded towards all the directions laying foundation to a strong empire. During the middle of seventh century they conquered small kingdoms in the Tibet-Sinkiang and Nepal borders. King Khri-srong lde-brtsan, who came to the throne in 755 CE again resumed the military expeditions. In 838 Ralpachan (815-38) was succeeded by his brother who reinstated Bon and persecuted Buddhism. During these times waves of migrations towards the west might have rippled one after the other. These were the early and great moments of expansion of Tibetan race and culture towards the west. Spiti might have been substantially influenced by all these long abiding movements. Many factors attracted the migrants to the west continuously.

Kullu and Spiti: Some traditions gathered from Kullu reveal that in the ancient times there was close contact between Spiti and Kullu. The two countries share a long common border formed by a high mountain range. Communication with each other was affected at least through two passes through which the shepherds, traders and other commuters passed regularly. The road starting at Jagatsukh in the upper Kullu valley passed through the villages of Prini and Hamta and crossing the Hamta Pass reached Chhatru or Old Khoksar in the Chandra valley. The route is straight and shorter than the modern route across Rohtang and Kunzom passes. It had great importance due to the linkage of Kullu with the commercially important regions of wool country like Undesh or Goggadesh, beyond Spiti, as the areas of Jangthang and Guge were known to the people of Kullu then. This route was actively followed till the Independence. The other route, equally important, connected the Parvati valley of Kullu with Pin valley in Spiti.

The kingdom of Kullu was founded by Bihangmanipal, a migrant prince, whose time is assumed to be circa first century CE. Jagatsukh was his capital. The prince in order to establish himself had to first uproot the existing chiefs including some called as Pitti Thakurs, the Chiefs from Spiti.

A few more references from Kullu shows Spiti in the early period of its history in a prominent position. The authors of the History of Punjab Hill States maintain, on the authority of the Vanshavali of Kullu that in very early times Spiti was probably ruled by the Rajas of a Hindu dynasty bearing the surname or suffix of 'Sena' and Kulu remained tributary to Spiti for two reigns.

Historians narrate that, 'during the reign of Raja Rudar Pal of Kullu, Chamba is said to have conquered Lahul and about the same time Kullu was invaded and subdued by the Raja of Spiti. The two invasions were simultaneous and probably Spiti and Chamba were allies in this invasion, which was made through Lahul. Now this is just almost the period when reference to Spiti are found in the Kulu annals, and two Rajas of Spiti are mentioned by name bearing the Sen suffix. One of these, named Rajendar Sen, is said to have involved Kulu and made it tributary, in the reign of Raja Rudar Pal 600-650 A.D.'. They were also allies in the subsequent war in which Parsidh Pal was the victor. Kullu then seems to have remained tributary to Spiti during this reign and that of Hamir Pal, the next Raja, the tribute money amounting to six annas in the rupee of yearly revenue. But on Hamir Pal's death, his son Parsidh Pal declined to continue the payment of tribute, and moved out with an army to oppose Chet Sen, the Spiti Chief. The battle was fought somewhere near Rotang Pass, and Parsidh Pal was victorious thus freeing itself from the dominion of Spiti.

The authors presume that in those early times Spiti must have been possessed of considerable resources and may have included in its dominion at least the Bashahar and Kulu Pandrabis Kothis on the right bank of the Satluj. Communication from Pin to Outer Saraj tract via the Bhabeh and Rupin Passes, along the right side of the Satluj, was not difficult, and the modern Rampur Shimla Road was not necessarily the line followed in early times.

In the temple of Parasu Ram at Nirmand in Outer Saraj, Kullu, there is a copper-plate deed granted by a Raja named Samudra Sena, and assigned on paleographic grounds to the seventh century. On the possible supposition the authors referred to above attribute the copper-plate to a Spiti Raja. They write, 'It seems not improbable that the copper plate referred to may have been granted by one of the earlier Rajas, bearing the name of Samudra Sena. Soon after the defeat by Parsidh Pal, Spiti was invaded by the Tibetans, and the pre-Buddhist Hindu dynasty was then probably overthrown. In this war Ladakh was aided by Sansar Pal of Kulu, and he received three villages in Spiti for the assistance, while the sons of Chet Sen, the Spiti Raja, were assigned a *jagir* (Hutchison and Vogel, 1920: 159). The authors of the Antiquities of Himachal Pradesh endorse the whole sequence of events regarding the Nirmand Copper-plate. They maintain that even in that early period in the time of Rudra Pal the tract around the Hamta pass was in the possession of the Piti Thakurs, as they are known to the compiler of the *Vansavali*. They made many incursions into the Kullu valley. Their names ended in Sena then one immediately thinks of the Sena family of Nirmand of the sixth-seventh century with names such as Varunasena, Sanjyasena, Rai Sena and Samudra Sena (Postel, 1985: 25). Handa suggests that the Nirmand copper-plate by inference points out to the existence of esoteric Buddhism prior to seventh century CE in Spiti and Kurpan valley in Saraj, where Nirmand is located (Handa, 1994:36). Evidence of the existence of pre-Lamaistic Buddhism in these parts of the Satluj valley has not come up yet.

Parsidh Pal of Kullu was followed by Harichand Pal, Subhat Pal, Som Pal and Sansar Pal. According to the chronicle another interesting event occurs in Sansar Pal's reign. It is said that sometime after Chet Sen's defeat by Kulu, Spiti was invaded by Gya mur orr presumably Ladakh or Rubshu, and the chief of Spiti was defeated and slain. The ruler of Gya mur orr then granted some villages in *jagir* to the chief's son, and three villages to Sansar Pal of Kulu, who assisted him, retaining the remainder of Spiti in his own hands. Possibly this note records the final overthrow and extinction of the pre-Buddhist Hindu dynasty in Spiti, when the country passed under Tibetan rule. Captain Harcourt is said to have reported that coins of this dynasty have been found in the valley but this has not been verified. Reference to Spiti in the Vansavali of Kullu compiled later on by Hardyal is met with for the first time in the period of Man Singh who invaded Spiti. Stories about the Piti Thakurs can be heard in Jagatsukh even these days which however may relate to some later period.

Jamlu of Hansa: Hansa is residence of a folk deity named Dabla Shagrtse. He is also identified with the Jamlu of Malana in Kullu. One story tells that Jamlu of Malana originally came to Malana from Spiti. At Hamta near Prini there is a temple dedicated to Jamlu where the devoties from Spiti pay their obeisance to the deity and they are not prohibited from going into the temple premises wearing shoes. Spiti possesses some other customs related to the tradition.

Zhang-zhung and Spiti: The regions around the mount Kailash and lake Mansarovar and the upper regions of Satluj and Sindhu has been known in the past by various names like Zhangzhung, mNgaris, Guge, etc. The areas were important commercially for from there came the valuable articles of trade like gold, precious stones, wool, pashmina, sheep of good quality, salt, borax, etc. and reached in the lower areas of the Himalayas and the Indian plains and in exchange were sent goods of produce and manufacture of these regions. Traders thronged from all the directions and Spiti was necessarily involved in the activities along with the numerous other groups of traders.

Division of mNgaris: sKyid-lde Nyima-mgon, son of dPal-khor-btsan (d. circa 910), fled from Tibet to mNgaris sTod, built a castle at Purang called Nyi-zung and lived there. He married two wives Pa-tsha-ba-za and Cho-ro-za. From Cho-ro-za he had three sons dPal lde rig pa mgon, bKra-shis lde mgon and lDe-tsug mgon. After his death the kingdom was divided among the three of his sons in about middle of the tenth century CE. Each became an independent king. The general agreement among the various sources is that the three divisions were Mang-yul (Ladak), Purang and Zhang-zhung. In some references it occurs that Zanskar and Spiti formed a separate kingdom. The Chronicles of Ladak record, "The younger lDe-gtsug-mgon received Zanskar sgo gsum, sPi-ti spi lcogs....". From here one Shak Thubpa migrated to Padum and then he became ruler of the whole of Zanskar.

The Age of Rinchhen Zangpo: Rinchhen Zangpo (958-1055), the great translator was born in Guge. He began his studies from his childhood and venerated many teachers. Then he went to Kashmir and studied under many learned *pandits*. Besides translating many Sanskrit books himself into Tibetan, he got prepared and trained a class of translators. He got constructed many monasteries where he conducted *Chhoskhor* and brought *lotsavas* and *pandits* together and laid foundation of a great tradition. Tabo is attributed to Rinchhen Zangpo. Lhalung belongs to his tradition. The force of the movement must have continued after him for long period. Besides many other small monasteries, which have disappeared, are attributed to Rinchhen Zangpo.

Spiti and Ladak

Spiti had been continuously under Ladak since long unknown time. It must have occurred quite early. Bashahar and Kullu, the strong neighbouring states of Spiti, were the competitors of Ladak. bLa-chhen Utpala (c. 1125-1150) was a predominant ruler among the early kings of Ladak and the period of his reign was the earliest occasion in the history of Ladak, when it could annex Spiti to its territory, as it did with some other trerritories. He is said to have united the forces of Upper and Lower Ladak and subjugated all the vassal chiefs. As regards the expansion of Ladaki power, the Ladaki Chronicles maintain that bLa-chhen Utpala in the early period of his reign invaded Nyung-ti (Kullu) and extorted from its king a treaty by which Kullu was bound to pay tribute perpetually. The conquest included gLo-bo (Mustang in Nepal), Purang, etc. Lahul is not mentioned among the areas conquered, but it is presumed that Lahul also came under Ladak from this time. Lahul lies between Ladak and Kullu. Thus Spiti too might have come under Ladak and once it became tied up with Ladak it continued to remain under its rule till the modern times. But the character of the Ladaki rule was lax. In this regard it is remarked that, 'Spiti was left very much to itself. The administration of the Leh Governor was loose.' 'Spiti seems always to have been at the mercy of its neighbours, especially Ladak, Bashahar and Kullu.'

Zainul Abidin

Rajtarangini records that Zainul Abidin, the king of Kashmir (1420-1470) invaded Goggadesh (Guge) and saved a golden image of the Buddha from the hands of the Yavanas (Muhammadans) in Saya-Desa and took over Kuluta (Kullu) which apparently at that time was occupied by Ladak. It is presumed that the expedition mentioned in the above stanza took place sometime in the last or fifth decade of Zainu'l-Abidin's reign i.e. between 1460 and 1470 CE. Vogel's note maintains that Kuluta was probably occupied by Ladak at that time which is in agreement with Ladaki history. The king of Kuluta was in a loose way a vassal of the kings of Leh. The route taken by Zain ul-Abidin was that taken by the Ladaki king, Tshe dbang rnam rgyal, later on when he went to Guge and Purang and returned to Ladak by way of Kulu and Lahul.' Spiti too most probably might have been involved in the imbroglio.

Piti Thakurs in Kulu

Mr. Howell while he was Assistant Commissioner in Kullu, gathered that in the 16th century CE certain forts above the Kullu valley like Jagatsukh, Bamar, Dirot, Diabangi, Guwari and several above Chhaki Nala were held by the widely known Piti Thakurs. At Jagatsukh the remains of the fort were visible clearly on a spur above the village. 'His place of worship was the Prini temple at the foot of the approach to the Hamta pass of the great god Jamlu. In this temple to this day alone of all the temples in Kulu the Spiti men go to make offerings; all other races must take their shoes off in the temple precincts, but lamaists go in fully shod'. In fact the Piti Thakurs held the left bank of the Beas with the approaches to the Hamta and Chandarkhani passes, and all the by-paths by which these could have been turned. Their "forward policy" was no doubt a sheer necessity, if they were to protect their trade' (Howell, 1918: 71).

Hutchison and Vogel note that 'The Tibetans of Spiti seem to have been in the habit of making incursions into Kulu and they seized territory to the south of the high passes, but being unable to live at a lower altitude than 7000 to 8000 feet they never advanced into the main. They were still in possession as late as the reign of Sidh Singh, A.D. 1500' (1933-II: 432-433). They further presume that there can be little doubt that the trade route was in use in the time of Sidh Singh and that the Tibetan officers called by the Kullu people, Piti Thakur, held control of the country through which it passed. Their hold must have been strengthened by an invasion of Kullu from Ladak, about 1500 CE during the reign of Tshewang Namgyal I in 1530 by whom Kullu was subdued and its chiefs were made to feel weight of his arm. It was probably soon after this invasion that the Tibetan officers or petty chiefs were finally driven out of Kullu by Sidh Singh, and we hear no more of them. In Kullu some families are found settled in different villages tracing their origin from Spiti.

The Ladaki Rule: Evidences confirming Ladaki rule over Spiti start becoming available from sixteenth century onwards almost continuously.

The earliest evidence of the Ladaki rule over Spiti relates to Tashi Namgyal (1555-1575). This is from Spiti itself (Ann. II-B). The document is a colophon to a religious work from a private house which was copied during the ceremony performed after the death of a person in the household. According to it Tashi Namgyal, king of Ladak, resides at Leh in his palace named 'sPang-'gang-rtse'. The palace of Singe Namgyal was known as 'sLel-chhen rtse'. Petech writes that Tashi Namgyal erected images at bLe-chhen sPang-gang (Leh). Francke has shown in his work on the History of Ladak a photograph of the palace of the king in ruins. Gaga sTanpa rGya-mtsho is Kharpon who ruled over Spiti and resided at Yang-mkhar-rtse i.e. Dankhar. Gaga Thubs-stan is Kharpon of Pin who resides in the palace in Pin. These are references that we learn from the formal salutations offered to the concerned authorities. It is notable that there is no reference to either the Nono of Kyuling or that of Guling. But possibly the Kharpon of Pin might have been from the family of Nono of Guling. The Kharpons are addressed as Gaga and the Kharpon appointed in Pin is the only instance. Dankhar is written as Yang-mkhar-rtse. Howell's Munshi is reported to have similarly found at Kyi a *farmana,* certificate, issued by the Ladaki king Tashi Namgyal concerning the application of funds collected at the Kyi monastery.

Another evidence, an inscription from Alchi, Ladak, describes the feats of Tashi Namgyal and says, "you have defeated your enemies of Mon-kha, the Hor and others. From Rudok and Spiti as far as Suru and Dras, upto Nang gong, Nubra and Zangskar, the realm of Nga-ri is under your dominion" (Snellgrove and Tude, 1980-II: 149). Tucci found a colophon at Brang-mkhar which mentions the name of king Tshedbang rNam-rgyal (1575-1595) and his minister 'Bum-pa-lde (Petech, 1977: 32). Gergan writes that this king in 1580 changed the date of celebrating the

New Year festival in Ladak. At that time the Dung-'gyur of Lhalung in Spiti was also founded. Singe Namgyal (1590 to 1642) reigned from Bu-ran, Guge, Zans-dkar, Spyiti, and Burig, as far as the Maryum pass in the east. He is said to have assigned the monastery of Tashigang to the lamas of Pin. During this period we observe Ladak in strong position and defeated the king of Guge. We have evidences of series of names of Kharpon posted by the Ladaki kings at Dankhar confirming the Ladaki rule over Spiti.

Senge Namgyal had three sons bDe ldan rnam rgyal, Indra Bhoti-rnam-rgyal and bDe mchog rnam-rgyal. lDe-ldan Namgyal (1642-1694) united under his sway Guge, Ruthog, Spiti, etc. In around 1648 the administration of the kingdom of Ladak was divided among three brothers. The eldest one became king of Ladak. The second one according to the teacher sTag tshang's advice was made ruler of Guge. The youngest brother bDe mchog rnam rgyal received Spiti and Zanskar and he ruled there. Dechhog Namgyal issued a decree under his seal from Dankhar (Ann. I-A). Thereafter we find evidences which prove Ladak governing over Spiti continuously. It has already been stated above that Tucci found a group of inscriptions with the name of the king Nyima Namgyal (1694-1729) at mKhar-rtse, stated to be at Kaza (Kaja).

The Decree of Dechhog Namgyal was issued by the Kharpon Namkha Gyaltshan from Dankhar in context of levying certain kind of revenue and its allocation among the astrologer and the monastery of Pin. The document may be dated as 1671 CE. There is another document available (Ann. II-C) relating to the rule of Dechhog Namgyal. This document says that the palace of Dankhar (now spelt as Brang-mkhar) belongs to king Dechhog Namgyal and Namgkha Gyaltshan, who is now elevated to the post of Kahlon, resides here. This is the only instance that a Kahlon is stationed at Dankhar. The document was evidently prepared during the reign of Dechhog Namgyal, but some years after the first one as above which was composed in 1671. The present document does not give any date, but may be placed at 1680.

The Tibeto-Mughal War of 1681-83

In the last quarter of the seventeenth century Ladak was involved in a grave entanglement which developed into an international war and resultantly put Ladak at a great loss and much weakened. The war remained active for almost three years from 1681 to 1683. Ladak lost in the war a considerable portion of its territory including the whole of Guge. Petech informs that the cession of territory included also Spiti. Spiti soon returned under the loose suzerainty of Ladak (Petech, 1977: 78-79). Spiti then indeed fell in the share of Bashahar, an ally of Gadan Tshewang in the war. A similar reference by Gerard that Bashahar possessed Dankhar fort for two years some fifty-five years back (Gerard, 1841: 147), agrees undoubtedly with the above fact. A faint reference to the occasion also comes from Trebeck who notes that Spiti is said to have been formerly included in Bishahar, 'subsequent to the Lassen conquest of Chan-than (Moorcroft, 1841-II: 67). After this war the wool trade of the Trans-Himalaya came under the control of Kashmir and Bashahar.

The whole of the above narration may be compared with that given by JD Cunningham whose description is based on oral sources. It is a typical example of folkway of preserving history. The historical facts of various periods keep on rolling into a single legend and changing the flavor of the story with the progress of the time. Events are mostly actual but they are misplaced and jumbled up, much of them indistinguishable. He writes that Jangthang, having headquarters at Tsaparang, was then an independent kingdom ruled by a Hindu Rajput Raja, whose kingdom included Spiti. The king in a war with the Ladakis called Lhasa in aid. But before the arrival of the reinforcement, the king was killed or he died. The Lhasa force advanced and expelled the Ladakis but as Tsaparang family was extinct the Lhasa authorities retained the country in their own hands. A treaty was formed with the Ladaki Raja and he married the daughter of the Lhasa Commander. 'The district of Pitti was given to Ladakh as the bride's dowery and twenty houses in the neighbourhood of Menser or Misser were added to it. A Raja named Kehar Singh of Bissahir, was at this time on a pilgrimage to the Mansorovar lake; he formed a friendship with the Lhasa leader and perhaps gave his countenance to the usurpation of Chapran; for this time two villages on the left bank of the Pitti river are said to have fallen under Bisseher' (JD Cunningham, 1844-148: 231). Cunningham assumes this event to have occurred towards the beginning of the last century i.e. of eighteenth century. He also adds, according to another version, that Spiti was given to Ladak on a different occasion.

Spiti and the War

Although the position of Spiti was very insignificant in comparison to the states involved in the above referred international war, yet Spiti could not escape the events and it had to show its presence. We find no direct evidence to the fact but an old song, which is almost oblivious, has preserved the picture safely and distinctly.

These days we know a very popular and entertaining song current specially among the younger generation in Ladak and the adjoining areas of Zanskar, Lahul, Spiti and Kinnaur, the initial words of which are 'no-mo ang-mo le, si-ki ang-mo le.' This song borrows the initial sentence, a part of the theme and the melody in whole from an old song from Spiti. The song is charmingly melodious and captivating. The new song is found at least in two versions, and the compositions are not comparable in vigor with that of the original. People rarely know that there exists an old song in Spiti and that these new songs have originated from it.

No-mo dbang-mo lags, No-no gnyis-kod lags: Song commemorating the war

The song from Spiti indicates involvement of Spiti in the war, (Ann.3-A). The story depicts the scene of departure of two princes of the family of Nono of Spiti to the war in Ladak. Their sister is bidding them farewell. The three characters are: two brothers, Phuntsog and Dondub, one elder and the other younger, and one sister named Siki Angmo (Shis-skyid dbang-mo), who in age falls between her two departing brothers. Since the two brothers are addressed as No-no, they certainly belong to the family of the chiefs of Spiti. The three are standing at the door of their own palace and their sister is bidding farewell to her two beloved brothers. The intelligent and sympathetic sister gives some advice to her two brothers as to how to go to the war, how the way is, etc. It is a conversation between the two brothers and their sister.

Siki Angmo tells: "You should wear good clothes and should ride the blue Mongolian horse. For use in the war you should carry good matchlocks manufactured in Lahore. You should be very careful to cross the Dooling bridge, which is very bad and you should go dismantling the bridge of Ban-go." Dooling cannot be identified properly. Some people presume that it may be in Spiti. Ban-go is the same as Bas-go of Ladak, where one of the battles of the war was fought. The battle of Basgo is famous and there are several songs prevalent in Ladak. The song is evidence to the fact that Spiti participated in the Tibeto-Mughal war of 1681-83.

The song certainly relates to Spiti but it appears to have been composed by a Ladaki musician. Although the song has both appealing subject and melody, it is the melody which made it survive for long period and flourish.

About the arms manufactured in Lahore we understand that, "The arms, which are principally made at Lahore, consist of swords, spears, match-locks, muskets, pistols and armour, the latter being composed of helmets or skul-caps, coats of mail, breast-plates, gauntlets and shields" (Steinbach, 1846: 87). The song reveals that during those times the Mongolian horses were in use in these areas and was considered as superior and might have been choice of the royal riders.

Spiti, the Common Property: A proverb from Ladak reveals the type of relationship that Ladak and Khunu (Bashahar) possessed with Spiti during the long past. In reality although Spiti was under the possession of Ladak, but the following expression of Ladaki view reveals how precarious the possession had been. It says:

> *Spyi-ti spyis (phis) ma yin*
> *gNam-mjug khu-nu'i bchol-ma yin* (Abdul, 2004: 52)

It means that Spiti between the two states of Ladak and Bashahar is like *spyi-ma,* a common property or two neighbours having a common boundary. These are always cause of contention. It may also be interpreted that it is like a property kept in trust, *bchol-ma,* with Ladak by Khunu. There was a custom in the trans-Himalayan regions that some families, who possessed less land and did not have enough fodder to feed all their cattle during the long winter, used to keep some of their cattle in trust with some other family. They reared the cattle during the winter and returned them to their owners after the close of the winter season. They received the valuable manure and were paid in kind in the form of labour during the summer. Similarly some families who immigrated with all their members during the winter to lower areas also kept their assets in trust with a family in the village. The assets were returned after the return of the owner. The conditions of the assets in which the owners received on their return is a subject of anybody's guess. Apparently the rule of Ladak over Spiti was frequently interrupted by Bashahar. Gerard

(1830) and J.D.Cunningham inform that Spiti made some payments to Bashahar in the form of tribute.

Kullu and Spiti: Kullu evidently had been much stronger than Spiti. But before the strong contenders like Ladak and Bashahar, the position of Kullu was a bit precarious. We have seen that Man Singh invaded Spiti and fixed a regular tribute. Hutchison and Vogel write that 'Some time after 1680 Spiti was invaded by Raja Man Singh of Kulu, who exacted tribute. Nawang Tshering the famed lama from Zanskar who had been then travelling in Lahul, Kullu, Kangra, etc. during these days, gives a reference to this event which he dates in the year of sTag (Tiger) which may be put equivalent to 1698 CE. Hardyal also says that Man Singh captured Spiti, raided the monasteries and left the administration in their own hands. As Ladak was in stronger position, Kullu was left with no other option.

According to one source from Kullu, Man Singh marched through Lahul. During this time he must have fixed the boundary of Lahul with Ladak at Lingti, as Francke says. Then through Baralacha pass he went to Piti, exacted tribute and fixed a regular tribute which continued to be paid to Kullu till the time Spiti was taken over by the British. Thus Kullu did not have opportunity to rule over Spiti independently. Hutchison and Vogel affirm that Spiti was never a part of Kullu.

C.A. Dane, Asstt. Commissioner, Kulu, who visited Spiti in 1884, noticed ruins of an old building in Pin valley at the junction of Pin and Buldur Nallah, known to the local residents as Nyungti Khar (Kullu Fort). In his view it was built by Jagat Singh which he is supposed to have built as a barricade against the invading Bushahri forces, as the legend runs that Jagat Singh reached Manikaran first on his retun journey and donated the spoils to the enrichment of the temple of Raghunatha there. Hutchison and Vogel mention two such forts instead of one and assigns them to Man Singh. They write, 'The two forts, the ruins of which may still be seen at Sumdo at the foot of the Bhabeh and Rupin passes, near the Pin river, are known as Nyungti Khar, and may probably have been built by Raja Man Singh.' Here it appears that the first proposition of Mr Dane is more probable. The forts must have been built during the period of Jagat Singh or early. But regarding the second part of the statement, the task is generally assigned to Man Singh.

An Incursion from Kullu: Trebeck has recorded an instance of a raid from Kullu into Spiti which took place during his stay there in 1822. During the time Kullu was under the Sikhs and Kullu was facing extreme financial constraint in meeting their increasing demands. Trebeck writes that with the objective in mind to collect funds for meeting out the exactions of the Sikhs during the time of Ajit Singh, Kullu made a foray into the territory of Spiti. He gives the circumstances of the dispute with Kulu in the following manner. 'About six years ago (1816?) when Khaga Rabgi was the governor of the district, attempts were made by the Gadhes or shepherds of Chamba, Kulu, and its neighbourhood to export shawl wool to the Muchna hills by way of the Parang Pass. As this was a contraband trade an order was received from Leh to have it seized. The order was executed but none of the animals were injured, nor was any violence offered to the shepherds.

'This deterred the traders from speculating again in the same way, and the authorities of Ladakh had no application made to them by the Raja of Kulu for the restitution of the property confiscated. Indeed, the occurrence seems to have remained unnoticed for more than four years, as both the Rajas were on friendly terms, and an agent from Kulu was residing at Le when we arrived at that city'.

But somewhat more than a year since Moorcroft and Trebeck reached at Leh (Sept. 1820), 'A large peasantry treated by a near connection of Sobha Ram, entered Spiti by the Lossar Pass and meeting with no resistence took possession of everything which was worth carrying away and had not been concealed. They advanced no further than Rerik, and destroyed several houses by lighting large fires in the rooms. The gonpa of Kih was much injured. The property taken off consisted chiefly of yaks, horses, and other live stock, but an estimate cannot be made of the amount of the loss'.

There were some preparations to retaliate on Kullu. Trebeck notes that on the 15th of August, 1822, orders were received from Leh stating that it was the purpose of the Kahlon to levy an armed force for the purpose of retaliating upon Kulu, for the foray lately commited by that state on Ladak, and ordering the people of Piti to prepare to meet him near Khoksar. He threatens death to any one who shall run away, should any fresh attack be attempted before his arrival; but this is only intended to give confidence to the people, for he knows very well, should they ever be persuaded to take the field, the first shot from a Kulu matchlock would put the whole Ladaki force to flight.

Dogra Rule

Zorawar Singh, the General of Gulab Singh of Jammu, conquered Ladak in 1834 and alongwith it Spiti, its dependency. There is no information if any force had been sent to Spiti. Perhaps there was no need. Major Hay writes that till the year 1839 the revenue from time within memory, was always paid to the Raja of Ladak. The Dogras might have made some amendments in the traditional Ladaki system of revenue collection like partial conversion from grains to cash and some enhancement in the rate of collection. In 1839 the revenue was raised abnormally to rupees 2000 per annum. This might have been done for accumulating funds for preparation for the expedition to Tibet in 1841, because it was again reduced to rupees 1031 in 1844 after the war was over. During the expedition of 1841 Spiti was put under the supervision of Rahim Khan. According to CL Datta he was Kiladar (literally Zongpon) i.e. Kharpon. Ghulam Khan, his son-in-law, is said to have engaged himself in plundering monasteries and temples. JD Cunningham writes that gold and silver were saved for his master, while he himself carried out the work of indiscriminately destroying clay idols, pictures, paintings and books. Ghulam Khan accompanied the force to Tibet.

Major Hay further writes that, the annual revenue of rupees 1031, besides some other in kind, for 1844, 45 and 46 was paid to the Thanader at Ladak. 'During these three years the Sikhs are said to have further plundered the country of 4000 rupees, also 60 *ghoonts* and much other property'.

During this period Tabo escaped the destruction of the Dogra, while some other monasteries in Spiti were ravaged.

Spiti vis-a-vis Kullu and Bashahar

The payment of tributes to Kullu and Bashahar might have continued as before even after 1839 as JD Cunningham reports in 1844 that 'Kulu, a Lahore dependency, demands from the whole of Pitti including the houses attached to monasteries, one *ju* or *jao* of gold, equal to 8 or 9 rupees, and also 4 pieces of woolen' (JD Cunningham, 1844-147: 211). He also says that the division of Pin paid 32 pieces of woollen and one sheep to Bashahar. Major Hay also writes that prior to 1839 Spiti paid annually to the Raja of Busahir 30 pieces of cloth as tribute. There is no source confirming if they held any control over any part of the territory of Spiti.

The Sikh Incursion: The Sikhs from Lahore after they had annexed Kullu in 1840 sent up a force to plunder Spiti in 1841. A few straggling plunderers from the Sikh force who ventured up too high were surprised and killed. The Sikhs retired when they had got all the plunder they could get, and did not attempt to annex the country to Kullu or separate it from Ladak, because Spiti was already under Gulab Singh.

Annexation by the British

In 1846 the whole Alpine region of the Punjab between the Ravi and Indus, including Ladak and Spiti, was transferred to Raja Gulab Singh of Jammu. But Spiti was exchanged for some other territory and added to Kullu with the object of securing a road to the wool districts of Jangthang. In the same year when A. Cunningham and Vans Agnew were on a tour for survey work, the latter by the summary settlement of Spiti fixed the revenue at rupees 753 per annum. The British Government gave the charge of collection of the revenue of Spiti to the Raja of Bashahar for three years, who was asked to pay Rs.700 per annum as revenue for the years 1846-47-48.

In the autumn of 1849 Major Hay went to Spiti and took over the charge of the district. 'He spent the best part of the winter there, and submitted a valuable report.' He reports that 'Mansuk Das, Vazir, made an offer to Mr. Edwards, the Superintendent of hill states, to continue farming Spiti, upon an increased rent of 1000 rupees, and I believe he recommended to the Board that his offer should be accepted, but I think it very objectionable, for the Spiti people believe that he only took the sum fixed for the three years with a view of obtaining a longer lease, when they were apprehensive that it was his intention to exact more from them.' Major Hay later on was appointed Assistant Commissioner, Kullu who remained in the office from 1853 to 1857 and stayed perhaps for the longest period.

Hay entrusted the Nono, the hereditary Wazir of Spiti, with the task of administration of the area and he was granted a *jagir.* On the death of Nono on 22 July, 1864 his son Tanzin Namgyal became Wazir. The allowance of Nono was raised to Rs. 282

yearly on the basis of six annas per rupee of revenue. After this C.U. Aitchison, Under Secretary, reported to the Secretary of the Punjab Government to draw a few simple rules for the guidance of Nono, on the basis of Penal Code and the Code of Criminal Procedure. In 1873 a set of rules were prepared for the guidance of the Nono and were notified from the Fort William on 20 February, 1873 to be effective from first April, 1873. Nono was formally vested with honorary magisterial powers and a reader was provided by the Government to assist him in his judicial work.

It is told that 'Tanzin Namgyal, the Nono of Spiti, was also an honorary magistrate but he had no civil powers and could only fine upto rupees ten on the criminal side. He is not much burdened by his honorary labours, and is but seldom called upon to exercise the very limited powers he enjoys'.

Indegenous defence device

Spiti was extremely weak and vulnerable to the raids and incursions by even small groups from the neighbouring states. It was sparsely populated with very poor resources. Gerard writes, 'Speetee has frequently been the scene of war; but their contests were never bloody and resembled the forays of the Scottish of the old being sometimes setting fire to a village'.

Harcourt expresses surprise and notes that, 'Spiti, so very poor a country, should ever have been deemed worth the trouble of conquering, and that its inhabitants, who only can be approached by most difficult passes, should have been unable to retain their independence. But it would seem that an invading army had only to appear, for the Spiti men to at once submit and even had they been a warlike race, it would have been difficult, with such a scanty population to guard all the passes for any length of time; and it must be remembered they were exposed to enemies on all sides, who never dreamt of declaring war or giving any time for preparation, invading the valley simply because it was their pleasure to do so.' Small parties of raiders came frequently to plunder the houses and monasteries and excaped with the loot. Larger incursions were also not rare.

In order to face such precarious situations the residents of Spiti had adopted several methods.

a) Francke has recorded an incident which he says goes back to circa 1647. It is a story of enmity created by the Ladakpas with the Pitipas. At that time Ladakpas used to come to Spiti, snatch and take away all the belongings, valuables and jewelleries of the women. The residents of Spiti would flee to the mountains. They took all their valuables with them to the hill side and hid there. The Jo and the rich men of Spiti have still their valuables hidden in the hills. Once the Ladakpas came and stayed in Spiti in the winter. On the arrival of the festival of Losar, the Pitipas executed a plan and took all the Ladakpas to each house. There they beat and killed the guests. Some of them fled away over the roof of the Dankhar fort and the people pushed them away, some others fled up the hills. They died there of cold, they being drunk.

b) The monasteries in the time of emergency functioned as virtual fort and garrison. The large monasteries are situated at strategic locations. They have capacity to accommodate a large number of residents. They maintained large store of grains and other provisions and also had arrangement for regular supply of water. They had secure rooms for hiding a number of persons for several days. For regular water supply, they were linked underground with water sources. About the Kyi monastery Vitali reports that, 'At Kye monastery it is reported that recently, during the work to prepare Kye Gonpa for the great ceremony of the Kalachakra initiation given in year 2000 by H.H. the 14th Dalai Lama, the monks discovered an ancient secret tunnel connecting the peak of the hill, upon which Kye Gonpa is built, to its base, so that the water supply could be assured in continuity. This system reminds one of a similar secret tunnel, one of the technological devices set up at Tsaparang, the citadel monastery capital of the ancient land, last kingdom of Guge in West Tibet. The period, in which Tsaparang was built, is the same as that when sTod Sherab Zangpo and his disciple established their foundations (including that Kye) in the stretch of lands from Spiti to Nubra.'

c) A similar device is stated to have existed in Pin valley. Opposite to the village of Sagnam, across the Pin river, there is a small village named Khar of about fifteen houses. Between this village and the river there is a small hillock lying parallel to the river. Over the hillock there is a lhakhang, and there are stone blocks, parts of walls and roof, all forming ruins of a structure, of an old fort. People say that the local deity does not allow anybody to pick stones from here. It is told that the people had laboured to dig out a large space where provisions and water could be stored. Several persons could live there for quite long time. At the base of the hillock towards the village and at the level of the village there is an opening of a tunnel which it is told links with the river on the other side. This was an effective device of defence. It is told that people from whole of the Pin valley used to come here for their safety. It is possible that similar structures existed at Dankhar and Tangyut.

In Lahul and Kinnaur the method adopted for conveying the message of arrival of the enemy forces was a little different. There are square stone structures raised at varying distances at prominent places over the ridges. Fire was lit over them and the message was relayed to the next post. The difference may be due to the topographical conditions.

The Ladaki Administration

Ladaki functionaries: Spiti remained under Ladak since the earliest time known and Ladak had a permanent administrative office headed by a Kharpon established at Dankhar, the capital of the region. References to the names of certain kings of Ladak and their representatives posted at Dankhar are available from various sources.

During this period there were two grades of authorities in Spiti. The representatives of the Raja of Ladak had its own staff and enjoyed higher status. The other office of the local functionaries headed by the Nono of Kyuling was subject to the authority of the former.

Gerard (c. 1830) writes that a Garpon or Governor stays here at Dankhar on the part of Ladak Giapo. But his authority is little more than nominal and he receives the tribute. Trebeck tells that the authority of the Raja of Ladakh, or rather that of the Kahlun, is absolute, and is exercised through a chief, who seldom visits Piti, except at harvest time, to collect the revenue. The office is therefore discharged by a deputy, who is rarely a person of much influence, and whose measures are completely controlled by the Gatpos, corresponding with the Sianas of Garhwal, and Mukhyas of Bashahar. Kahlon was of the rank of minister at Leh who was, among others, incharge of the administration of Spiti.

We get a fairly good picture about the kind of establishment that existed at Dankhar from a document issued from here in 1671 (Ann. I-A) under the authority of the Ladaki king Dechhog Namgyal, by the occupant of the office of the chief of Spiti, Kharpon, mKhar-dpon, named Nam-mkh'a rGyal-tshhan. The other offices mentioned are Zongpon (rdsong-dpon), who was junior to Kharpon in rank, Manager (gNyer-las-byed) and extra-Manager (Phyir-dpon). Later the European visitors name some different offices. It is evident that at Dankhar there was a castle (*mkhar*), residence of the Kharpon. It was also a fort (*rdsong*) in charge of Zongpon, besides the impressive monastery. In the fort earlier there might have been a garrison for there is mention of armymen in the Dechhog's document. But there was no Garpon posted here ever.

From the Chronicles of Ladak we observe that Ladaki princes were given charge of the administration of the vassal states like Dechhog having Zanskar and Spiti, and Tashi Namgyal having similarly Purig, Zanskar and Spiti. It may be that they did not stay regularly at Dankhar but they must have been visiting occasionally. Therefore the mKhar might have been called Yang-mkhar, the other castle. In the time of Trebeck the district was in charge of a Kahlon.

It is observed that sometimes confusion arises in the use of the three similar terms of Garpon, Kharpon and Zongpon as they are sometimes found used interchangably. *dPon* here means officer, distinct from an artist-painter. *sGar* means tent and sGar-dpon is an executive of a camp of army. *mKhar* means castle or palace and *rdsong* means fort. Both Kharpon and Zongpon were posted at Dankhar but there was no Garpon.

The Kharpons at Dankhar

Study of the history of the Kharpons resident at Dankhar is helpful in understanding the history of domination of Ladak over Spiti. Although there is a brief break in the continuity of availability of evidences beginning from the period 1555-1575 onwards, yet it hardly affects the fact that there was no break in the Ladaki rule over Spiti during the whole length of this period and it was continuous. The first evidence, a colophon to brGyad-stong-pa (Annx. II-B), mentions the name of Tashi Namgyal (1555-1575), king of Ladak. At this time the Kharpon at Dankhar was bsTanpa rgya-mtsho. This is the first name of a Kharpon that we know of.

The document also mentions a Kharpon residing in Pin, named Thubs-bstan. This is the only reference about a Kharpon residing in Pin. The document is not dated but may be placed c. 1565.

Gergan writes that the next king Tshe-dbang rNam-rgyal (1575-1595) raised the Dung-'gyur at Lha lung in Spiti in c. 1580 as is known from the che-brjod. At this time Ga-ga Tanzin Namgyal, father and son, stayed at Dankhar, as mKhar Pon (Gergan, 1976: 367). Reference to the king is found made again. Petech informs that 'A colophon found by Prof. Tucci at Brang-mkhar mentions king Tshe-dbang rNam-rgyal and his minister Gaga 'Bumpa lde' (Petech, 1977: 30). We don't know the exact designation of Gaga 'Bumpa lde. From the epithet 'Gaga' given to him, he may be taken for Kharpon, who lived prior to Tanzin Namgyal, also a Kharpon, under the same king.

Petech writes from a colophon to a book from Sa-bu that during the time of Singe Namgyal (1616-1642) there was one bsTan-'dsin ram-rgyal as Kharpon in Dankhar. Petech presumes that he could not have been the same as the half-brother of Singe Namgyal. This may be true because the office of Kharpon was lower than that of even Kahlon. This fact is corroborated from an inscription discovered from the village of La-ra in Spiti propitiating the king Singe Namgyal at the *rGyal-sa* (capital) *Gra-khar rdsong* (Dankhar) and alongwith it the name of Ga-ga bsTan-('dsin) rNam-rgyal is also restated (Gergan, 1976:371).

Hutchison and Vogel write on the information from Francke that Senge Namgyal held Spiti and a subordinate, i.e. Kharpon, Gaga Chhering Namgyal was posted at Dankhar Fort. From the above it may be derived that Gaga Tanzin Namgyal, who is mentioned by Gergan as Kharpon posted at Dankhar during the king Tshebang Namgyal continued during the time of Singe Namgyal also and Gaga Chhering Namgyal was appointed after him, who could be son of the predecessor if we go with Gergan as above.

Dechhog Namgyal: During the reign of Dechhog Namgyal the post of Kharpon was held by Namkha Gyaltshan which we learn from a decree issued by him in 1671 from Dankhar on behalf of the king (Ann. I-A). In a colophon to Zamatog, (Ann. II-C) names of the above two persons appear again. It writes that Dharamraj lDe-mchhog rNam-rgyal is residing at Dankhar. Nam-mkha rGyal-mtshan is now designated as Kahlon who by then might have been promoted. But as there is no Kharpon mentioned, he might have been continuing to reside at Dankhar and carrying on the responsibilities of Kharpon.

G. Tucci found in an inscription the name of Nima Namgyal (1694-1729) who caused renovation of the Sa-kya-pa monastery of Kaza or Tangyut.

After Nima Namgyal, Gergan notes, the kingdom was divided into two parts. Purig, Zanskar and Spiti were given to Tashi Namgyal (1734-1758), second son of Nyima Namgyal, who is said to have recorded victories against the Mon (Kullu or Chamba), Hor, Ruthog, Spiti, Suru, Hembab, Baltistan, Nubra'. Mention of Spiti here holds no significance.

Francke informs that on one of the *mane* walls of Kaza, the name of the capital of Spiti is spelt as Drag-mkhar-rtse. A nobleman, Gaga Sod-nams is mentioned as having held the office of resident at the castle but the name of the king of Leh is missing. Sonam may be presumed to have been a Kharpon.

Trebeck informs that in about 1816 Gaga Rabghi was the governor of Spiti, who may be taken as Kharpon. He in 1822 names the chief of Spiti as Sultan Begh, who may be taken as Kharpon. As Sultan Begh was staying at Leh, the office at Dankhar was held by Gaga Khan, the manager, who could have been Zongpon. Gaga Khan later on might have been promoted as Kharpon as the Getey document (Ann.II-D) evidences, which document could have been of around 1830. In 1841 Rahim Khan was Kiladar i.e. Kharpon. JD Cunningham says that Khaga Khan was the father of the Kharpon, not named, who was holding the post during his time in 1843. He says that Gaga Khan was a Buddhist and his real name was Tashi Dondub (JD Cunningham, 1844-147: 214). He also writes that, 'Sultan Begh was of a family of Shia Mahometan settled near Leh, his grand-daughter or great grand-daughter married Gholam Khan subsequently made Chief of Pitti, an active partisan of Sikhs, and he died in the war in 1841'. CL Datta clarifies that Rahim Khan was made Kiladar i.e. Kharpon of Spiti (CL Datta, 1973:132). Others like A.Cunningham, Francke etc. also hold that Rahim Khan was made the chief of Spiti and Gholam Khan, son in law of Rahim Khan, engaged himself in plundering the monasteries and he went with the forces in the war to Tibet where he died in 1841.

The officers posted at Dankhar may be shown in tabular form as follows:

Name of the Ruler/ Authority	Name of the Kharpon	Remarks
Tashi Namgyal (1555-1575)	bsTanpa rGyamtsho	
-do-	Thubs-bstan	Kharpon in Pin
Tshe-dbang Namgyal (1575-1595)	'Bum-pa-lde	(Minister, as per Petech)
Tshebang Namgyal	Tanzin Namgyal	
Singe Namgyal (1616-1642)	Tanzin Namgyal,	continued.
-do-	Chhering Namgyal	(Son of Tanzin Namgyal?)
Dechhog Namgyal 1671 CE	Namkha Gyaltshan.	
Dechhog Namgyal	Namkha Gyaltshan.	He is now designated as Kahlon, c. 1680.
Francke Auth.	Sonam (?)	
Trebeck Auth. 1816.	Rabgey	

Trebeck Auth. 1822.	Sultan Begh (Chief = Kharpon?)	Gaga Khan, (Manager= Zongpon?)
Getey Colophon c. 1830	Gaga Khan (Tashi Dondub)	
CL Datta Auth.	Rahim Khan	Kiladar, Kharpon, 1841.
JD Cunningham	Son of Gaga Khan	1843

From the fact that all the Kharpons are addressed as Gaga and a number of their names, except the one at the beginning and the others in the latter part, end with the second name Namgyal, which is the surname of the kings, it may be presumed that they mostly belonged to the Jo class, the class of the kings of Ladak and a few of them might have been related to the king's family. The posts of Kharpon and Zongpon both continued till 1841 and must have continued till 1846, the end of the Ladaki and Dogra rule.

Staff during Trebeck's visit: Trebeck gives detail of the officials resident in Dankhar castle during his time: "The house belonged to the Taoche, or head of the carriers, and he with Khaga Khan, the manager of the district, and the Paon or scribe, paid me every civility, in the absence of the Chief of the Piti, Sultan Begh whom I had left at Le." As indicated by Trebeck and JD Cunningham the 'Chief'may be assumed equivalent to Kharpon and manager to that of Zongpon.

Taoche: JD Cunningham commenting on the narrations given by Trebeck says that *taoche*, or *tagotcheh*, or *dogotcheh*, is simply the deputy of the resident manager particularly charged with the collection of the revenue under the Karrpan or griot, chief or manager, and he also collects the porters and beast of burden for the use of the Raja and proceeds in person with them if any are required. The two narrators have assigned Taoche different duties in their descriptions. Togochhe or Tabochhe was a middle level functionary, below the Zongpon. Trebeck stayed in the house of the Tabochhe. The term itself is indistinct. It occurs in Ladak, from where it reached Spiti. There also it is found written with different spellings and the attributed functions also are numerous and indefinite.

Lyall writes that under the kings of Ladak, a family in the village of Mane held the hereditary office of Togochi of Spiti. He acted as secretary and keeper of the records, and was associated with the wazir on an almost equal footing in all State business. During the time of Lyall the post was held by Sonam Tobgye who had been in the habit of assisting the Nono as a secretary. Lyall appointed him as Patwari of Spiti, and recommended his receiving forty *khal* per annum out of the '*nethal*' collections (Lyall, 1975: 117). The picture becomes more complicated. It appears that Togoche who worked earlier for the Kharpon later on during the British period worked for the Nono. Trebeck is correct in explaining the meaning of Taoche as 'Head of carriers' which may be rendered as rTa-dpon-chhe (=mule-officer-great, the Great Mule Officer). The Senior Officer incharge of mules. As the designation indicates, principally he must have been in charge of making arrangement of ponies. Ponies were required in a good number for use of the king, the officials and for carriage of *Ne* to Leh and for carrying supplies to the places of conflicts, etc. He was head and he might have had several other junior functionaries under him. In those days this was an important portfolio.

Pon: Trebeck mentions a *Pon* who functioned as scribe. We have not noticed this post earlier, nor we see it afterwards. JD Cunningham clarifies the point saying, Paon is not known as the word for scribe in Pitti or its neighbourhood, but the individual alluded to by Mr. Trebeck, is still remembered as a skilful carver, etc. He was the eldest son of Khaga Khan above mentioned.

The word *dPon* of the lexicons meaning officer or head has been explained above. Here the term is employed as is used in local tradition, as painter-artist, which expression is not found in the lexicons. They are professionals who paint *thankas* (cloth hangings), statues, walls, pillars, etc. in the monasteries and private houses. They are literate and are also skilled in carving wood blocks for printing books. The present incumbent was not actually an employee but he was there for he being the son of the Kharpon.

Local administration and the officials: Nono of Kyuling was the head of the local functionaries. The local staff did not have separate office and they all assembled at Dankhar. They brought the revenue collections here and through the Nono handed over to the Ladaki authorities. An annual fair of accounting was held at Dankhar.

Gadpo: Two kinds of authorities functioning under the Nono were Gadpo Chhenmo, the Senior Elder, and Gadpo Chungun, the Junior Elder. Trebeck writes that Gadpos corresponding with the *sianas* from the households acted for a month in turn as elders of the villages. They met five or six times in a year to discuss the interest of the district. Those from the distant seldom attended unless there was some urgent matter to discuss.

i. Gadpo Chhenmo: There was a *gadpo* appointed at *kothi* level who was known as Gadpo Chhenmo, the Senior Elder, thus numbering five in all. The traditional method of appointment to the office of Gadpo Chhenmo as it is said was, 'by the vote of the *gatpos* of villages with the concurrence of the Nono'. Later on during the British period the procedure of selection got reformed and is described as, 'They have considerable influence and some of them are men of character. They were selected by the Nono who first takes the opinion of the people and the village *lambardars* and such appointments are placed before the Assistant Commissioner for ratification (as in the case of the heads of monasteries). These officials held office at the pleasure of the people, who have been known to depose the whole five of them owing to embezzlement of public funds, but the present incumbents have continued for periods varying from two to seven years, and deposition is rarely resorted to.'

As regards his function, 'The gadpo chenmo received the land revenue from the village lambardars and checked it before they passed it on to the Nono to see if it was correct. They also are in charge of the begaar, and also act as a privy council for the Nono in all matters which come before him'. Later on they appear to have been relieved of the burden of collection of *khral,* revenue and then their importance was much reduced. It is said that, 'They have nothing to do with the collection of the revenue, but are in charge of the *begaar* arrangements, and receive and account for the collections of supplies for travelers'.

Trebeck notes that, 'if a dispute arises between individuals, the parliament of Gatpos must settle it; if a robbery is committed, they must inquire into it; and if the thief be discovered, award him punishment. The consequence is that thefts are constantly perpetrated with impunity'. 'The remuneration of the gadpo chenmo before the British period was the loan of a horse and 5 dre (or de) of barley meal daily, from their kothi, when on actual service: this was commuted in 1891 to 40 khals of barley per annum. This arrangement was not however accepted by the people and the *gadpo chenmo* could only collect 20 khals. In 1917 Government compensated their loss by assigning them one tenth of the land revenue, namely, rupees 20 each'.

ii. Gadpo Chhungun: In each village there was a Gadpo Chungun equivalent to village *lambardar*. Trebeck reports, each household served by turn. These lambardar circles comprised one village if it was a large one, or two or three smaller villages. He collected the revenue of the village direct from every payee, great or small, and conveyed the sum due from the village to the Nono. After the settlements the office was made more functional. The Gazetteer writes that, 'These village *gatpos* hold office for a year only, or for two or three years. Whenever the landholders wish for a change, or whenever the man in office chooses to resign, they elect a new man, and report the matter through the kothi *gatpo* to the Nono. As remuneration, he gets five *de* of meal a day for the days in which he is actually employed in public service, and is also excused his turn of carrying loads from village to village, but not his turn of carrying loads across the passes, for which there is a different roaster. In kothi Pin two men do the work of village messangers and policemen, and are paid three *khal* of barley per annum apiece out of the *netal* collections; the office goes by the name of *laspa*, and is held by the landholders in turn' (Gazetteer, 1897- IV: 94).

The Moravians: The Moravian missionaries had no post in Spiti although they had been looking out for a suitable place. They served the area by providing educational and medical services from Pooh in Kinnaur and Kyelang in Lahul. Their members were frequenting with the British officers sometimes as interpreters. They were educating children from Spiti in their school at Kyelang. When Andrew Wilson visited the village Morang he found that the Mukhiya of the village was educated by the mission at Kyelang and he spoke Hindustani. Similarly many others had benefitted.

Chapter VII

The Traditional Fiscal System and History of its Study

The society in Spiti was liable to pay levy of three kinds to three different institutions: Land Revenue payable to the King; Contributions for the maintenance of the religious institutions to the Religious Organisation; and Payment to the village institution for meeting the expenditures of social and economic nature concerning the village. In volume all the three kinds of payments were almost equal and all were compulsory. The issues relating to the payments to the village institution, of course, was of local nature and could be solved at the same level.

For the other former two kinds of payments the whole of the region was concerned. The traditional system of collection of the two kinds of levies worked well till the end of the Ladaki rule, rather till the end of the Dogra rule who did not disturb the method of collection of the revenue. A problem of serious nature arose when the area came under the British rule and they introduced their own system of revenue collection.

The small, isolated and remotely settled society of Spiti, owing to extremely difficult environmental conditions had to struggle hard for its subsistence. In order to economise on all kinds of its scarce resources it had organized the social, economic and religious systems in a peculiar way. This unusual feature was to some degree manifested in its method of payment of revenue and other dues to the Raja and the great religious organization.

The inhabitants,instead of each unit paying its share of revenue of two kinds to the Raja and the religious institutions separately themselves, had divided the whole tax-paying population into two sections. One section paid only to the Raja and the other to the monastic organization. A section paying to one entity had basically no liability for the other. In a way the payments like that of state revenue and those of religious nature were mixed up. Contributions to the monasteries,as compared to other places, was quite heavy, which might have been instrumental for invention of the mechanism.

Whole of Spiti was administratively divided into five divisions. Of the five, four divisions paid *khral,* revenue, to the Raja. The fifth, *Chhos-gzhi*, was identified to pay, *bun,* religious contribution,exclusively to the monastic organization. From this it may be estimated that one fifth or twenty percent of the revenue went to the group of the five big monasteries. In fact the total amount going for the religious purposes was much larger than this. Another peculiar feature of the system, although not uncommon, is that most of payments were made in kind.The payment to the Raja was further segmented: bulk of the collection went to the Raja to Leh, a part of it was spent at Dhankhar under some administrative heads, and a part went infavour of Nono.

The British administrators then were unfamiliar with the whole of these complex customary practices of the society of Spiti. As soon as they took over the administration of the province, they made a summary settlement in 1847. Disregarding all the norms of customary practices, the levy was converted wholly into cash and distributed among all the inhabitants in the province. This fell as an additional burden on the residents of *chhoszhi kothi* who were paying *bun.*

The people were bound to follow the government orders. At the same time they could in no way ignore their obligations towards their religious institutions and for other liabilities. These made the system more complicated. The issue became a big cause of irritation for the inhabitants. Although from the point of view of the government they had simplified the system and also had lightened the burden. But practically as people were required to continue to make all kinds of payments, necessary to maintain the social and religious systems, all became over burdened, and a few, those of *kothi Chhoszhi*, were more burdened than all others. Thus dissatisfaction pervaded among all the residents. The people brought their problem before the authorities whenever they got opportunity but there was none who could understand them fully or bothered to do so or bring any relief to them. The first regular Settlement of 1853 did not give the issue any recognition.

In one way the issue could have been resolved by the people themselves, particularly the religious organization. The people did not venture to touch the issue perhaps due to the fact that traditionally *bun* was equated with land revenue.

The burden on the people being too heavy the issue kept on cropping up now and then. Ultimately government was compelled to look into the matter seriously and thoroughly. The government took more than two decades in understanding the problem fully and solving it to the complete satisfaction of both the people and the government, and also fulfilling the requirements of the religious organisation. Credit for all this must go to Mr. James B. Lyall. He gained deep understanding and knowledge on various aspects of the society. He, first as Assistant Commissioner of Kullu and then as Settlement Officer, district Kangra, of which Spiti formed a part, made painstaking effort in understanding the complex social, economic and religious systems of Spiti and its typical revenue system. Lyall's capability in understanding the primitive and typical societies like that of Malana in Kullu and Spiti was unique and highly praiseworthy. His reports, rather studies, are permanent documents and have always been guiding object and reliable source of reference for all his predecessors and scholars. After him not much material of value had been added either to that of Malana or Spiti.

Traditional System of Revenue Payment

The various forms of revenue paid by the farmers of Spiti traditionally to the king, the monastic establishment and the others may be put down as under: *Nethal*, tax collected in the form of grain which all went to the Raja of Ladak; *mKhar-gi-bun*, a part of the nethal, was collected by Nono which was not sent to Leh and *Bun,* the grain collection, which went in the account of the five big monasteries.

Nethal: Traditionally Spiti paid all revenue taxes in kind in the form of *Ne* (huskless barley) which was known as *Ne-thal* (*nas-khral*), barley-tax. *Ne* is principal crop not only in Spiti but in whole of the trans-Himalayan region. It is considered as a whole-meal grain and is of multifarious use. People used *tsampa,* flour of semi-parched grain of *Ne*, in a number of ways. Travellers could depend even for months long journey on it alone which could be used with *ja-thang,* milk-less salt tea. *Chhang*, native beer, used profusely on all occasions of social, religious and all kinds of gatherings is prepared from it. For the authorities of Ladak, which had been ruling over Spiti, for quite long time, *Ne* was preferable and for the monasteries in the province, no other substitute for it could have been better.

Trebeck who visited Spiti in 1822, during the reign of Ladak, reports that, 'the whole revenue of Piti is collected in grain, by a measure called *khal,* equal to eight *pakka*sers, and of the value of thirteen annas'(Moorcroft, 1841-II: 70-71). He further explains that some 2937 *khals* of *Ne* valued at rupees 2386 was being collected annually from 267 houses leaving aside about one third of the houses considered as unworthy of levy for having no land.Out of the total collection a part was used for local expenditure. He further says that trade was being done by barter and that money was almost useless.

The points emerging from the report may be summarized that revenue was collected all in kind and currency was not much in use. Out of the total collection a part was used for local consumption.Further, about one-third of the families were exempted from the payment of tax to the Raja, for various reasons.

JD Cunningham visited Spiti thereafter in 1843. His statement does not contradict that of Trebeck. He says that the revenue was collected all in kind, but he reports the data in monetary terms. He states that in 1841-42 there were 250 families out of which 52 or 53 families were appropriated to the five monasteries. Thus the sum demanded from the '197 or 198'houses was rupees 398 and 30 pieces of woolen. If we convert this sum at the conversion rate given by Trebeck i.e. thirteen annas for a khal, the figure of the grain collected works out at 490 *khals*. This is at great variance from the figures reported by the Trebeck. Cunningham is aware of this fact, as he writes, 'As my statement of the revenues differs greatly from the estimate of Mr. Trebeck. I may be wrong; that is, my informants may have purposely misled me.' It appears that here the data reported by Cunningham is more realistic and that of Trebeck is much inflated. We have seen that the highest figure of revenue levied on Spiti was rupees two thousand during the period of Dogras at the time of their expedition towards Tibet but this was reduced shortly to nearly rupees one thousand. The customary amount of levy under the Ladaki kings was much less. In 1843 Spiti was under the Dogras. When Alexander Cunningham conducted census in Spiti in 1847 he found that there were 1407 persons, 686 men and 721 women, living in 262 houses in 38 villages. The data on the number of houses given by the three authorities are nearly close to each other and equal to the rough figure of 250 households of the local tradition.

JD Cunningham further says that the whole of this tax was denominated as *mathal*. Besides the above, the Raja of Ladakh levied from all Piti a tax named *horthal,* and a second *mathal*, amounting to 36 and 18 rupees respectively. *Mathal*, *ma* equivalent to *mool,* root, in Hindi, means real, principal or the original tax. *Horthal* means the tax related to the country of Hor, i.e. the country about Yarkand in the neighbourhood of Ladak.

The two important terms *Ma-thal* and *Hor-thal*, if they ever existed in Spiti, lost their continuity within a very short time. JD Cunningham is the only authority to record these two terms. Both these terms existed in Ladak. Gergan informs that *Horthal* was not sent to Hor but it was collected in order to meet the expenditure for preventing influx of the enemies from the northern side of Ladak, including Hor, Yarkand, etc. (Gergan, 1976: 615). This must have been quite frequent. During the stay of *siddha* sTag-tshang Ras-pa from 1622 to 1651 in Ladak, the biography reveals that, at least three incursions occurred from the northern direction.Cunningham writes further that,'The Rajah of Ladakh further demands a quantity of iron, cotton goods, paper madder, etc. from the whole of the district for which he gives 50 rupees, taking however 200 rupees' worth of goods'.

Interdependence of Khangchen and Monastery

A. Support to the Monastery from the Lay Society: As we have seen above Trebeck says that about one third of the houses are considered as unworthy of levy for having no land. This is partly true and the fact has been explained by JD Cunningham who writes that out of 250 houses about 52 or 53 families were appropriated to five monasteries. These families paid only to the monasteries, the organization of the five big monasteries,instead of paying to the Raja. In fact there were also some households who possessed no land and were not required to pay any revenue.Besides, there were some small households who were not liable to pay either to the monasteries or the Raja. However, the society was heavily dependent on the support from the monastic system. "All younger sons of the landholders are forced by custom to enter the monasteries," (Gazetteer, 1898- IV: 97).The family relieved itself of its surplus population by sending all its sons other than the eldest one to the monasteries. In turn it had arrangement for supporting the monastic establishment both at individual level to the members of its family, and at the community level, by paying the regular collection, whether one has its members in monastery or not.

Monastery was not merely a religious institution. It was integrated into the complex social weband was a necessary innovation of the Spiti society. The distinctive system of primogeniture of Spiti developed with the cooperation from the large monastic establishment. In the monastery the child received education, training and grew up as a trained and educated lama who leads a celibate life. Some of them achieved higher status and went to Tibet and other areas for higher studies. The society supported in maintaining it in a number of ways.

i. Support to the members of own Family:

a. Da-zhing (grva-zhing): All the families who had their members in the monasteries had some arrangement to support them financially. The settlement reports maintain that in most holdings a plot of land equal to the measure from one to half a *khal* may be found in the occupation of the lama brother or uncle of the head of the family. It is known as *da-zhing*, monk's land and is ploughed and sown by the latter, but the lama provides the seed and gets the whole produce. On the death of the lama it reverts to the head of the family.

The gazetteer clarifies further that, "It is, however, only the second son who is entitled to claim da-zhing, and many do not take it from their elder brothers and have all in common with him, including their income from begging, funeral fees, etc. This is to the advantage of the elder brother, as a celibate monk's expenses are, of course, very small. When there are more than two brothers, the younger ones, though they cannot get da-zhing, are considered entitled to some subsistence allowance from the head of the family, but in return they do certain kinds of work for him in the summer, during which season only the elder monks remain in the monasteries. For instance, as long as they are *tsunpa* or *getsul*, that is, neophytes or deacons, and not *gelong* or fully ordained monks or priests, they will carry loads and do all field work except ploughing; when *gelong*, they will cook, feed cattle and sheep, and do other domestic services, but not carry loads or cut grass or wood," (Gazetteer, 1898-IV:83).

b. Da-Shag: The households who have their members as lamas own a cell called *Da-shag (grva-chhag),* monk's cell, in the monastery. Egerton informs, 'Each landholder's family has its particular 'Tasha' or cell in the monastery to which it is hereditarily attached, and in this all the monks of the family, uncles, nephews, and brothers keep their books, clothes, cooking utensils and other private property in them.'On the death of a lama, his private property, whether kept in his cell or deposited in the house of the head of the family, goes not to the monastery but to his family, first to the lamas of it, if any, and in their default, to *khang-chhen*.

Occasionally the households had to bear a part of their heavy incidental expenditures. Lyall writes, 'When a lama starts for Lhasa, to take his degree, his khangchhenpa is bound to give him what he can towards the expenses of the journey, but only the better to do men can afford it; many who go to Lhasa get high employ under the Lhasa Government, are sent to govern monasteries etc. and remain there for years; they return in only old age to their native monastery in Spiti bringing a good deal of wealth, of which they always give some at once to their families.'

ii.*Bun:* Contributions from the Community:There are monasteries almost in every village but of them the big five viz. Tangyut, Dankhar, Kyi, Tabo and Gungri (Pin) were recognized distinctly as institutions of importance of the provincial level. The households of *Kothi Chhoszhi* were assigned the responsibility of paying contribution to them. In turn they were exempted from the payment of revenue tax to the Raja. This payment to the monasteries was known as '*bun*'.

'*Bun*' is a shorter form of the word '*bu-lon*' which means debt. *Chhoszhi* means 'religious endowment', and appears to have been created with the special objective of supporting the chosen monasteries. The following table shows the amount of barley collected as '*bun*'from each *kothi* for each of the five different major monasteries and showing the number of lamas resident in each monastery. This data relates to the period, after the settlement made byLyall. However it gives good idea of the position existing before Lyall's settlement.The difference is that earlier the whole contribution came from one *kothi*, *kothi Chhoszhi* and presently it comes from the whole province.

(Quantity in *khal* and *de*)

Name of Monastery/ Kothi	Dankhar	Tabo	Kyi	Tangyut	Pin	Total
No. of Lamas	90	92	100	60	100	442
Amount of	Ne	collected				
sTod	73-17	10-10	60-00	9-12	–	153-19
Bar	–	–	14-00	87-16	–	101-16
Chhoezhi	120-00	134-19	379-14	222-00	–	856-13
Sham	137-14	53-05	–	–	–	190-19
Pin	–	–	–	20-00	81-10	101-10
Total	331-11	198-14	453-14	339-08	81-10	1404-17

Lyall states that in addition to the above, 57 *khals* more was also collected. Out of this 17 *khal* was paid to an old family of astrologers and 40 to the Pithug monastery in Ladak. According to Hay the assignment to Pithug came wholly from the village of Khikhyim.

iii. Own resources of the monasteries: In addition to the above the monasteries had their own resources for income.

a. **Land of Monastery,dGon-zhing:** The monasteries had their own landed property, income from which was wholly utilized for the benefit of the monastery. Lyall writes that, certain fields are the full property of the monasteries: they pay no revenue, and are generally either near the monastery to which they belong, or in adjacent villages. The land of the Dankhar monastery is cultivated by six tenants, landholders in Dankhar, who pay half produce as rent; that of the Pin monastery is cultivated gratuitously by the Nono of Pin; the men of *Chhoszhikothi*, as the special clients of the monks, cultivate the lands of the other monasteries, but the monks are expected to give the men who actually do the work something for their trouble.

b. It is said that just after the harvest, parties of five or six monkswere sent out on begging expeditions all over Spiti by each monastery. They go round from house to house in full dress, and standing in a row, chant certain verses, the essence of which is: 'we are men who have given up the world, give us, in charity, the means of life; by so doing you will please God whose servants we are.' The receipts are considerable, as each house gives something to every party.

c. A lama can acquire in the way of frees for attendance at marriages, reading scriptures in the houses of the villagers or other ceremonies or in the way of wages for work done in the summer.

d. '*Bul-ba* (offerings):The monks pay services on the occasion of death. They receive funeral offerings consisting of money, and clothes, pots and pans, grain, butter, etc. This forms a substantial amount as most of the valuable personal belongings of the deceased person alsoused to be offered as '*bul-ba.*

e. Trebeck reports the lamas also engaged themselves in trade, as during his visit a team under the leadership of the head lama of Dankhar had proceeded on a trade trip.

B. Functions of the Monastery towards the Society

The society recognized the importance and necessity of the large monastic establishment that it supported and maintained. The reasons must be more than mere faith. In return to the goods and services rendered by the society, the monastic system supported the society in its own way.

a. Extremely limited economic opportunities restrict a household from the division of its properties. Therefore the ownership of the household property descends from the eldest brother of one generation to the eldest brother of the next generation intact. The other brothers are sent to the monasteries which can accommodate in a large number. This is an important function the monastery does towards the society. Monks are bound to remain celibate.

b. Sometimes it may happen that the head of the family has no male issue and there is no immediate successor. At this moment the younger brother leaves the monastery to take the responsibilities as the heir of the household in place of his elder brother. Rose maintains that, 'once a monk always a monk', is not the law in Spiti. Supposing the head of a family to die and leave a young widow, with no son or a son of tender age only, then the younger brother, if there is one, almost always acts to leave the monastery, and there upon he is at once considered as his brother's widow's husband. She cannot object, nor is any marriage ceremony necessary. If there was a son by the elder brother, he of course, succeeds when of full age, and his mother and uncle retire to the small house, and the other sons, if any go into the monasteries in the usual way. A monk who throws off the frock in this way has to pay a fine to his monastery. Many decline to become laymen; this is a rule in the case of those who have attained to the grade of *gelong*. Where the lama brother declines, then it is agreed that in the lower part of the valley (i.e. *kothis* Pin and Sham), the father or widow mother can take a son-in-law to live in the house and succeed as son and heir, and no kinsmen (if there are any) can object. In the upper part of the valley this right does not appear to be so clearly established: the objections of near kinsmen are sometimes attended to, or a field or two given to them by way of compromise. Kinsmen, however, are, of course, very few, as the only way in which younger brother can found a separate family is by becoming son in law, and adopted son to another landholder. Such a man might claim on behalf of his younger son, but not on his own behalf or that of his eldest son, as it is a rule that for each holding or allotment there must be a separate resident head of the house to do service for it, as well as pay the revenue. Sometimes an illegitimate descendant of the family who has been living on the estate as a yang-chung pa, will claim as a kinsman and succeed, but he cannot be said to have any absolute right or title (Rose, 1883- III: 27).

c. The monks work at their home mostly as an occasional labourer during the time of pressing demand for work, or for begaar, etc.

d. The monks render the usual function of the religious services to the households.

e. Monasteries are places of social gatherings, religious and social functions and festivals, which were not few.

f. At the times of emergency the monasteries served as place of refuge like forts.

Revenue under the Dogras and modification in the system

As we have seen above Trebeck and JD Cunningham both report that revenue during the time of Ladaki rule was collected all in grain. Since 1834-35, as Ladak came under the Dogras,Spiti, the dependency of Ladak, also came under their rule. According to Major Hay, the king or Gyalpo of Ladak prior to 1839, took as revenue from Spiti Rs.396 cash, 200 *khals* of grain, 100 mundis or iron crowbars, 34 pieces of barmur cloth, and 132 *shugu* or paper. The crowbars or iron to make them came from Bashahar and were paid out of the common fund. The other manufactured articles could be made in every house. We observe that according to Major Hay before 1839 the revenue of the state constituted partly cash and partly grain. This dual system might have been introduced by the Dogras.

The conversion from grain collection to cash might have been done to the extent of the amount of grain used to be sent to Leh. The part of collection in grain which was consumed in Spiti towards public purposes and also *bun* perhaps remained unchanged. JD Cunningham's report is, of course, slightly different. Besides, there must have been some increase in the amount of collection.

Major Hay further records that from 1839 to 1843 the *thanedar* at Leh took the revenue of Spiti. For the first two years rupees 2,000 plus two ponies and 35 sheep were exacted. For the last three years the cash was reduced to rupees 1,031 but 100 iron crowbars were added and the number of sheep were increased to sixty.

Propositions of the British Government

The British took over the charge of the district in 1846. Alexander Cunningham and Vans Agnew visited the area in 1847. Agnew also conducted a Summary Settlement of the revenue system of Spiti fixing it at rupees 753 per annum. The amount was much reduced from the amount paid to the Dogras. This was to be collected entirely in cash and was distributed on all the landholders in the five *kothis* equally, including the *Chhoszhikothi*. The responsibility of collection of the revenue was assigned initially to Mansukh Dass, Wazir of Bashahar state.

Thereafter Major Hay visited Spiti in 1849 and spent the whole winter there in studying the area with the objective, as stated, of future revenue settlement. He makes no reference to any kind of problem faced by the people in paying the revenue.

Nethal and *Bun*

As we know that the principle form of the revenue collected from the four *khalsa kothis* which went to the Raja at Leh was known as *nethal.*Besides this they were also paying a small amount of grain to the Nono which was known as *mKhar-gi-bun.* After the conversion of the *nethal* into cash after the summary settlement this latter term came to be known as *nethal.*

The Difficulty and the Cause: After the Summary Settlement the system of collection of the revenue from the point of view of the tax-payers became much complicated. On the part of government they had finished the job considering to have lightened the burden of the people of Spiti and to have simplified the whole system. The entire collection was consolidated into one form of cash divided on all the households proportionately in all the five *kothis*. As was the custom, besides the regular payments of revenue the four *khalsakothis* continued paying the partial *nethal* which was collected by the Nono. The fifth *kothi, kothiChhoszhi*, in addition to the regular revenue equal to all others, continued paying *bun* to the monasteries at the same rate as they had been paying traditionally. As the government had ignored touching all kinds of traditional payments, the people could not stop the paymentsof their own will as they were essential from their point of view. Thus all were overburdened, but those of *Chhoszhikothi* were burdened more than all others.

Lyall notes, 'the collection of pun and ne-thal went on as before; the pun continuing to go to the monasteries and the ne-thal being expended by the representative of government in Spiti, the Nono on public purposes. No alteration was made in the grain collection after the Regular settlement but the redistribution of the cash revenue affected under Mr Barnes' orders had an oppressive effect upon the land owners of ChhoszhiKothi. They had previously fixed a light cash revenue but a very heavy pun contribution to the monasteries. By the redistribution their cash revenue was considerably enhanced while they continued to pay the same amount of grain to the monasteries as before'.

Lyall explains how this issue was ignored during regular settlement saying that,Barnes at the regular Settlement of 1851-52 maintained the status quo as fixed by Vans Agnew. He sent a *tehsildar*, his representative, who visited Spiti, roughly divided the amount of rupees 753 upon all the five *kothis* with reference to the number of holdings in each. He perhaps was unaware or ignored the payment in grain and Barnes made the holdings in *Chhoszhi* pay cash as much as those of other *kothis*, though they paid ten times as much grain to the monasteries. Not to pay the grain to the monasteries would have been sacrilege and would have been resented by the whole community.

About the works of the tehsildar deputed to Spiti by Barnes,Lyallwrites that, 'I think he must have heard of the grain payment, but he was in a great hurry, and seems to have considered that they could not be taken into account, so without making any report to Mr. Barnes, he made the holdings in Chuzie pay as much as those of other kothis. The Chuzi men paid, the grain as before, though with much grumbling, which no officer of Government seems to have heard or understood.'

It is not that the fact that some houses were exclusively attached to the monasteries and they were not paying any tax to the king, was not known earlier, as we have already noticed.

Efforts towards removal of the difficulty

The exercise in understanding the cause was long drawn and took very long time. A few travelers and administrative officers put their effort of their own to thrash out the problem. The fiscal system of Spiti was rooted in the intricately woven web of the social structure, religious organization and the economic system. Therefore in order to reach at the root of the cause, understanding of the whole social system was essential.

Egerton, Deputy Commissioner, Kangra, visited Spiti in 1863 and remained there for two months. Besides pursuing the specific problem of revenue payment emerging before the administration time and again, he was interested in studying the area in its different aspects. Egerton summoned a meeting of the monks, head of each of the five large monasteries, and the zamindars in 1863 at Dankhar. The monks were called upon to attend the meeting in their full dress. He placed the problem before them.According to Egerton, Lyall had brought the problem to his notice stating that the grain rates were not paid voluntarily and the matter was under his investigation. Egerton proposed that instead of grain rates or tithes, the monks should consider to accept a fixed allotment of land and that government could not sanction the collection of a compulsory grain tax, and could not interfere if the payments were upheld. But if the zamindars chose to make over a certain amount of land for the maintenance of the monasteries, they could do so, and the government would take the appropriate action. Egerton says that the monks seemed to relish the idea but the very zamindars unanimously objected to the proposition. They urged that under the present arrangements the monks had a direct interest in the welfare of their parishioners helped them in their fields and in carrying travellers' baggage, did any bit of handicraft required, and in short were, to some extent, dependent on their parishioners: whereas by the proposed arrangement, the monks would be quite independent; they would cease to look after their welfare, spiritual or temporal, and would no longer take a share in their labours (Egerton, 1864: 30).Egerton felt impressed by the arguments adduced by the zamindars.

The problem remained as it was.In fact the problem came up before Egerton in the reverse form, as he says that the farmers were not paying the grain payments to the monasteries voluntarily. Egerton's sympathy was naturally sided with the dazzling sight of the monastic performances and the problem of those who were maintaining the monasteries and were the real sufferers remained unnoticed and was ignored. He could not understand that the burden being too heavy the farmers were not in the position to pay and not that they were unwilling to pay. Egerton's gift to Spiti, however, survives in his monumental work.

Lyall's Efforts

Lyall visited Spiti in 1862 when he was Assistant Commissioner of Kullu. He was aware of the grave problem and some other grievances of the people of Piti. After the visit he submitted a report recommending that the '*bun*', the assigned grain which was being paid by the landlords of *Chhoszhikothi* to the religious institutions, should be lumped together with the grain collection made from the residents of other four *kothis*, although it was in small quantity, and the total sum should be redistributed equally on all the landholders of the five *kothis*. All other kinds of collection which the Nono was levying should be stopped, but Nono and all the concerned workers should be properly compensated and paid for.

The Problem Aggravated: Lyall says that his proposals were not fully understood by the officers who had never seen the country, and no definite orders were passed for some years. Eventually when the government came to implement the provisions of amendment as proposed above by Lyall, the Nono was given remuneration for his job, further he was given to understand that he must not collect the *nethal*. But the monasteries were left to collect the *'bun'* as before, although it was not formally recognized as assigned revenue. The arrangement made the situation worse by comparison, for it was the four *khalsakothis* to whom *nethal* was remitted. Their burden was lightened to the extent they were paying the *nethal* collection to Nono. The burden of the *Chhoszhi* men remained the same, and in comparison to the others the difference became much wider.

Lyall's suggestion was judicious and equitable. If the recommendations of Lyall had been accepted and implemented,without disturbing the existing system of cash levy, the *nethal* and *bun* also would have been distributed similarly among all the taxpayers of the five *kothis* equally.The result would have been that all the tax-payers of the five *kothis* would have been paying *nethal*, *bun* and cash payment in equitable measure. This would have rooted out the cause of the problem at this stage.

Change in Collection and the final settlement: Thereafter Mr Forsyth, Commissioner of the Division, again represented the case to Government in 1866 and as revision of Settlement had then commenced, Mr Lyall, Settlement Officer, was assigned the responsibility to reinvestigate the case. Lyall was already well aware of the nature of the problem. He studied all the aspects of the problem thoroughly again.

Lyall, with Mr Forsyth's concurrence, revised the *nethal* collections, not in part, but in whole, without disturbing much the traditional distribution system, and recommended their assignment in part to village officials and in part to other purposes to which they were applied by custom in former days. The *nethal* which was to be spent in Spiti and the *bun* which was to go to the monasteries were all redistributed among all the five *kothis*. Lyall says the cash assessment of *Chhoszhikothi* was reduced by more than one half and the amount was distributed over the other kothis. Thus cash assessment and *nethal* collection were redistributed equitably on all individual tax-payer of the whole district. Finally the grievance of the men of Spiti especially those of *Chhoszhikothi* were removed.

The following table shows the amount of collection of the cess in various kinds of cash and grain for the monasteries and on the government account from the different kothis after the assessment made by Lyall, as he reports.

Name of Kothi/ Particulars	Pin	Sham	Bar	Chhoezhis	Tod	Total
No. of villages Attached to kothi	14	7	11	7	11	50
1. No. of Jeolas	63	55	53	64	61	296
2. No. of houses	171	126	117	184	161	759
3. Arable land a. khalsa (acre)	323	221	194	203	178	1119
b. muafi (acre)	12	18	22	10	3	65
4. Assessment a. Cash (Rs., Anna)	219-17	180-4	156-0	91-2	166-0	813-3
b. Bun (khal, de)	101-10	190-19	192-13	856-3	120-2	1461-07
c. Nethal (khal, de)	99-5	157-5	87-9	12-0	100-12	456-11

Lyall explains about the utilization of the amount of *bun* in the monasteries and says that it is not divided among the monks for everyday consumption in the separated cells. It is used in public kitchen on the occasion of certain festivals which last sometimes several days during which special services are performed in the chapels.

Holdings or allotments other than those of the *thalpa* or revenue paying landholdings:Lyall further informs that a family of hereditary astrologers (*Jhoba*) hold two allotments at Tashigang, granted to them by the kings of Ladak free of demand for revenue or begaar. The land at Dankhar is incharge of the Nono. The holdings of the Nono in his village were rent free. The Nono of Pin possessed rent free holding but it was not more than equal to an ordinary holding. There are two families who, in addition to their revenue paying allotment also hold good sized plots rent free under the name of *manzhing* (medicine field). They are *amchie* or hereditary practitioners of the art of medicine and this land was granted to them in support of the art. Many of the landholders practice medicine, but only these two families hold *manzhing*.

Contribution to Pithug: Settlement Report (1887-92: 32) records that a contribution of 40 *khals* of *Ne* equivalent to rupees three was collected in Spiti as *bun* and was sent to Pithug in Ladak. This was collected wholly from the village of Khyikhim. But no payment had been collected by the monks of Pithug during the British period. Pithug claims to have been blessed by Nyi-ma Gungpa, Arya Madhyantika, who was an *arhata* and succeeded Ananda in the lineage of the seven upholders of the Doctrine of the Buddha. He went to Kashmir and subdued Nagaraj Audustathere. The monastery is also stated to have been founded by Rinchhen Zangpo. In the time of king Dag-pa Bum-de of Ladak it was converted into Gelugpa Order by Lama Lhabang Lodoe.

Begaar or forced labour: Begaar (free services) ordinarily implies the free and compulsory services provided by the landlords by way of labour towards the Raja or the government. In the medieval period to some extent military service also was levied in the form of begaar. During the British period there were large contingents of government officials, government sponsored and supported visitors, travelers, to whom such services were directed to be rendered. They had large quantity of loads and required large number of mules, labourers, ration, fuel and fodder. These were required to be arranged by the villagers which were identified traditionally from stage to stage within the respective area. The government also required the post bags to be carried in similar manner to distances and across the high passes. In the event of great demand the *khangchhenpas* could impress upon the *zurpas* for the supply of labour and also the monks. The villagers had also created common store wherein grains were collected annually and were supplied from there to the travelers.

Festivals:

Traditional Festivals of Regional level: The Gazetteer records that in the month of August or September the great fair called *Namkan Chhenmo* is held at Dankhar, at which horse races are also held. In November the ta'lsi(*khral-rtsi*) chhenmo, grand audit, is held at which the annual accounts of revenue collection (*rtsi-rug*) are rendered. Five days later the religious festival of dgu-gtor is celebrated at four monasteries of Kyi, Tabo, Dankhar and Pin at which are performed the *chham* or mask dances. At Tengyudgonpa a similar festival called 'jigs-byed (Bhairava) is held a month earlier.

Agricultural Activities and Amusement: The festival of Namkan was held in Spiti to mark the beginning of the important agricultural operations of mowing and harvesting. After the celebration of the fairuse of sharp edged instruments like sickle could be started which was otherwise banned from the time of beginning of the season i.e. sowing of the crops. After this the mowing of grass and harvesting of crops could be started. Namkan fair was held at two levels, at regional level at Dankhar which was called Namkan Chhenmo, Great Namkan, and at the village level in many vallages called Namkan Chungun, Little Namkan.

The Festival of Namkan Chhenmo: The Festival of Namkan Chhenmo is held at Balang-ri, situated near the village of Daimul near Dankhar on a high mountain. It is a beautiful place where during the summer season the villagers keep their cattle, sheep, goat, horses, etc. for grazing. There is a large plain where grass grows in plenty. This is perhaps for this reason that this mountain is called 'Balang-ri', 'mountain of cattle', in short also as Beng-ri.This mountain is supposed to be the residence of Lha (gods) and Dre (demons) and some also know it as sBas-yul, name of a mythical secret place.

In this festival horse race is a great attraction where about more than fifty participants take part. The fair used to be attended by the traditional peers like jhova, lamas, amchi, the wealthy people of the villages, and the other villagers who came in the best of their dresses. Women are prohibited from going to the mountain and participating in certain fairs.

Festival at Dankhar: Trebeck when he visited Spiti in 1822 witnessed the fair at Dankhar which was held on the 15th of August. He narrates: "On the fifteenth of August the approach of harvest was celebrated by a public festival, and at the invitation of Khaga Khan I joined the party at his residence. I found his room crowded by the men of the village. I had not been long seated before three of the company rose to dance to the tune played by the blacksmith, who had exchanged his anvil for a couple of drums. The performance precisely resembled what often witnessed at Le, the motion of the feet was extremely slow and spiritless, but was accompanied by various movements of the hands and arms and the waving of a woolen cloth in the form of a shawl, which latter is always used for the purpose by the more wealthy people in the north. At twelve o'clock everyone went home to saddle his horse and put on his smartest dress. After this had been done, the whole again assembled in the hollow below the village, where a piece of ground about one hundred yards long had been smoothed for the occasion. On one side of this a small mark was set up, and every one galloped his pony past, in general throwing at it with a stone, though one of the riders made use of a bow and arrow, and two others had their matchlocks. The last were admirable caricatures: both rode about as fast as an active person might hop, and fired with the muzzle of their guns within a few inches of the mark, which it is but justice to observe they always hit. In the afternoon, every inhabitant of the village, both male and female, met in a yard close to the fort. A second and larger batch of chang was in readiness, and the dancing was incessant, and much more varied and entertaining than any I had seen at Le'. The most pleasing part of it was performed by the women, who joined hands, and moved in a circle, with a regular step and much vivacity, singing at the same time. A *pas-seul* of an old shepherd was also amusing, as it had more of humour than vulgarity, and would have done credit to a clown on an English stage. Notwithstanding the rain which was falling the greatest part of the evening, the general mirth continued till dark unabated. On the following day eating superseded other occupations",(Moorcroft,1841- II: 75-77). This was perhaps one of the three fairs referred to by Major Hay, one of which as he says was held at Dankhar.

Namkanchungun: Similar festivals were held in many villages with slight variations a few days before the agricultural operations like mowing of grass and harvesting of crops can be started in the village. It is also a symbolic celebration praying for wealth and prosperity.

The festival is held in the month of July-August. The villagers gather in the best of their dresses in one of the houses. Every house has to host the festival by turn each year. They bring with them tsampa, ghee, chhang and arrack. On the second day they get up early in the morning and go up towards the moutain, singing throughout the way. At a fixed place there is the residence of the village deity of the wild, generally near a water spring where there are many kinds of flowers in full bloom. He says this is my place, these are my flowers, without my consent you cannot pluck them. He even threatens the people of dire consequences, in case they fail to follow his instructions. The deity is the first to pluck the flowers, then the people follow. They collect flowers of different kinds from different places. These are large *han mentog,* yellow *lata-mentog*, small *lama mentog*, etc. They wear the flowers on their heads. They offer tsampa, chhang and arrack to the deity which they had brought with them and then enjoy themselves, singing and dancing. They come back singing and dancing by the late evening carrying flowers of different kinds wrapped in *ling-tse*, women's shawl, carrying on their back to offer to the gods. In the village the musicians have gathered and are waiting for the arrival of the party from the mountain.

They all gather at the house of the chief of the village. They place the flowers in his chapel. On the next day there is a horse racing. People bring their horses from the grazing land and decorate them with saddles with new carpets. They celebrate the fair in the *ulthag*, the thrashing ground, of the chief. The old men dance with swords in their hand and then starts the horse race. Some figures of *tsampa* are prepared for target. Then they sing song. They shout as they run, throw arrows and pelt stones on thetarget. In the evening they come in the best of their clothes and decked with ornaments when they drink, eat, sing and dance.

The next day is considered as sacred day. The village deity, at some places called Jor-lha or Jho-ku-lha, is propitiated. The *lha-tho* is decorated with animal horns and fresh branches of *shugpa* which has to be brought by the house in which there is a sick person. The *labdad*, priest, pays prayer. A lama also pays prayers and *lungta,* prayer flag, is raised. On the next day the work of mowing and harvesting in the fields can be started. The villagers have obligation to do work firstly at the house of the important persons in the village like *amchi, jhoba, Nono,* etc. Customarily one person from each household also goes in the household where there is a sick person. They get divided if there are more than one such house in the village. This is done so that their work is not left behind. Customs of such celebrations have now ceased to be held in many villages. In Kaza it is said to have been stopped about in the year of 1973.

Musical Instruments: Important folk musical instruments common in Spiti are:*mda-man* (paired kettle-drum), *surna*(trumpet), *dab* (large sized tambourine), and string instruments of *gogpo* and *piyang*. The former three instruments are played by the *beda* class, the professional musicians and the latter two by the amateur players from chha-zang class. *Dab,* of the size of about half meter of diameter, is played by women. *Daman* and *surna* are played by men. Gogpo and Piyang, two string instruments, are played by men. Gogpo receives its name from a bird of the same name which is slightly bigger than crow. Base of the instrument is round resembling the bird's body. It has six strings and produces heavy sound. Piyang, a three stringed instrument like a guitar, smaller than *gogpo*, has base with a shape resembling a sitting cat and produces pitched sound like that of a cat. The word *piyang* is formed from two words *pi* (from *pi-shi* = cat) and *dbyangs*(voice) i.e. voice of cat which is nearly so.

Annexure-1

I. Documents

A. Decree of Dechhog Namgyal

ས་སྐྱོང་སྤྲིའི་དབང་པོ་ཆོས་རྒྱལ་ཆེན་པོ་སྲི་སྤྲཚོག་ནམྤྲ་རྒྱལ་གྱི་བཀའ།

རང་རེའི་སྤྲང་འོག་དུ་རྡོགས་པ་ནམྤྲས་ལ་དཙལ།སྡོད་ནམྤྲ་གྱི་ཕེ་བ་སྤུད་དང་།དཔང་འཁྱོར་གཉིས། ཀྱི་ཞིང་ཁང་ཐུགས་སྟག་པ་ལ་ཡིན།ཨུ་རྒྱན་གི་དུས་ཀྱི་སྤྲཚོད་པ་ཆེན་པོའི་ཚེ་ཆུ་ངཙལ།ས་སྟུགས་སྐེང་སྤྲི

དགེ་ཚོ་ཆེན་པོ་ལ་དཙལ་བ་ཡིན།དེ་ནམྤྲས་ལ་སྟག་སོས་ལུག་སོས་ཤོག་ཁྲལ་འདོར་ན་ཁྲལ་རི་གང་ཡ ང་སྤྲིད་པ་ཐུགས་ལ་བསྟགས་པ་ཡིན་བསླལ་ནམྤྲ་གནས་གྱི་བར་དུ་ཐུགས་ལ་སྟགས་པ་ཡིན།སྤྲཁར་དཔོན་རྫོ ང་དཔོན་རྣན་སྤྲི་དསྤྲངས་སྤྲུག་སྤྲི་གཉེར་ལས་བྱེད་ཕྱིར་དཔོན།ཁི་ར་དྲག་གཞན་ཡུལ་སྤྲི་འི།འདི་ལ་ཟེར་རི་སོགས་པ གང་ཡང་སྤྲིད། བདེ་བར་གནས་ཙུག།། སུས་ཀྱང་སྐྱེ་ར་ཆེར་སྤྲིད་པ་ཡིན། སྐྱེ་ར་ཆེར་བྱེད་ན་ཚར་རྡབ་ཆོད་དྲག་པོ་རྫེ་ལ་ཡོང་།ལྕུགས་སྤྲོ་ཕག་གི་ཟླ་བ་ ༡པའི་ཚེ་བ་བཅུ་གཉིས་ཕོ་བྲང་ཆེན་པོ་ཡང་སྤྲཁར་རྩེ་ནས་དཙལ།

ཞུ་བ་པོ་སྤྲཁར་དཔོན་ནམྤྲ་སྤྲཁའ་རྒྱལ་སྤྲཚན་ཡིན།

B.Contract for sharing the crops from the fields of Guling monastery

པདྨ་ལྷུན་གྲུབ་ལ་ཁལ་ལྔ་སོ་གཉིས་སུསྤྲ་ཆ་གཉིས་བི་ཀ་ནས་ཆེ་ཙུ་བོན་གྲང་ལ་གུ་ལིང་ལ་ སྤྲང་ལང་ཅེ་ལ་ཞེས་ཡིན།འུ་བ་ལེན་ཅེ་ན་ཁལ་བྱེད་དང་ཕེ་དང་གསུམྤྲ།སྡོད་ནམྤྲ་ན་ཆེ་རིང་རྡོ་རྗེ།

C. Collection of revenue for the monasteries

པི་ཏི་ཁུ་ལ་གྱི་ས་དགེ་སྐྱིང་གསུམྤྲ་གྱི་ཟླ་སྤྲ་ལས་སྟེ་ནམྤྲས་ནས་ངེས་དགོས།

སྔོན་དུ་༸གཞུང་བདེ་སྐྱཆོག་གི་ཞབས་དྲུང་ལ་གང་སྐྱེ་ནས། དགོན་རྙིང་གི་····བསྟུ་ལེན་བྱེད་པ་ལ།
རེ་གཉིས་····འདོད་ཀྱི་སྣ་བར་གང་དྲན་བྱེད་པར་ཉམས་པ་ཐོབ་པ་····བཞི་ཆ་གོང་གི་ཟླ་སྤྲ་སྤྱི་ལ་དངུལ་སྲང་ཉི་

ཤུ་ཙ་ལྔ་དང་ཞོ་དྲུག་སྐར་ལྔ།སྐྱིད་པ་ཟླ་སྤྲར་དངུལ་སྲང་དྲུག་དང་ཞོ་དགུ།བར་ཀྱོག་ཟླ་སྤྲར་དངུལ་སྲང་དྲུག
དང་ཞོ་དགུ།ལག་དཔེ་ཟླ་སྤྲར་དངུལ་སྲང་གསུམ་དང་ཞོ་དགུ།

ཧྲ་སོ་ཟླ་སྤྲར་དངུལ་སྲང་བདུན་དང་ཞོ་དགུ།བྱང་གླིང་ཟླ་སྤྲར་དངུལ་སྲང་དྲུག་དང་ཞོ་བདུན་དང་སྐར་བརྒྱད།
གོང་སྦྲིག་ཟླ་སྤྲར་དངུལ་སྲང་གང་དང་ཞོ་གང་སྐར་ཕྱེད་བརྒྱད། གྱི་ཉི་ཟླ་སྤྲར་དངུལ་སྲང་སྤྲིད་ཞོ་དགུ་
བཅས་སྤྲོབས་པར་༸གཞུང་ཞབས་སྟན་རྣམས་སྡེ་སོར་བཀའ་སྟན་རི་སྤྲུས་པའི་དགོངས་དོན།གཞི་རི་སྤྲ་སོ་
སོའི་དགོན་རྙིང་ཆེ་ཆུང་ལ་སྐར་སྤྲི་བྱི་སྐར་ཚོམ་ཆེ་ཆུང་ཉམས་ཆེ་ ། བྲིས་ཕྱག་བྱེད་པ་ལ་བར་དང་རང་གང་དྲན་བྱུས་པར་སུ་སྤྲ་ཧྲད་ནས་དེ་ལ་འབྱུང་
སྤྲ་བྱས་ན་སྤྲི་སྤྲུན་པ་ངེས་པ་བགྱིས། སྤྱི་བྱི་ཟླ་ཚེས་ལ།

D. mKhan Rinpochhe

ཡི་དེ་ཁྱལ་ཟླ་སྤྲ་ལས་སྡེ་ཐུན་སྤྲོངས་ནས་ཡིན་སྤྲོགོན་ཞུང་ཞབས་སྐྱེར་ལོ་སྣང་ཆགས་ཀྱི་ཞབས་དཀུ་ལ་འབུལ་དོན་
ཀྱིསྐོར་ལ་སྟར་རྒྱན་དགོན་ཆེ་ཆུང་གི་ཟླ་སྤྲར་འབབས་ཆུང་ནང་ཚོགས་འབྲི་པ་འཆང་སར་གྱོར་རྒྱན་ལུགས་པར།འདི་ལོ་ཟླ་སྤྲ་རེ་གཉིས་ནས
དང་པའི་བྲིགས་ཅན་པ་སྤྲ་ལུགས་ལྟ་བུའི་དགོན་ཆེ་ཆུང་པོ་ངས་ཀྱི་ཟླ་སྤྲར་འགོ་སྤྲེ་པ་རྟགས་འདུག་པས་འོས་སྤྲིན་ཡིག་འཚོ་བཅས།།ཕྱག་ཆད
སྟར་རྒྱན་བཟང་པོའི་རྒྱན་བཞིན་ཟླ་སྤྲ་འི་དངུལ་འབབ་དགོན་ཆེ་ཆུང་འདི་དག་འབབ་བྲི་པ་སྟར་བཞིན་ཕོངས་པ་བགྱི།།ཚེས་སུ་ཟླ་ཚེས་ལ།།

The title of the letter is torn out. Outside, the letter is addressed to:

སྤྲཁན་རིན་པོ་ཆེ་སྐུ་ཞོག་ཁྲི་ཆེན་ལ་དང་བཉེན་གྲགས་ཀྱི་ཁྱབ་བདག་ཆེན་པོ།།

II. Colophons to Sacred Books

A. Colophon to Zamatog-I

ཀ་ དོན་གཉིས།

ཨོཾ་སྭསྟི། པདྨ་ཧཱུྃ། ཕྱག་རྡོ་རྗེ་ཆེན་པོ་སྤྱན་རས་གཟིགས་དབང་ཕྱུག་ལ་ཕྱག་འཚལ་ལོ།ཕྱག་རྡོ་རྗེ་ཆེན་པོའི་རྟེན་པ་དར་རྒྱལ་བསྟན་པའི།
སྔོན་ཡང་དག་པར་རྫོགས་པའི་སངས་རྒྱ་མྱ་ངན་ལས་འདས་པར།བྱང་ཆུབ་སེམས་དཔའ་རྣམས་ཀྱི་སྤྱོ་ཆོག་

འཕགས་པ་སྤྱན་རས་གཟིགས་ལ་བཀའ་སྩལ་པ་ང་འི་སྟོན་པ་ལ་ཞུགས་པ་ལ་།བྱང་ཕྱོགས་ཁ་ཅན་གྱི་རྒྱལ་
ཁམས་ཞེས་བྱ་བ་བྱང་ཆུབ་སེམས་དཔའ་ཁྱེད་ཀྱི་འདུལ་བྱར་གྱུར་པ།ཡུལ་ཕྱོགས་དེར་ཁྱོད་ཀྱིས་འགྲོ་བ
འི་དོན་གྱིས་ཅིག།དེ་སྐྱེས་པའི་སེམས་ཅན་ཐམས་ཅད་ཤིན་ཏུ་སྡེ་རགས་པ་འདུལ་བཀའ་བར་གྱུར་
པས་།ཐབས་སྣ་
ཚོགས་ཀྱིས་སྤྲུལ་ཅིག།དེ་སྐད་དུ་ལུང་སྟན་ནས།འཕགས་པ་སྤྱན་རས་གཟིགས་དབང་ཕྱུག་ལ་བོད་ཡུལ་བྱ་
བ་སྲིད་པ་ལ།བྱང་ཆུབ་སེམས་དཔའ་སྤྲེའུ་ཏ་ལ་སྤྲན་འཛུར་སྤྲུལ་ནས།
ཇོ་སྤྲོ་སྤྲོལ་སྤྲ་བྲག་སྲིན་སྤྲོར་སྤྲུལ་ནས།དེ་གཉིས་ལས་བསྐྱེད་ནས་རིགས་རྒྱུད་སྤྲིར་ཕེལ་ནས།
སྤྲི་ནམས་འདུལ་བྱ་ལ་བབ་པར་གཟིགས་ནས། (དོན་གསུམ།) ཕ་སྤྲེའུ་དང་སྤྲ་བྲག་སྲིན་སྤྲོ་རུ་སོང་ནས།
ཤིན་ཏུ་འདུལ་བཀའ་བར་འགྱུར་ནས།ཁྲིམ་ཉེར་ཅན་གྱི་སྤྲུལ་བལ་སྤྲོ་ཟ་ཁྲི་བཙུན་དང་།ཇོ་སྤྲོ་སྤྲོལ་སྤྲའི་སྤྲུལ་པ་རྒྱལ་
སྤྲོ་ཨོང་ཇོ་གཉིས་ཁབ་ཏུ་བཞེས།སྤྱན་རས་གཟིགས་ཀྱིས་སྤྲུལ་པ་སྤྲོན་སྤྲི་ས་སྟོ་རས་སྤྲི་ཁ་བྱུང་།རྒྱ་ནག་ནས་ཡི་གེ།སྨ
བས་བོད་ཡིག་ཏུ་རྒྱུར།ལྷ་ས་འཕྲུལ་ནང་དང་ར་སྤྲོ་ཆེ་ལ་སོགས་པ་ལྷ་ཁང་རྒྱ་རྩ་བཞེངས།རྒྱ་
གར་རྒྱ་ནག་བལ་པོའི་ཡུལ་གིས་སྤྲཁས་པ་ཊི་ཏ་ནམས་སྤྱན་དྲངས།ཡང་དག་པར་རོགས་པའི་སངས་རྒྱས་
ཀྱིས་སྒྲ་ཚབ་ལྷཤྭ་ཀྱཱ་སྦཱ་ནེ་གཉིས་རྒྱ་ནག་དང་།བལ་པོ་ནས་སྤྱན་དྲངས།སྤྲོན་སྤྲི་ས་སྟོ་རས་ལོ་ཚ་བའི་སྤྲ་ཚན་བུ་སྤྲཁས་པ
འགའ་ཡང་སྤྲབས་ནས།དམ་པའི་ཆོས་པོ་ཏི་དང་གླེགས་བམ་སྤྲང་པོ་སྤྲུར་རོ།།ཁྱད་པར་འཕགས་པ་སྤྱན་རས་གཟིགས་ཀྱི་སྤྲོད་རྒྱུད་ཨཱ་ཧཱུཾ་
གཅིག་སྒྲུར།
རྒྱལ་པོ་ཡབ་དང་ཡུམ་སྤྲ་དང་།ཇོ་སྤྲོ་དང་སྲས་པོ་དང་སྲས་སྤྲོ་དང་།འབངས་དང་།ནང་བློན་དང་།ཕྱི་བར་བློན་དང་།ཕྱི་བློན་དང་ཕྱི་འཁོར་ད
ང་།ནང་འཁོར་ལ་སོགས་པ་ཡང་རང་རེ་འི་བློའི་རི་སྤྲ་པ་དང་།སྟོད་ཀྱི་རི་སྤྲ་པ་དང་སྤྲར་ནས།ཐུགས་རྗེ་ཆེན་པོའི་གདན་སྤྲ་པ་བཤད
།འཁོར་ཐམས་ཅད་ཕྱིར་སྤྲི་ལྡོག་པའི་སྲིད་པ་ཐ་སྤྲ་བྱང་ཆུབ་སེམས་
དཔར་འགྱུར་ཏོ།དེ་ནས་རྒྱལ་པོ་དུས་ཕྱི་སྤྲའི་འགྲོ་དོན་ལ་དགོངས་ནས།ཐུགས་རྗེ་ཆེན་པོའི་སྒྲུབ་སྐོར་སྤྲང་དུ་གསུངས། (དོན་
བཞི།) ལོ་ཚ་བ་སྤྲོན་སྤྲི་བས་སྤྲ་སྟོ་རས་སྤྲི་རྗེད་པའི་གཟུངས་ཐོབ་པས།དེས་སྤྲུལ་པའི་རྒྱལ་པོ་ཅིག་གསུངས་ཡི་གེ་བྲིས་སོ།རྒྱལ་
སྟོན་པར་ཤེས་སྤྲང་འ་དེ་ཐུགས་རྗེ་ཆེན་པོ་ཡིན་པས་ལོ་ཚ་བ་ནམས་ལ་
བཀའ་ཆེ་སྤྲས་སྟད་ནས།ང་འི་བཤད་པའི་ཆོས་འདི་ནམས་དཔེའ་གཉིས་སུ་བྲིས་ཅིག།ཅིག་ཆུ་དར་སྟོན་པོ་ལ་
བྲིས་གསེར་དངུལ་གི་བྲིས་ལ།ཁྲ་སྤྲ་ཁྲུ་སྤྲ་གི་དཀོར་སྤྲཛོད་དུ་རྒྱལ་བུ་ཡི་ཟླ་གཏེར་དུ་སྤྲོས།ཅིག་རྒྱ་ཤོག་ལ་
དྲིལ་དུ་སྤྲིལ་ལ།ཐུགས་རྗེ་ཆེན་པོའི་ལྷ་ཁང་གི་རྣ་འབྲིན་གྱི་ཞབས་འོག་ཏུ་སྤྲོས།

གང་ཟག་སྡིགས་ཀྱི་གྲུབ་པ་ཐོབ་པའི་གང་ཟག་གིས་སྙིང་ནས་རང་གི་འདུལ་བྱའི་ཆོས་སུ་གྱུར་ནས།དེ་ནས་ལས་འབྲེལ་ཡོད་པའི་སྐྱེས་བུ།སྐྱེ་བ་སྦྱང་པོར་སྦྱངས་པའི་སྐྱེས་བུ་སྒྲུབ་པ་རྩོན་པ་ནི།བྱང་ཆུབ་སེམས་འབྱོངས་པ་ཅིག་ལས་དང་བསྐལ་བ་ཡིན་གྱིས།དེ་ལ་ཤོག་ཏྲིལ་སྟོག་ཅིག། དེ་ཉི་མ་ལྷོ་ཕྱོགས་ནས་ནུབ་དང་།བྱང་ཕྱོགས་སུ་རྒྱས་པར་འགྱུར་རོ།དུས་དེ་ཙ་ན།ཨོཾ་མ་པ་དྨེ་ཧཱུྃ།ཞེས་པའི་ཡི་གེ་རང་འབྱུང་དུ་ཆར་བ།འོངས་པས།སྐུ་རང་འབྱུང་ཆར་བ་འོང་།ཐུགས་རང་འབྱུང་ཆར་འོང་།བྱང་ཆུབ་སེམས་དཔའི་ལམ་ལ་གནས་པ་ལྷ་ཞིག་ཀྱང་ཡོད།ཐུགས་རྗེ་ཆེན་པོའི་བསྟན་པ་ལ་ཕོད་ཅིག། བྱང་ཆུབ་ཀྱི་སེམས་སྦྱོངས་ཅིག། འགྲོ་བ་ཐམས་ཅད་ལ་ཕན་སེམས་ཀྱིས་སྐྱོངས་ཅིག།། དེའི་དུས་སུ་སངས་རྒྱས་ཤཱ་ཀྱ་ཐུབ་པའི་སྟན་པ་མར་འགྲིབ་ལ།(དོན་ལྡཱ།)འོངས་པས།གཞུང་གི་ཆོས་བཤད་མི་བྱེད་པར་མན་དག་གིས་སྤྲུལ་པ་ཆོས་ལ་རྟེགས་སུ་བྱེད།ཆ''''དང་ཆེ་བས་དར་སྐྱེན་བསྒྲུབ་པ་ཉམས་སུ་མི་ལེན་པས་ནུབ་རྒྱན།ཆོས་ཀྱི་ཁ་འཛིན་ཆེ་ལ་སྒྲོ་བསྐུར་འདེབས།ཆོས་པ་རྣམས་ཀྱི་སྙིང་དུ་བདུད་ཞུས་ནས།ཅིག་ལ་ཅིག་ཐོད་སྟོང་གཅིག་བརྗོད་སྡིགས་པ་རྣམས་ཀྱི་སྙིད་''དུ་དམ་སྲི་ཞུགས་ནས།ཅིག་ལ་ཅིག་མ་ཐུ་འཁྲན་''བྱེད། སྐྱེས་པ་རྣམས་ཀྱི་སྙིད་དུ་འགོད་པོ་ཞུགས་ནས།དཀྲིའ་བྱེད་འཁྲུག་པ་བྱེད།བུད་མེད་རྣམས་ཀྱི་སྙིད་དུ་དི་མོ་ཞུགས་ནས་བཟའ་ཐབ་བྱེད་རང་སྲོག་རང་གིས་གཅོད།བྱིས་པ་རྣམས་ཀྱི་སྙིད་དུ་ཐེབ་རང་ཞུགས་ནས།ཕྱོད་ལོག་བྱེད།ལྷ་ཀླུ་གཉན་པོ་རྣམས་ཁྲུགས་ནས།ཆར་ཆུ་དུས་སུ་མི་འཕེབས།སྐབས་སུ་མ་གི་འོང་།སྲི་ཀུན་བསོད་ནམས་འགྲིབས་པའི་དུས་ནས་འོང་བའི་དུས་དེ་ཙམ་ན་བདེ་སྐྱིད་འཛོམ་པར་འདོད་ན།ཐུགས་རྗེ་ཆེན་པོ་སྤྱན་རས་གཟིགས་དབང་ཕྱུག་ལ།གསོལ་བ་ཐོབ་ཅིག།

B. Colophon to brGyad-stong-pa

ཨོཾ་སྭསྟི་སིདྡྷཾ།སྐུ་གསུམ་མངོན་དུ་གྱུར་པའི་བསྟོན་པ་སངས་རྒྱས་དང་། སྡེ་སྣོད་གསུམ་གྱི་ཕྱུག་པའི་དམ་ཆོས་དང་།བསླབ་གསུམ་ཀྱིས་མཛེས་པའི་དགེ་འདུན་སྡེ། སྐྱབས་གནས་དཀོན་མཆོག་གསུམ་ལ་གུས་ཕྱག་འཚལ་ལོ། ཨེ་མ་ཧོ། ཆོས་སྐུ་སྣང་བ་མཐའ་ཡས་འོད་དཔག་མེད། རི་བོ་ཏ་ལར་མགོན་པོ་སྤྱན་རས་གཟིགས།རྡན་ཀོ་ཤར་པདྨ་འབྱུང་གནས་སྐུ། མཁྱེན་རྩེ་ནུས་ལྡན་བླ་རུའི་བཞབས་ལ་འདུད།ཨེ་མ་ཧོ། སྟོན་པ་ཤཱཀྱ་ཐུབ་པ་དེ། འགྲོ་དྲུག་གཡོངས་ཀྱིས་བརྒྱན་དུ་མཛེས། སྒོ་གསུམ་གུས་པས་མཆོད་པ་ལ།ཀུན་ཀྱང་བརྩོན་པ་ཆེ་བར་མཛོད།རང་འབྱུང་སངས་རྒྱས་རྡོ་མཚར་ཆེ། ཡིད་ལ་སྨོན་མ་པས་མགོ་རིར་འགྲོ། ཨེ་མ་ཧོ། འཕགས་པ་སྤྱན་རས་གཟིགས་དབང་དེ། བོད་ཁམས་

གསྲོངས་ཀྱིས་བརྒྱན་དུ་སྤྲཛེས། འཁོར་བ་དོང་སྤྲུགས་སྤྲཛད་པ་ལ། ཀུན་ཀུང་སྤྲི་བོར་འཁྲུར་བར་སྤྲཛོད།
ངན་སོང་སྐྲི་སྒྲོ་བཅོད་དོ་སྤྲཚར་ཆེ། ཡིག་དྲུག་དྲངས་པ་སྤྲུབོ་རིས་འགྲོ། ཀྱི་ལེགས།གཏེར་བསྟོན་པདྨ་གླིང་
པ་དེ།སྤྲུལ་སྐུ་གཡོངས་ཀྱིས་བརྒྱན་དུ་སྤྲཛེས།དུས་གསུམ་སྤྲ་ཆོས་འཁོར་སྐོར་བ་ལ།ཀུན་ཀུང་དད་པ་ཆེ་བར
་སྤྲཛོད།སྤྲཚན་སྤྲུབོས་ཙམ་ཀྱི་སྤྲུབོ་རིས་འགྲོ།ཀྱི་ལེགས།རྗེས་བཙུན་གླིང་བཟང་གྲགས་པ་དེ།
བསྟན་འཛིན་ གཡོངས་ཀྱི་བརྒྱན་དུ་སྤྲཛེས།བསྟན་པ་བཞི་ནས་སོས་ པ་ལ།ཀུན་ཀུང་བཀའ་དྲིན་ཆེ་བར་སྤྲཛོ
ད།བདུད་རྩིའི་བཅུད་བདུས་དོ་སྤྲཚར་ཆེ། ཀྱི་ལེགས།དྲིན་ཅན་རྩ་བའི་ བླ་སྤྲདེ། སྤྲི་བོ་གཙུག་གིས་བ
རྒྱན་དུ་སྤྲཛེས། སྒོ་གསུམ་སྤྲ་གུས་པས་བསྟོད་པ་ལ། ཀུན་ཀུང་བཀའ་དྲིན་ ཆེ་བར་སྤྲཛོད།
བྱིན་བརླབས་དངོས་གྲུབ་དོ་སྤྲཚར་ཆེ།ཡིད་ལ་བསམ་པ་སྤྲུབོ་རིས་འགྲོ། ཀྱི་ལེགས། གླིང་
གི་སྤྲ་ཆོག་འགྱུར་ལྷོའི་འཛམ་བུ་གླིང་། སྟོང་གསུམ་སྤྲི་འཛིད་ཤ་ཀྱི་རྒྱལ་པོའི་ཞིང་། བསྟན་པའི་འབྱུང་
གནས་ རྡོ་རྗེ་གདན་གྱི་བྱང་།ཀུན་དགའ་བོ་དང་འོད་བསྲུངས་ནསྤྲ་གཉིས་ཀྱིས། ལན་གསུམ་སྤྲ་ བར་དུ་
བསྐུས་ནས་ཡི་གེར་བྲིས།དེ་རྗེ་སྤྲུལ་པའི་ཆོས་རྒྱལ་ནསྤྲ་གཉིས་ཀྱིས། ཆོས་ནསྤྲས་སྤྲ་ལུས་རྒྱ་ནས་ བོད་དུ་བསྒྱུར།
ཆོས་རྒྱལ་ལོ་པན་བོད་ལ་བཀའ་དྲིན་ཆེ།ཀྱི་ལེགས། ཁ་བ་ཅན་དུ་དསྤྲ་ཆོས་དར་བའི་ཞིང་།
དགྲ་བཅོསྤྲ་བཞུགས་གནས་ཏེ་སེ་གནས་གྱིས་སྤྲགུ་ལ།། སྤྲ་གྲོས་བཞུགས་གནས་སྤྲ་པང་གཡུ་འི་འགྲསྤྲ།
སེང་གེ་ཁ་འབབས་འབྲུག་པའི་གཡས་ཕྱོགས་ན།ཕོ་བྲང་ཆེན་པོ་བླ་ཆེན་སྒང་འགངས་རྩེར།
སྤྲི་དབང་ཆེན་པོ་བཀྲ་ཤིས་ནསྤྲ་རྒྱལ་གྱི་དབུ་མོག་སྤྲབོ་ཞིང་ཆབས་སྲིད་རྒྱས་འགྱུར་ཅིག།ཀྱི་ལེགས།
ཁོང་གིས་ཆབ་འོག་རྒྱལ་ས་ཡང་སྤྲཁར་རྩེར།སྤྲཁར་དཔོན་ཆེན་པོ་ག་ཏ་བསྟན་པ་རྒྱ་སྤྲ་ཚོ་ཁོང་ལ་བསྟོད།ཀྱི་
ལེགས།ས་ལ་འབུར་དུ་ཐོན་པའི་སྤྲིན་སྤྲཁར་ཆེན་པོ་འདིར། སྤྲཁར་དཔོན་ཆེན་པོ་ག་ཏ་ཐུག་བསྟན་ཁོང་ལ་སྟོད།
ཀྱི་ལེགས། ཡུལ་དགེ་བཅུ་འཛོམ་པའི་སྤྲིན་གྱི་ལུང་པ་རུ།ཕུ་རུ་རྩི་བཅུད་རྒྱས་ཤིང་སྤྲདོ་རུ་འབྲུ་ནསྤྲས་སྨིན།
ས་ལ་འབུར་དུ་ཐོན་པའི་གཞུང་ཡུལ་བརྟགས་ནསྤྲས་ཀྱི་སྐྲིད་ཡུལ་འདིར།ཆེ་སྟོན་བསོད་ནསྤྲས་བསགས་པས།ད
ལ་འབྱོར་སྤྲི་ལུས་ཐོབ།ཆེ་སྟོན་སྤྲིན་པ་བཏང་བས།ལོངས་སྤྱོད་ཤུགས་ལ་འབྱུང་།ཆེ་སྟོན་བཟོད་པ་བསྒོམ་སྤྲ
པས།ལུས་ལ་ནད་ཚ་སྤྲིད།དསྤྲ་ཆོག་ལས་འབྲས་ཡོད་པས་དསྤྲ་པའི་ཆོས་ལ་སྤྲོས།སྤྲི་རིགས་ཁྲུངས་བཙུན་སྐྲ་ཡི་

བརྒྱུད།དད་ལྡན་ཡོན་གྱིས་བདག་པོ་ཆེ་རིང་འགྱུར་ར་དང་།བསོད་ནསྤྲས་ལྷུན་གྲུབ་གཉིས་ཀྱིས།ཡ་འདྲེན་བླ་

སྤྲའི་སྐུ་ཆེ་སྟན་ཕྱིར་དང་།དྲིན་ཅན་ཕ་སྤྲའི་དྲིན་ལན་བསོབ་ཕྱིར་དང་།རྒྱལ་བློན་ནསྤྲས་ཀྱི་དབུ་མོག་སྤྲབོ་ཕྱིར་
དང་།རིགས་དྲུག་སེསྤྲས་ཅན་སྤྲཐར་ལསྤྲ་སྒྲོད་ཕྱིར་དང་།ཕྱི་སྤྲ་བྱང་ཆུབ་གོ་འཕངས་ཐོབ་ཕྱིར་དང་།རང་གི་

འགལ་རྐྱེན་བར་ཆད་ཞི་ཕྱིར་དང་། དམྲ་ཆོས་ཁྱད་འཕགས་རྡོ་རྗེ་གཅོད་པ་སྨྲ་བུ་བདུན་དང་རྒྱ་སྟོང་གསེར་གསུ་སྨྲ་སྤྲངས། བསགས་པ་ཆོས་ཕྱིར་གཏོང་བ་ངོ་སྨྲ་ཚར་ཆེ། ཀྱི་ལེགས། ཀོང་རྗོའི་རྒྱུད་འཛིན་དགའ་བའི་དཔལ་སྨྲ་ཆེ།

སྨྲོངས་ལ་ཕྱུལ་ཆགས་ནི་བཙུན་ལྷའི་ཕྱས། ངག་འཇམ་གསུང་སྐན་ལྷ་སྨྲི་དབྱངས་ཅན་འདྲ། ལྷས་ན་བཞིན་

སྐུ་ག་ལྷ་སྨྲི་ཡིད་འཕྲོག་འདྲ། དད་ལྡན་ཡོན་གྱིས་བདག་སྨྲི་སློབ་བཟང་བུ་ཁྲིད་ཀྱིས། སྨྲིའི་ཟས་ལ་ལྷའི་བདུད་རྩི་ར་སྤྲར། སྨྲ་ཚོད་གནས་གཉིས་བར་བྱེད་ངོ་སྨྲ་ཚར་ཆེས། ཀྱི་ལེགས། པའི་སྨྲ་ཚོག་འགྱུར་ཆེ་རིང་ལྷུན་གྲུབ་དང་། སྨྲའི་སྨྲ་ཚོག་འགྱུར་སོ་ནམ་དང་། ནོའི་སྨྲ་ཚོག་འགྱུར་ཤེ་རབ་དབང་འཛིན་དང་། ཆེ་རིང་ཆོས་འཕེལ་གཉིས། གསུངས་རབས་འདི་ལ་ཞབས་ཏོག་ལེགས་པར་སྨྲོད།། ནོ་སྨྲིའི་སྨྲ་ཚོག་འགྱུར་ཆེ་རིང་ཆོ་འཛོམ་དང་། པདྨ་བུ་འདྲེན་དང་། བུའི་སྨྲ་ཚོག་འགྱུར་ཆེ་བསྟན་དོན་གྲུབ་དང་། ཆེ་དབང་བསྟན་འཛིན་དང་། བཀྲ་ཤིས་བཟང་པོ་དང་། བསམ་གྲུབ་ཆེ་རིང་དང་། ནོ་སྨྲི་ཙུང་དུན་བཅས། ཕ་སྨྲ་བཞིན་དུ་ཆོས་ལ་དཀར་བར་སྨྲོད།། ལྡོན་པའི་སྨྲ་ཚལ་དུ་འདབ་ཆགས་ཇ་བཞིན་འདུས། སྨྲང་རྩེ་རོ་ལ་བོང་བ་འདུ་བ་བཞིན།། ངང་པ་སྨྲ་ཚོ་ནས་འོ་སྨྲ་ལེན་དང་སྨྲ་ཚུངས། དཀའ་རུ་དགེ་རྩེས་བྱེད་པའི་དད་ལྡན་ནམ་སྨྲས།

C. Colophon to Zamatog-II

ཨོཾ་སྭ་སྟི་སིདྡྷཾ། སྐུ་གསུམ་སྨྲ་སྨོན་དུ་གྱུར་པའི་སྟོན་པ་སངས་རྒྱས་དང་། སྡེ་སྣོད་གསུམ་སྨྲ་གྱིས་ཕྱུག་པའི་དམྲ''''། སློབ་པ་གསུམ་སྨྲ་གྱིས་སྨྲོས་པའི་དགེ་འདུན་སྡེ། སྐྱབས་གནས་དཀོན་སྨྲ་ཚོག་གསུམ་སྨྲ་ལ་གུས་ཕྱག་འཚལ་ལོ། ཨེ་སྨྲ་ཧོ། ལྷ་སྐྱོན་གིས་སྨྲ་སྨྲ་གོས་སྐུ་སྨྲ་དོག་དཀར། རྫོགས་སངས་རྒྱས་ཀྱི་དབུ་ལ་བརྒྱན།

ཐུགས་རྗེ་ཅན་གྱི་འགྲོ་ལ་གཟིགས། སྨྲ་གོན་པོ་སྤྱན་རས་གཟིགས་ལ་ཕྱག་འཚལ་ལོ། ཀྱེ་ལེགས། གླིང་གི་སྨྲ་ཚོག་གྱུར་ལྷོའི་འཛམ་བུ་གླིང་། ཁབ་ཅན་ལྗོངས་དམ་ཆོས་དར་བའི་ས། དགྲ་བཅོམ་བཞུགས་གནས་ཏི་སེ་གངས་ཀྱི་སྨྲ་གུ་ལ་ཁྱད་པར་ཅན་ལྡབ་ཆུ་བོ་འགང་ག་འབབ་པའི་ཡོན། པོ་ཏང་ཆེན་པོ་རྒྱལ་ས་བྲང་སྨྲ་ཁར་རྩེ་ར། ཆོས་རྒྱལ་ཆེན་པོ་འདི་སྨྲ་ཚོག་གནམ་རྒྱལ་གྱི། དབུ་མོག་སྨྲ་བོ་ཞིང་ཕྱབས་སྲིད་རྒྱས་འགྱུར་ཅིག། བོད་གི་བཀའ་བློན་ཆེན་

པོ་ནམ་སྨྲ་སྨྲ་ཁའ་རྒྱལ་སྨྲ་ཚན་སྐུ་ཆེ་སྟན་གྱུར་ཅིག། ཀྱི་ལེགས།

ཡུལ་ལ་གཡང་ཆགས་སྐྱིད་པའི་སྤྱིན་གྱི་གཞུང་ཡུལ་དུ།ས་ལ་འབུར་དུ་སྨྲོན་པ་རྒྱག་ནམྲ་ལུང་པ་འདིར།
སྔོན་སྦྱངས་བསོད་ནམས་བསགས་པ་སྤྲི་ལུས་རིན་ཆེན་ཐོབ།ལས་དད་བཀའ་བ་ལྡན་པ་དམ་པའི་ཆོས་ལ་སྤྲོས།སྤྲི
ན་པ་ཕྱོགས་སྤྲིད་བཏང་བ་འོངས་སྤྲོད་ཤུགས་ཡ་འབྱུང་།སྤྲི་རིགས་ཁྱུངས་བཙུན་ཆེན་སྤྲང་ཡེར་རྒྱུད།

ཡོན་གྱི་བདག་པོ་ནམྲ་སྨྲཁའ་རྡོ་རྗེ་འོ་རི་གིས།ཡ་འདྲེན་བླ་སྨྲའི་སྐུ་ཆེ་སྣན་ཕྱིར་དང་།དྲིན་
ཅན་པསྨྲའི་དྲིན་ལན་སོབ་ཕྱིར་དང་།རིགས་དྲུག་སེམས་ཅན་ཐམས་ཅད་སྒྲོད་ཕྱིར་དང་།ཁྱད་པར་སྨྲ་ཆེ་ལ་འདས་པའི་ཡ་འདྲེན་དུ།
དམྲ་ཆོས་ཁྱད་འཕགས་སྨྲད་སྤེ་ཟ་སྨྲ་རྟོག་སྦྲངས།བསགས་པ་དོན་ཆེན་སྨྲཛད་པ་ཨེ་སྨྲ་ཧོ།ཨོང་རྫེའི་རྒྱུད་
འཛིན་དགའ་བའི་དཔལ་སྤྲོ་ཆེ།ལྷས་ན་སྤྱིན་སྡུག་ལྷ་སྤྲོ་ཡིད་ཁྲིག་འདྲ།ངག་འབྲུམྲ་གསུང་སྣན་ལྷ་སྤྲོ་དབྱངས་ཅན་འདྲ།
སྨྲཛངས་ལ་འཕུལ་ཆགས་ནེ་བཙན་ལྷའི་སྲས།ཡོན་གྱི་བདག་སྤོ་བཀྲ་ཤིས་འཛོམྲ་པ་གིས།སྤྲི་ཡི་
ཟས་ལ་ལྷའི་བདུད་རྩི་ར་སྨྲར།སྨྲཆོད་གནས་གཉིས་པར་བྱེད་པ་ཁོང་ལ་སྟོད།ཀྱི་ལེགས། བུའི་སྨྲཆོག་གྱུར་
འགའ་ར་བཀྲ་ཤིས་དང་བཀྲ་ཤིས་དོན་གྲུབ་དང་བཀྲ་ཤིས་རྒྱ་སྨྲཚོ་གསུམ་གི། ཕ་སྨྲ་བཞིན་དུ་ཆོས་ལ་དཀར་
བ་སྨྲཛོད།སྣ་སྨྲའི་ཆོག་གྱུར་སོ་ནམྲ་སྐྱིད་གི།གསུང་རབས་འདི་ལ་ཞབས་སྟོད་ལེགས་པར་སྨྲཛད།ལྗོན་པའི་
ཚལ་དུ་འདབ་ཆགས་ཇ་བཞིན་འདུས།སྤྲང་རྩེ་རོ་ལ་བོང་བ་འདུ་བ་བཞིན།ངང་པ་ཆུ་ན་འོ་སྨྲ་ལེན་དང་ཚུངས།
དཀར་རྟུ་དགེ་རྩེ་སྨྲཛད་པའི་དད་ལྡན་ལ། བྲང་སྨྲཁར་ནམངས་རྒྱས་རིན་ཆེན། བཀྲ་ཤིས་ཕུན་ཚོགས་དང་
རྒྱ་སྨྲཚོ། ཀླ་སྨྲ་ཤེས་པ་སྤྱིན་ན་ཚེ་རིང་བ། བྱམྲས་པ་རྒྱལ་སྨྲཚན།སྨན་ལྷ། ཚེ་རིང་བཀྲ་ཤིས།དབང་ཕྱུག།
བཀྲ་ཤིས་ཕུན་ཚོགས། ཁྲི་ལ་དུ།ཀུང་ག་དོན་གྲུབ།ཀ་འཛིན། ཚེ་རིང་རྒྱལ་སྨྲཚན།ཕུན་ཚོགས།
བཀྲ་ཤིས་རྒྱ་བ་སེ།ལ་པདྨ།ལྷོ་རོ། འགའ་ང་བཀྲ་ཤིས།པོ་སྤྲོ་སྨྲཆོག།བཀྲ་ཤི་དོན་གྲུབ།། །།བཀྲ་ཤིས།།

D. Colophon to Dorchhod, rGe-te

ཨོཾ་སྭ་སྟི་སིདྡྷཾ།སྐུ་གསུམ་སྨྲོན་དུ་གྱུར་པའི་སྟོན་པ་སངས་རྒྱས་དང་། སྡེ་སྣོད་གསུམ་ཕྱུག་པའི་དམ་ཆོས་
དང་།བསླབ་པ་གསུམ་གྱི་སྨྲཛེས་པའི་དགེ་འདུན་སྡེ། སྐྱབས་གནས་དཀོན་མཆོག་གསུམ་ལ་གུས་ཕྱག་ འཚལ།
ཀྱི་ལེགས། གངས་ཅན་ཞིང་དེ་སོལ་བྱེད་ཅོང་ཁ་པ།། སྨྲོན་རྟོགས་རིག་པའི་དབང་ཕྱུག་ རྒྱལ་ཚབ་རྗེ།།
སྨྲད་སྡུགས་བསྟན་པའི་བདག་པོ་མཁས་གྲུབ་རྗེ། རྒྱལ་བ་ཡབ་སྲས་གསུམ་ལ་གུས་ཕྱག་ འཚལ། ཀྱི་ལེགས།
སྨྲཁའ་སྨྲཉསྨྲས་འགྲོ་ལ་སྨྲཁྲིན་རྗེ་རབ་དགོངས་ནས། གྲངས་སྨྲིད་གསུམ་དུ་
ཚོགས་གཉིས་རབ་རོགས་ཞིང་།སྟོང་གསུམ་སྨྲི་འབྱེད་ཞིང་དཔལ་གྱུར་པ།འདྲེན་སྨྲཆོག་ཤཱཀྱའི་ཏོག་ལ་གུས་ཕྱག་འ
ཚལ།ཀྱི་ལེགས།སྨྲཐུན་པའི་སྨོན་ལམྲ་དགེ་ཚོགས་བྱུང་ཞིང་།སྤྱད་པ་སྤྱོད་ཆེ་ནམྲ་ཡང་སྤྱི་དལ་ཡང་

།བསྐལ་བཟང་གཅིག་ལ་སྤྲཛད་པ་སྤྲབར་ཕྱིན་ནས།རྫོགས་པའི་སངས་རྒྱས་སྟོང་ལ་གུས་ཕྱག་འཚལ།ཀྱི
ལེགས།གླིང་གི་སྤྲཆོག་གྱུར་ལྷོའི་འཛམྦུ་བུ་གླིང་། དགྲ་བཅོམ་སྤྲ་བཞུགས་གནས་དེ་སེ་གངས་ཀྱི་སྤྲགུ་ལ།
སྤྲ་གྲོས་གཞུགས་གནས་སྤྲ་སྤྲང་གཡུ་འི་སྤྲཆོ།སེང་གེ།ཁ་འབབས་འབྱུག་པའི་གཡས་ཕྱོགས་འདིར།།ཡོ་བྲང་ཆེན་པོ་ཆེ་
ཆེན་དཔལ་ཁར་རྩེར། ཆོས་རྒྱལ་ཆེན་པོ་ཆེ་དཔལ་སྣ་སྤྲ་རྒྱལ་གྱི། ཨུ་རྨོག་སྤྲབ་གྱུར་ཅིག། ཁོང་གི་
སྤྲང་འ་ཞབས་སྤྲཛང་པོ་སྤྲི་དེ་འདིར།རྫོང་སྤྲབ་བརྟན་པ་རྒྱལ་ས་གྲང་ཁར་རྩར།རྫོང་དཔོན་ཆེན་པོ་ག་ག་
ཁན་ཡབ་སྲས་ཀྱི་སྐུ་ཚེ་བརྟན་གྱུར་ཅིག།དགོན་པ་ཁྱད་དུ་འཕགས་པ་ཉོར་བུ་དགེ་འཕེལ་ནས།དཔོན་སློབ་ཆེ
ན་པོ་ཡེ་ཤེས་རྒྱལ་ཀྱི་ཆོས་བཙུན་སྤྲབ་ཞིང་འཕྲིན་ལས་རྒྱས་ཅིག།ཡུལ་ལ་གཡང་ཆགས་སྐྱིད་པའི་རྒྱེ་དེ་འདིར།
ཕ་རུ་རྩ་ཚུ་འཛམ་སྤྲ་ཞིང་སྤྲར་རུ་བྲུ་སྣ་སྨིན། སྤྲི་རིགས་ཁྲངས་བཙུན་རུས་ཆེན་རྒྱ་ཤིང་། དད་ལྡན་ཡོན་གྱི་
བདག་པོ་དཀོན་སྤྲཆོག་གི་རང་གི་འགལ་ཀྱེན་བར་ཆད་ཞི་ཕྱིར་དང་འཆི་སྤྲ་རྒྱལ་བའི་གོ་འཕང་ཐོབ་ཕྱིར་དུ།
དསྤྲ་ཆོས་ཁྱད་འཕགས་རྡོ་རྗེ་གཅོད་པ་དང་ཕ་ཡོན་དང་།ཤེ་ག་བཤགས་བཅས་སྤྲ་བུ་སུ་སྤྲ་བཞངས།བསགས་པ་
ཆོས་ཕྱིར་བཏང་བ་འདི་སྤྲཆར་ཆེ། དད་ལྡན་ཡོན་གི་བདག་སྤྲོ་དཔལ་སྤྲཛིས་ཡི་སྤྲི་ཟས་ལ་ལྷ་ཡི་བདུད་ རྩ
ི་སྤྲར། སྤྲཆོད་གནས་གཉིས་ངེས་པར་བྱེད་པ་འདི་སྤྲཆར་ཆེ།།བུ་ཡི་སྤྲཆོག་གྱུར་ཆེད་ཆེ་ལསྤྲ་དང་།
བཀྲ་ཤིས་ལྷུ་འགྲུབ་དང་། ནོ་ཙུ་ཀུན་ནསྤྲས་གསུང་རབ་འདི་ལ་ཞབ་ཏོག་ལགས་སྤྲཛད།གསུང་རབ་ཀཀ་དགེ་
རྩེ་འབྱུང་གྲངས་ལ། སྤྲགོན་པ་ཉོར་བུ་དགེ་འཕེལ་ནས། སྤྱོན་སློབ་ཡེ་ཤེས་ནསྤྲ་རྒྱལ་ཀྱི་བསོལ་བྱ་དྲ་ བཀར།
ཀ་ཆེན་ཆེད་ཕུན་ཚོགས་ཀ་ཆེན་སྤྲ་ཉི་ཀྱི་བསོལ་བྱ།ཨུསྤྲ་སྤྲཛད་སོལ་བྱ། དེན་དགེ་ཞུ།། སྤྲིང་འབྲིད་དགེ་ཞུ།

III. བཀའ་ཤོག། Kashog, Message,

A. King's Message རྒྱལ་པོའི་བཀའ་ཤོག།

དེ་ན་ཡང་བློན་པོ་འགར་གྱིས།།རྒྱལ་པོའི་དྲུང་དུ་ཕྱིན་དེ།། རྒྱ་ནག་གི་ལྷ་གཅིག་དེ་ཡང་བདེན་འདྲེན་བ།།
བཀའ་སྤྲནང་ངར་ཞུས་སོ།། ཡང་རྒྱལ་པོ་གསེར་གྱི་དོང་ཙེ་བདུན་བཀུར་ནས།། འདི་ལ་ཞུ་སྟེན་བཀྱི་
ཅིག་གསུངས་སོ།། རིན་པོ་ཆེ་བདུན་གྱི་ནི་ཁྲབ་ལ་པདྨ་ར་གའི་ཕྲ་རྒྱབ་བ་གཅིག་སྐྱུར་ནས།།
འདི་ལྷ་གཅིག་དེའི་རིན་དུ་ཕུལ་ཅིག་སུངས་སོ།།སེར་ཕྱེ་བྲེ་གང་སྐྱུར་ནས།།འདི་གང་དགོས་སུ་ཐོང་ཅིག།
རྒྱལ་པོ་དེ་དཀའ་ལུང་སྤྲི་འདྲ་བ་གསུམ་དུ་འདུས་ནས།།དེའི་དུས་སུ་འདི་སུསྤྲ་རེ་རེ་བཞིན་གཏོང་ཅིག

གསུང་ནས།།བཀའ་ཤོག་གི་ཤོག་རི་ལ་གསུ་སྲྲ་བསྐུར་རོ།།འཕྲུལ་གི་ཡོ་བྱད་གོས་དང་རྒྱན་ལ་སོགས་པ་ཧ་སྲྲོ་དང་།།དྲི་ལ་སོགས་པ་ལ་བཀལ་བ་འི་ཁལ་སྲྲང་པོ་རྫངས་སོ།།ཉིན་སྲྲཚན་དང་ལསྲྲ་ཕྲང་གང་དུ་ཡང་།།རྗེ་ཙུན་སྲྲོ་ལ་སྲྲ་ལ་བསོལ་བ་འདེབས་ཀྱིན་གསོང་ཅིག་གསུངས་སོ།།དེ་ན་སྲྲགར་གྱི་རྒྱལ་པོ་བཀུར་བ་ཐསྲྲས་ཅད་ཁྲི་ར་ཁལ་ནསྲྲས་དོང་།།བློན་པོ་ཧ་བ་བརྒྱ་དང་ལྷན་གཅིག་ཏུ་སྲྲེ་པོ་ཕྲེའི་ལོ་ཟླ་བ་བཞི་པའི་ཚེ་རྒྱད་ལ་སྐར་སྲྲརྒྱལ་དང་སྲྲཛོ་སྲྲ་བ་རྒྱ་ནག་ཏུ་ཆེས་སོ།།དེ་ན་རྒྱ་ནག་གི་བཟི་སྲྲ་ཆུང་བཀྲ་ཤིས་ཁྲི་སྒོ།།རྒྱལ་རྗེ་ཐང་ཐྲུང་བཞུགས་པའི་པོ་བྲང་གི་སྒོ་དྲུང་དུ་སླེབ་བོ།།དེ་ན་སྲྲེ་ཁྲི་འདུསྲྲ་ཚོ་ཙསྲྲ་ཡོད་པ།།ལོགས་དེ་ལ་ཉེན་ལསྲྲ་རེ་ཡོད་པ་སྒོ་སྲྲོ་ཆེ་བཞི་ཡོད་པ།།སྲྲཐོང་བ་ཙསྲྲ་ཀྱི་སྣངས་ཤིང་འཇིགས་པ་ཅིག་འདུག་གོ།།དེར་རྒྱ་གར་ཆོས་ཀྱི་རྒྱལ་པོ་ཧ་བརྒྱ་ཐསྲྲ་པ།།རྒྱལ་སྲྲོ་ཀོང་འགྱུར་འདོད་པ་ལ་སླེབ་བོ།།གེ་སར་དམག་གི་རྒྱལ་པོ་……།།སྟག་གཟིག་ནོར་གྱི་རྒྱལ་པོ་……།།ཧྲ་ཏ་ཧོར་ཀྱི་རྒྱལ་པོ་……།།སྲྲཐའ་ཁོབ་བོད་ཀྱི་རྒྱལ་པོ་……།།སྲྲེ་རིགས་སྲྲེ་འདྲ་བའི་སྨྲ་བོ་ལྔ་ལྔ་རྒྱ།།རྒྱལ་རྗེ་དྲུང་དུ་དུས་གཅིག་ཏུ་སླེབ་བོ།།དེར་རྒྱ་གར་བ་ནསྲྲས་ཤར་སྒོ་ཡོངས།།གེ་སར་བ་ནསྲྲས་ལྷོ་སྒོ་ན་ཡོད།།སྟག་གཟིག……།།ཧོར་བ་ནསྲྲས……།།བོད་བློན་ནསྲྲ་བྱང་ཤར་ཚསྲྲ་སུ་གནང་ངོ་།།དེར་བློན་པོ་བཞན་སྲྲ་ནསྲྲས་ཀྱི་ཞུ་རྟེན་འཛལ་ཕྲད་བྱེས་སོ།།

B. བློན་པོ་འགར་གི་བཀའ་ཤོག། Message of Minister mGar

ཀ།། ཤོག་བྲིལ་དང་པོ། First Message

ཤོག་བྲིལ་དང་པོ་རྒྱལ་པོ་ལ་ཕུལ་བ།རྒྱལ་པོ་ཁྱེད་ནས་གཟིགས་པས་ཐེང་ཤོག་ལ་གསེར་གྱི་ཡི་གེར་བྲིས་པ་རྒྱ་ནག་གི་ཡི་གེར་འདུག་དེ། ཁྱོད་རྒྱ་ནག་རྒྱལ་པོ་ལ་ཁྲིམས་ཡོད། ང་བོད་ཀྱི་རྒྱལ་པོ་ལ་ཆོས་ཁྲིམས་མེད་དེ། རྒྱལ་པོ་ཁྱོད་དགེ་བ་བཅུ་ཡི་རྒྱལ་ཁྲིམས་ཡོད་པ་དགའ་ནས་བུ་མོ་སྟེར་ན། ངས་སྐུ་ལུས་ཀྱི་བགོད་པ་ལྔ་སྟོང་དུ་སྤྲུལ་ནས་དགེ་བའི་ཁྲིམས་ཉིན་གཅིག་ལ་བཅད་ནུས་པ་བྱེད། དེ་ལྟར་བྱས་ནས་བུ་ སྦྲོ་སྦྲི་སྟེར་ན།། ངས་སྤྲུ་ལ་བའི་དམག་ཁྲི་ཕྲག་ལྔ་བཏང་ནས་ཁྱོད་གསད་ལྷ་གཅིག་འཕྲོག། ཡུལ་ཁམས་ཐམས་ཅད་བཅོམ་ནས་བཞག་གོ།རྒྱལ་པོ་ཤིན་ཏུ་སྐྲགས་པར་གྱུར་ནས། སྐྲགས་ཀྱང་སྤྲི་སྐྲགས་པ ལྟར་བྱས་ནས། ཁྱོད་བོད་ཀྱི་རྒྱལ་པོ་དེ་ལ་ཁ་སོ་ཤིན་ཏུ་ཆེ་བ་འདུག།། ཁྱོད་བོད་ཀྱི་ཡུལ་ན་གཙུག་ལག་གཅིག་པའི་ནུས་པ་ཡོད་དམ་མེད།། ཡོད་ན་བུ་སྦྲོ་སྟེར།། སོང་ལ་དྲིས་ཤོག། གསུངས་སོ།།

ཁ། ཤོག་བྲིལ་བར་སྤྲ། The Middle Message

ཡང་སྤྲགར་གྱི་ཤོག་བྲིལ་བར་སྤྲ་དེ་རྒྱལ་པོའི་ཕྱག་ཏུ་ཕུལ་ནས། འཕྲིན་རི་རི་ལ་བོད་དུ་འགྲོ་བ་སྦྱི་འོང་བས། རྒྱལ་པོ་ཁྲིད་ཀྱི་གསུང་དེའི་ལན་དུ་གཟིགས་པར་ཞུ། རྒྱལ་པོ་ཁ་ཕྱིད་ནས་གཟིགས་པ་འདི་ལྟར་རོ། ཁྲིད་རྒྱ་ནག་ཡུལ་ན་ཆོས་དང་གཙུག་ལག་ཁང་བརྩིག་པ་ཡོད། ང་བོད་ཀྱི་རྒྱལ་པོ་ལ་གཙུག་ལག་བརྩིག་པའི་ནུས་པ་སྤྲིད་དེ། རྒྱལ་པོ་ཁྲིད་གཙུག་ལག་ཁང་གཅིག་པ་ལ་དགའ་ནས་ལྷ་གཅིག་སྟེར་ན། ངས་སྐུ་ལུས་ཀྱི་བཀོད་པ་ལྔ་སྟོང་དུ་སྤྲུལ་ནས་གཙུག་ལག་ཁང་བརྒྱ་རྩ་བརྒྱད་བཞེངས་ནས་སྒོ་ཐམས་ཅད་ཁྲིད་ཀྱི་ཕྱོགས་སུ་བསྟན་པར་བྱའོ།།དེ་ངོ་སྤྲཚར་སྤྱི་ཆེ་འསྤྲ།། དེ་ལྟར་བྱས་ཀྱང་བུ་སྤྲོ་སྤྲི་སྟེར་ན། ངས་སྤྲུལ་པའི་དསྤྲག་ཁྲི་ཕྲག་ལྔ་གཏང་ནས་ཁྲིད་གསད་ལྷ་གཅིག་འཕྲོག། ཡུལ་ཁམས་ཐམས་ཅད་བཙོསྤྲ་ནས་བཞག་གོ།རྒྱལ་པོ་དེ་ཤིན་ཏུ་སྐྲགས་པར་གྱུར་ཀྱང་སྤྲི་སྐྲགས་བ་ལྟར་བྱས་ནས། ཁྲིད་ཀྱི་རྒྱལ་པོ་དེ་ཁ་སོ་ཤིན་ཏུ་ཆེས་བ་འདུག།ཁྲིད་ཀྱི་ཡུལ་ན་འདོད་ཡོན་ལྔ་ལ་ལོངས་སྤྱོད་པ་ཡོད་དསྤྲ་ སྤྲིད། ཡོད་ན་བུ་སྤྲོ་སྟེར་སྤྲིད་ན་སྤྲི་སྟེར། ད་ལན་སོང་ལ་དྲིས་ལ་ཤོག།

ག། The Last Message ཤོག་བྲིལ་ཐ་སྤྲ།

ཡང་བློན་པོ་སྤྲགར་གྱི་ཤོག་བྲིལ་ཐ་སྤྲ་དེ་རྒྱལ་པོའི་ཕྱག་ཏུ་ཕུལ་བ། འཕྲིན་རི་རི་ལ་རྒྱ་ནས་བོད་ལ་ འགྲོ་བ་སྤྱི་འོང་བ། རྒྱལ་པོ་ཁྲིད་ཀྱི་གསུང་དེའི་ལན་འདི་གཟིགས་པར་ཞུ། རྒྱལ་པོས་ཁ་ཕྱིད་ནས་ གཟིགས་པ།། ཁྲིད་རྒྱ་ནག་རྒྱལ་པོ་ལ་ནོར་ལོངས་སྤྱོད་ཡོད། ང་བོད་ཀྱི་རྒྱལ་པོ་ལ་དེ་བཞིན་སྤྲིད་དེ། རྒྱལ་པོ་ཁྲིད་ནོར་ལོངས་སྤྱོད་ཡོད་པ་ལ་དགའ་ན་བུ་སྤྲོ་སྟེར་ན། ངས་སྐུ་ལུས་ཀྱི་བཀོད་པ་ལྔ་སྟོང་དུ་སྤྲུལ་ནས་གསེར་དངུལ་གྱི་ལོངས་སྤྱོད་ཆེ།། འབྲུ་དང་དར་ཟབ་གོས་དང་རྒྱན་དང་ཟས་ནོར་གྱི་ལོངས་སྤྱོད་བཞན་རྣམས་སྤྲོ་སྦྲང་དུ་འདུས་ནས་ལྟན་པར་བྱའོ།།

Annexures-2

Translations

I. Documents

A. Decree of Dechhog Namgyal

Decree of the Lord, the Protector of the country, the great Dharamraja sDe-mchhog rNam-rgyal.

This (decree) is addressed to our own subjects. The houses and fields of two households of Phi-ba sTud and dPang-'byor, of village sTod-nam (in Pin) have been allocated (to the astrologer). The great prayer (festival of) Tshe-chu (tenth day of the fifth month, the day of birthday of Guru Padmasambhava) is being celebrated since the time of Urgyan (Padmasambhava). For the assembly of the monks of the sa-ngags snying-ma (monastery) the levy of mule, sheep and paper have been charged (from the other households).

All should bear in mind that anybody who defaults in the payment will be recovered from him without discrimination from the beginning. Kharpon (Castle officer), Zongpon (Fort-officer), old men, the public, soldiers, the manager, the officer for the external tasks, hunters and other important persons of other villages, none will have any objection. It should be left undisturbed.

None will have any concern. Anybody doing so will be punished with the harsh thrashing. This order was issued on the

12th day of the 3rd month of iron-female-pig year at the great palace of Yang-mkhar-rtse (= Dankhar).

Petitioner: mKhar-dPon, Nam-mkha' rGyal-mtshan.

Note: The document may be dated 1671 CE.

B. Contract for sharing the crops from the Fields of dGuri monastery

From Padma Lhundub five khal of barley, two thirds, from (the field of) Bikane. Manglang-rtse (field) of Guling has been given on sharing basis for revenue as *bun* for the festival of Tshe-chu. From Tshering Dorje in sTod-nam from the field of U-ba Len-tse half khal, and two and half (half of Ne).

C. Collection of revenue for the monasteries

Share of each monastery from the amount of cash collected from the public has been fixed on the basis of the tradition followed earlier under the administration of Dechhog, as learnt by hearing or whatever was in memory.

The shares of the teachers of each of the three sects of Sakya, Gelug and Nyingma of the province of Spiti should be known properly. The amount of cash collected from the public for the monasteries has been divided as was the practice earlier under the administration of the king bDe-mchhog, learnt as is in memory and is heard from the others. (The shares of each one is given as under). Fourth part is for the lamas generally,... as above, equal to 25 srang, 6 zho and five skar; for sKyid-pa Lama 6 srang and 9 zho; Bar-kyod Lama 6 srang and 9 zho; Lag-pe Lama 3 srang and 9 zho; Ta'-so lama 7 srang and 9 zho; Byang-gling Lama 6 srang, 7 zho and 8 skarma; Gong-mig lama 1 srang, 1 zho and seven and half-skar; and for lamas of Pin nil srang, 9 zho only. Each will receive in this manner.

These sums were received traditionally by the various small and big monasteries. By consensus everybody should feel satisfied. No amount of dissension, not even equal to the seed of *tila*, should be borne in mind. Written in the fire-mouse year.

Note: The document was framed in the fire-mouse year after Dechhog's rule which thus may be placed in 1756 CE. The three sects mentioned here are as they exist today. The document mentions seven important monasteries as sKyid-pa, Ta'-so, Gongmig, Pin, Bar-kyod, Lhag-pe and Jangling. The first four may be identified as Kyi, Tabo, Tengyud and Pin, the rest of the three cannot be identified, one of them may be that of Dankhar.

D. mKhan Rinpo-chhe

The document concerns the yearly accounting of the receipt and distribution of the offerings from the public for the Pin monastery, and others.

The document was written in the year of iron-bird, 1741 (?).

The letter is addressed to: The renowned and honourable mKhan Rinpochhe.

II. Colophons to the sacred books: The texts given below are taken from the colophons given in different books which in local language is called *zab-byong (=zhabs-sbyong)*. Generally these books are copies prepared at the occasion of death ceremony of some important persons. They are informative documents and some of them contain important historical data. They mostly record the names of the ruling kings or the local chiefs, names of members of the family of the deceased, its lineage, names of persons presenting offerings and they are often dated. In the most common samples they list the names of the guests with the description of the customary offerings they brought.

It is to be noted that none of the documents given below makes mention of either of the Nono of Guling or that of Kyuling, or any other chief of local origin. Only in one of such documents, not given here, a name of a Nono of Guling as Chhus (=Chhos) ṣnyid has been found. Here names of two nuns also have been mentioned. But it cannot be dated.

A. Colophon to Zamatog -I, Advent of the Doctrine in the Region

Ka. (Meaning two). Aom mani padme hum! I bow to the great compassionate Lord Avalokitesvara. The manner of expansion of the Doctrine of the great Merciful One is explained as follows. Formerly when Samyaksambuddha attained *mahaparinirvana,* he instructed Arya Avalokitesvara, excellent among the Bodhisattvas, stating that: 'In order to initiate the inhabitants of Himavata, in the region of northern direction, into my Doctrine, Oh! Bodhisattva, you will have to perform certain worldly acts there. The beings there having been difficult to discipline since former times, you will have to apply several methods.' Lord Arya Avalokitesvara took incarnation in the form of a Hanuman, a monkey, in Tibet. Goddess Tara got herself incarnated in the form of a spirit of rocks. Their offsprings were born as human beings and then their generations expanded. Then they saw that now the proper time has arrived to tame the beings. (Meaning three). The two, father monkey, and mother, spirit of rock, found the task difficult to perform. Therefore Khri-btsun, the princess of Nepal, the incarnation of Bhrikuti and princess Ong-jo, incarnation of Devi Tara, were brought in marriage (to Srong-btsan sGampo). Thonmi Sambhota, incarnate of Arya Avalokitesvara, learnt the language of the men. He learned writing in China and converted it to Tibetan. He built a hundred monasteries including 'Khrul-nang of Lhasa and Ramoche. Learned Pandits were invited from India, China and Nepal. The Samyaksambuddha caused to bring two images of Shakyamuni from China and Nepal.

Thonmi Samhbota learned some skills of translation and translated many books of the Excellent Doctrine, specially the twenty-one *sutras* and *tantras* of Arya Avalokitesvara. He explained his own thoughts, the teachings of the *pitakas* and the teachings of the *mahakarunika* (the great merciful) to the king, queens, princes, princesses, the subjects, all the ministers and all the persons concerned. All the members of the circle attained the birth of the Bodhisattva in their next life without liable to rebirth. The king performed tasks keeping in view the life in the next world. He delivered many discourses on the meditation of the *mahakarunika*. (Meaning four). Lotsava Thunmi Sambhota, having received the boon of non-forgetfulness, put down to writing whatever the incarnated king spoke. The king, with the power of foreknowledge, knowing himself as incarnation of the *mahakarunika,* left words of transmission for the translators.

The king advised that his discourses should be written in two ways. One should be written on blue sheet in gold and silver, and kept hidden in the chest of the prince in the treasury of Khram-khrum. The other one written on paper should be rolled up and placed hidden under the foot of the image of Hayagriva in the temple of Mahakarunikạ. A person who attains perfection will discover the concealed treasures and preach them. Those who discard the worldly affairs and practice during the course of several births will attain the perfection to become a Bodhisattva. This is one paper roll. Thus the sun shines more brightly in the west and northern direction than in the south. At that time the letters of *Om mane padme hum* will be born spontaneously. The body and spirit will be born spontaneously. Many will be led to the path of Bodhisattva. Thus they will be initiated into the Doctrine of the Mahakarunika. One should practice Bodhisattva doctrine and serve all the beings with caring mind.

(Meaning five). At one time the Doctrine of the Buddha Sakyamuni may become weak. At that time the true meaning of the Doctrine will not be explained but imaginary forms of the teachings will be preached. The Doctrine will stop from further expansion and will diminish immensely. Many learned persons will be slandered. Demons will enter in the minds of the faithful ones. Each one will be querrelling with the other. The minds of women will be defiled who may be led to suicidal path.The ferocious gods and Nagas will quarrel with each other. Rains will not come in proper season. Occasionally there will be drought. The prosperity of the people will diminish. Hence while desiring for happiness and pleasure, pray to the benevolent Lord Avalokitesvara.

Note: This colophon to a sacred book is unlike any such other. It displays many old characteristics in regard to subject matter, language and style of presentation. The subject treated is Avalokitesvara and his doctrine of *mahakaruna,* the great compassion. It hints at a weakening phase of the Doctrine. It uses some ancient technical words like *sku-tshab* for *sku* (image); *lha-khang* for *dgonpa, tsug-lag khang* (monastery); *shog-dril* (paper-roll) for *gleg-bam, pothi* (book); etc. Paragraphs are divided by numbering. It says that Sambhota built many *lhakhang,* temples, but makes no mention of Padmasambhava and Rinchhen Zangpo. Towards its end the text has subjects resembling to those of folk religion like the scarcity of rain, occasions of draught and prosperity of the people.

For the evolution and development of the Doctrine, language and literature in Tibet the author praises only Lotsaba Sambhota which is written as Sambhora and erroneously says that he studied in China instead of saying in India. Further, although he writes many things about the king which certainly relate to Srong-btsan sGam-po, but he misses to name the same. Perhaps it is copied from an older document and the text could belong to the period of the first expansion of the Doctrine.

B. Colophon to brgyad-stong-pa, Tashi Namgyal:

....

....

The Excellent Doctrine has spread in Himavata. Kailash, like a neck, is the holy residence of the arhats. The Naga king Anavatapta has his residence in the holy turquoise like green lake of Mansarovar. The great king Tashi Namgyal resides in the great palace of sPang-'gang-rtse, in Leh, situated on the left bank of Sindhu. May his head be held high and may his kingdom expand. Hello. mKhar-dpon Ga-rga bsTan-pa rGya-mtsho, under whose rule lies this area, resides here at Yang-mkhar-rtse, Dankhar, the capital. We pay reverence to him. Hello!

Ga-rga Thubs-bstan, the mKhar dPon, resides here at the great palace of Pin which is like an engraving on the earth. Reverence to him. Hello! Here in the Pin valley the ten virtues are spread. In the upper parts of the valley fruits grow abundantly and the grains ripe in its lower parts. The prosperous village of Tsag-nam is situated in the middle of the valley. The beings here have received the human life by the merits amassed in the former life. They have increased prosperity due to their donations made in the former life. Due to forbearance in the former life they are disease free. They revere the good Doctrine by the solemn vows.

They originate from (Sha?)-kya lineage. The faithful lord patrons Tshering Byor and Sonam Lhundub have: for the health of the upright teachers; return of the kindness of the parents; reverence of the king and the ministers; preparing the path of salvation of the beings of the six realms; attainment of the Bodhisattva path in the next life; and for the removal of their own obstacles, prepared copies of the works of the Excellent Doctrine viz. *Vajrachhedika*, small and larger versions; *Astasahasartika*, and *Suvaranaprabhasutra*. There are numerous donors. Hello!

Originating from the lineage of Kongjo, the landlady, offspring of the goddess, possessed with melodious voice like that of the goddess of learning, attractive to look at, the faithful Lozang Buthid, she mixed elixir of the gods in the meal of men. Wonderful. Hello!

Father Tshering Lhundub and mother Sonam, two younger brothers Sherab Yangzin and Tshering Chhos-phel, served very well during the discourse. The young daughters Tshering Chho Zom and Padma Budren and sons Tshhetan Dondub, Tshewang Tanzin, Tashi Zang-po and Samdub Tshering all express happiness towards the Doctrine like the parents. The faithful ones have gathered like the birds gathering in a garden, like the worms gathering on honey, and have served well like the swans separating milk from water.

Note: King Tashi Namgyal (1555-1575) resides in his palace sPang-'gang-rtse at Leh. Gaga Tanpa Gya-mtsho is Kharpon at Dankhar and Gaga Thubstan is Kharpon in Pin. This is the earliest evidence of Ladaki rule over Spiti and the Kharpon is addressed as Gaga since the beginning. This is the only evidence regarding the Kharpon of Pin.

C. Colophon to Zamatog -II

Aom hail to the *siddhas*! The Excellent Doctrine manifested in three forms; the Buddha, the teacher; the enriched three *Pitakas*; and the Organisation adorned by the three teachings, I bow with reverence to the three precious ones, the place of refuge. E ma ho! The god, spotlessly white, adorned with the Sambuddha on the head, looks upon the world with compassionate eyes, I bow to the Lord Avalokitesvara. Hello!

Just as Jambudvipa, situated in the south, is excellent among all the continents, so is Himavat, where the Excellent Doctrine has spread; and similar are the mount Tise (Kailash), the neck like snowy mountain, which is the sacred dwelling place of the Arhats; and the great palace of *dharamraj* 'De-mchhog gNam-rgyal, situated in Brang-mkhar, the capital, on the left bank of the river Ganga (Spiti river). May his crown remain high and the kingdom expand vastly. The great bKa'-blon, rNamkh'a rGyal-mtshan, may his life be strong. Hello!

The village of Tsagnam, as if raised in relief, is situated in the middle of the prosperous and happy valley of sPin. Here the inhabitants have received the birth of precious human life as a result of working for the welfare of the others in the former life; and the hardworking and faithful followers uphold the Excellent Doctrine. They are generous in giving alms, yet there is no decrease in their enjoyment of the wealth. The race originates from the great lineage of *mang-yes*.

Namkha Dorje Ngore, the patron, has for the health of the teachers; for repaying the debt of the kindness of the loving parents; for the emancipation of the six kinds of beings; and specially with the objective that the deceased mother may be lead to the higher path, the *Zamatog sutra* of the well developed Excellent Doctrine has been raised. For the accumulation of the merits, a great purpose has been done. E ma ho!

The patroness Tashi Zom, who is an ideal of happiness, attractive to look at, possessed of melodious voice like that of Sarasvati, having a courageous son like miraculously powerful god bTsan, has added elixir of the gods in the food of the human beings. She has performed the services so perfectly, we pay reverence to her. Hello!

The good sons Ga-ra Tashi, Tashi Dondub and Tashi Gya-tsho, may show pleasure in the Doctrine like their parents. Sonam-sKyid, the excellent daughter-in-law, has served nicely, during this period of discourses. The donors have joined here like the birds in a garden; like the worms on the honey and like swan separating milk from water, the faithful ones are doing the acts of welfare. They are: from Dankhar Sang-gey Rinchen; and Tashi Phuntshogs and Gyatsho, the learned lama from Pin, Tshering-ba, Tshering Tashi, Wangchug, Tashi Phuntshogs; and at Khyil Kunga Dondub, Ga-zin, Tsheing, Gyal-tshan, Tashis de, La Padma, nGo-ro, Ga-nga Tashi, the Excellent daughters. Tashi Dondub, etc., etc. Manglam!

Note: This is the second document after the Annex. I.A dealing with the king Dechhog Namgyal.

D. Colophon to rDor-mchhod, from Getye:

Among all the continents Jambudvipa in the south is the best. Tise (Kailash), like a snowy neck, is the place where the arhats reside. Mansarovar, the turquoise like lake, is the residence of the naga Anavapta. The great king Tshepal Namgyal resides in the palace called dPal Khar rTse in Leh which is situated on the left bank of the river Sindhu. May his crown be held high. Spiti lies under his excellent rule. Here at the high and strong fort of Dankhar, the capital, resides the great Zong-pon Ga-ga Khan, father and son. May they be healthy. The well developed monastery of Norbu Gephel is situated here. Here resides the great teacher Ye-she rGyal, may his high teachings expand. Here at the prosperous village of rGe-te, in its interior there is abundance of water and grass, and there ripen numerous grains at the end of the valley. Originating from the high clan of rGya-shing, the faithful landlord Konchhog of the flourishing and enjoying village of rGe-te, for the removal of the obstacles in attaining the status of the Jina, in the next life, the works of the Excellent Doctrine of Aryavajrachhedika , the three were copied. Reading it will benefit in the removal of sin. The donations made in order to accumulate the merits were wonderful. The landlady, Pal-zes served food so delicious as if the god's elixir was mixed in the human food. The prayers were wonderful. The excellent sons Tshering Tshelam and Tashi Ludub and the younger brother served well for these religious services. There were numerous persons who made offerings for the recitation here. From the monastery of Norbu Gephel, the teacher Yeshe Namgyal gave tea and a meal. 33 more persons are named. Of them 19 gave only tea, eight gave only chhang, one gave chhang and tea; and the remaining four gave chhang and a meal.

Note: The present document belongs to the period of king Tshe-dpal (+don-grub) rNam-rgyal (1802-1840) of Ladak. It mentions Gaga Khan as Zongpon. Trebeck informs that in c.1816 the office of Zongpon was held by Gaga Rabgey and in 1822 it was held by Gaga Khan. The date of the document may be placed sometime nearby the latter date, c. 1830.

1. The text was perhaps composed on the occasion of the death of a monk, who might have belonged to Dankhar monastery. Most of the donors are monks and they mostly hail from the monastery of Dankhar except one who is from Kyi. The offerings are only tea and *chhang*.

2. In the task of composing the text the work appears to have been shared by two authors. The first part which deals with the religious aspect is written by a *gra-ba,* a monk and the second part which deals with the secular aspect is written by a *skye-bo*, a layman.

3. The monastery of Dankhar as a monastery belonging to the Gelug sect is named as Norbu Gephel which name is shared by Kyi monastery.

III. A. King's Message

Then, again, the Minister mGar went before the king (of Tibet) and requested the king to order him to go to China and bring the princess. The king sent seven golden coins and told him to offer them as present. A cloak, studded with seven hundred precious stones and a jewel of *padmaraga,* was also sent. The king instructed that this may be presented as the gift of marriage. One *dre* full of gold grains was sent for miscellaneous expenditure. The king's instructions were collected in three different paper-rolls, and the minister was advised to present them one by one at the appropriate moment. The king gave many articles of urgent need like clothes, ornaments, etc. loaded on camels and mules. The king bade to offer prayers day and night to goddess Tara on the way and wherever needed. mGar took whatever the king had sent. The minister together with one hundred horsemen set out at the auspicious moment on the 8th day of 4th month in fire-male-monkey year (636 CE) on journey to China. Then they reached at Tashi Khri Go, the main gate of the King Thang rdsung's palace in the capital city in China. There were one lakh men and dogs there. Each side of the palace was equal to a day's walk in width and there were four big gates. They appeared wonderful and awful to look. There the hundred horses of the king of India were present who had come to take the princess Kongjo. The king of Gesar, king of soldiers; the king of Tazig (Persia), king of wealth; the king of Bhata Hor (Turkistan); the king of Tibet, of the borderland; people of different races and five hundred camels and mules, had assembled before the king at one time. The Indians came through the eastern gate. The people of Gesar came through southern gate. Tazig. The people of Hor. The minister and men from Tibet stayed on the direction of north-east. Then the other ministers made presentation of their gifts.

B. Three Ka-shog, Letters, of mGar, Minister of king Srong brTsan sGampo

mGar (d. 667 CE) was Minister of the king Srong-brtsan sGampo (r. 629-650 CE). As we have seen above he is supposed to have gone to the city of Khrang-An, in China, and brought Wun-shing Kong-jo, princess of king Tha-e Tsung (r. 626-649 CE.), of China in marriage for the prince Srong-brtsan sGampo in 636 CE. The princess of Nepal was brought in 634 CE. Other sources give the dates of marriage of the king slightly later.

Here are given the three bK'a-shog letters containing the statements of the Minister mGar containing the probable questions that would have been asked by the king of China from the party sent by Srong-brtsan sGampo asking for the hands of the princess in marriage and answers thereto. Each successive letter discloses the answer to the question contained in the previous letter. The answers were prepared beforehand by the minister as he had prophesied the questions. The answers were devised for each of the three occasions and placed before the Emperor of China as if these were the answers given by the king of Tibet himself. The letters express the ingenuity of the minister of the Tibetan King.

i. The First Letter

On presenting the first paper-roll to the king of China, the king looked on it and opened the blue sheet on which was written in golden letters in the Chinese character.

"You possess the Doctrine. O! king of China. I, king of Tibet, have no tradition of Dharma. O king, you have the tradition of the ten royal virtues, so you may be pleased to give your daughter to me.

I will turn my body to the incarnated five thousand miraculous forms and I can establish the law of the ten virtues in one day's time. If you don't give your daughter in this manner, I will send five thousand miraculous soldiers who will kill you and bring seizing your worthy daughter, and capture whole of your kingdom."

The king became greatly frightened. Even though he was frightened, he pretended as if not to be so. "You the king of Tibet speak, too high. Do you have strength to construct Viharas in your country? If you possess the capacity, I will give my daughter. Go and bring the massage," Ordered to the envoy.

ii. The Middle Letter

Then the middle paper-roll of mGar was presented in the king's hand. One cannot go to Tibet for one and only one massage. O King, look for the answer to your querries. The king was surprised and looked in the manner:

"You have Dhamma and have got constructed Viharas in your country. I the king of Tibet have no strength to construct viharas. O king, becoming happy to construct Viharas thus, you could also extend the hands of your princess. I turning my body to five thousand forms, will construct one hundred and eight Viharas and show all their doors towards you. Will not curse you. If you don't give your daughter in this way, I will send five thousand fantom soldiers, who will kill you, snatch your daughter and destroy your kingdom".

The king becoming extremely frightened yet pretended not to be so. "The mouth of your king is very loud. Is there the practice of five *kámaguòha* in your country? If there is, I will give my daughter, otherwise not. This time go and bring the answer."

iii. The Last Letter

Then again handed over the last roll of paper written by the Minister mGar, stating, for each massage one cannot be sent from China to Tibet. For this, O King, see the answer to your question.

"O the king of China, you are wealthy. I am not so. If you are pleased with your wealth, give the hands of your daughter to me. I will multiply my body miraculously to five thousand times and accumulate wealth of grain, silk, cloth, jewellery, in your front."

Note: The above two documents consisting of the King's Message and the Minister's Message are literary compositions taking subject from history. They form part of folk drama and are also samples of early marriage songs extent in Tibet and the countries lying along its borders in the north and west-north.

Annexure-3

Other Topics

A. No-mo Ang-mo le, Si-ki Angmo le:

A Song Commemorating the occasion of War of 1681-83

Although the position of Spiti was very insignificant in comparison to the states involved in the above war, yet Spiti could not keep itself aloof from the events and had to participate. Below is given a song indicating the occasion of participation by Spiti in the Tibeto-Ladakhi-Mughal war of 1681-1683. The song has an appealing composition and is charmingly melodious. Besides, references to the matchlock manufactured at Lahore and the blue horses from Mongolia are interestingly rare and valuable. The original song, given here, is now rarely known. But the melody survives in the new compositions in the hearts of people, and is extremely popular in Ladak, Zanskar, Lahul and Spiti. The talented author of the long lasting melodious composition appears to have belonged to Ladak. Here is the song:

No-mo dbang-mo lags. No-no gnyis-kod lags

No-no gnyis-kod lags. Phun-tshogs don-grub lags.
Phyu-ba phu-dung bsnams de skyod dang.
No-no gnyis-kod lags.

nGa-ti no-mo lags. shis-skyid dbang-mo lags.
Mgo-dbang gyu-zungs gsnams de skyod dang.
No-mo dbang-mo lags.

No-mo dbang-mo lags.
Dpal gyu-yui ga-'u bsnams-la zhu.

No-no gnyis-kod lags.
Phun-tshogs don-grub lags.
La-ao-ri du-bag bsnams-de skyod dang,
No-no gnyis-kod lags.
La-ao-ri du-bag bsnams-de skyod dang,
Phun-tshogs don-grub lags.

No-mo dbang-mo lags.
Don-grub la gzigs te ci la bshums.
No-mo dbang-mo lags.
Gser gyi sor-gdub bsnams-la skyod cig.

No-no gnyis-kod lags
Du-ling zam-pa mi-bzang yod
Gzigs la skyod
No-no gnyis-kod lags
Ban-go zam-pa gcad de skyod
No-no gnyis-kod lags.

Hor rta sngon-mo la phyibs-de skyod.
No-no gnyis-kod lags

Sa-de la-dvags gzhung la skyod lags.
No-no gnyis-kod lags.

No-mo dbang-mo lags. Shis-skyid dbang-mo lags.
No-no gnyis-kod lags. Phun-tshogs don-grub lags.

Translation

In the story of the song there are three characters: two brothers, Phuntsog and Dondub and one sister Shis-skyid dBang-mo. In age the position of the sister is in the middle of the two brothers. They are present at the door of their palace. The moment is the departure of the two brothers to the war in Ladak. Here follows the translation:

Oh dear brothers, Phuntsog and Dondub! You should wear your long cloaks.

Oh dear sister, Shis-skyid dBang-mo! We request you, you should wear turquise studded headdress.

Oh brothers, I request you to take with you the matchlock manufactured in Lahore.

Oh dear sister! Why do you cry while looking at Dondub? Oh, sister! You should wear the golden ring.

Oh brothers! Duling bridge is bad, go carefully. You go breaking the bridge of Bango (Basgo). Oh brothers! Go riding the blue Mongolian horse. Thus go to the land of Ladak. The modern songs as are widely current in the region draw strength only from the melodic tune of this old song.

B. Hong glu, Song of Grain Thrashing

Hong: Hong means heap of thrashed grains, which has not yet been separated from chaff. Zambala is considered as the god of grain. His character appears to be different from the Jambhala of Buddhism. Possibly there was a god of grains, who had no name, or had an ancient name and might have been replaced by the new name under the influence of Buddhism.

Hong la skyod ul-thag sgo-mo ru
Di ring di-ru hong la skyod
Gangs har tikche tsam shig bur u-ru
Mtsho-mo ma-bang zam zhig chi li li
Shar rdorje ri ki kha-do-ma di-ring i-ru hong la skyod.
Khyim ser lung be dang ze sal
Sgan-mo du-i chhar bab sal

Pray, come, god of Hong! Come at the threshold of the auspicious thrashing ground; Must come here today for Hong, the occasion of separating grains from chaff.

Let the wind blow bur-ru-ru, so powerful like that seals the hollows of the glaciers,

Or chi-li-li, which creates ripples on the surface of the lake Mansarovar!

Oh dakini of the eastern quarter! We invoke you to help us in our hong!

Oh rich wind of household, grant us flour for meal;

Let there be rain of grains!

The prayer is long. Thereafter they sing taking the name of each part of the plough and the names of the plough-men.

C. Biography of Guru Jangsem Sherab Zangpo-Translation

I bow to Manjunath Lozang Dagspa (Tsongkhapa), the teacher and the pupils, and Lama Jangsem Sherab Zangpo. References to the life and excellent deeds of Sherab Zangpo have been collected here and is being presented like an ornament for further propagation among the faithful ones. sTod Jangsem Sherab Zangpo was direct pupil of reverend Tsongkhapa, about whom it was so forecast in the Kadam Legbam that the smaller number of his deeds will be exhibited in the form of monasteries and the larger number as worship in the four directions. Having served the former Jinas exceedingly well and concentrating his mind on the Excellent Bodhisattva, he secured unlimited power from the prayers. He took birth here contemplating to propagate the Doctrine of the great Tsongkhapa in this region. Jangsem Sherab Zangpo, took birth in the village of Khrigse, in the upper region of Ladak.

2. The nature of righteousness being manifested in him from the childhood, he imbibed great faith in the Doctrine. He studied and recited Vajrachhedika. With the good propensities of the former lives, he looked upon his home as the ground producing numerous faults and as a prison of ill desires. Therefore thought was arising continuously in his mind for going to the Snowy Valley of Bod (Tibet) for the study of the Doctrine. Accordingly he requested his parents who in turn enquired from the local deities

whether they should allow their son to go to Tibet or not. The priest revealed that this youth will be happy to be in Tibet. He will meet the teacher (Tsongkhapa), the mine of knowledge, and his pupils. Comprehending the whole literature he will be the holder of the knowledge in the northern land (of mNgaris). The pure and good practice of Gadan will flourish. These future happenings were thus explained clearly. Therefore, Tashi and Palzom, father and mother, being pleased, invited a trader from Sham (southern area of Ladak) on a feast (and sent the boy with him).

3. The trader took the two companions of travel with him upto the border of Gangri, Kailash. There they visited Gangri and took its circumambulation. Then the Sham-ma, the trader from Sham, handed over the young novices to a trader from Tibet requesting him to take them with him.

They went living by making collections from the rDogpa nomads and crossed the district of Lha-tse. On reaching Lha-sa they visited the statue of Shakyamuni, etc.

There he saw an old lady who was bowing before them and taking circumambulation of the statue of Jo-bo Rinpochhe (Munindra,The Buddha). He asked from her, at present who is the most learned lama in Tibet. Gadan was, at that time, founded only recently. The lady folded her hands and saluted towards Gadan. She told, presently the teacher in whom all the three qualities of scholarship, learning and righteousness are found assembled is only Lozang Dagpa. Gadan is the great seat of the Excellent Jina where he resides delivering discourses on the Excellent Doctrine to the fortunate ones. So it is said.

4. The young boy, as soon as he heard the name of Je Rinpochhe, felt the hairs of his body trembling with happiness and his eyes were filled with water. Then he came to Gadan. As soon as he saw the Lord Tsongkhapa, Jangsem was filled with

unlimited happiness as if having had seen Bodhisattva Chhos-'phags (*Dharmodgatah*). Whatever was spoken, he took as if it was a direction made to him. From the Je Lama, he solicited many discourses on *Sutra* and *Mantra*. From Prince Darma Rinchhen and mKhas Grub Gelegs dPal Zangpo, etc. he listened the essence of philosophy and made himself clear of the doubts. At Lhadan Mon Lam Chhen-mo he took vow of the Excellent Doctrine and received name. He listened discourses on Paramita, *Vinaya*, the three baskets and on *Mantra*, and reflected over them and became an excellent scholar. He took vow of accomplished Gelong. Among the six direct pupils of Je Tsongpkhapa, he became one of the holders of the banner of the Doctrine, who protected the Doctrine completely.

5. These six are: sTod Sherab Zangpo, sMad Sherab Zangpo, Guge Ngag dBang Dagspa, Lhopa Gyaltshan, Sangey Lama Paldan Sherab, and Danma Yontan Palwa. Even though he had not yet taken vow, Jangsem, the perfect one, protected the discourses on the Mantras like his eye balls. It is stated here. In the vast land of Mangyul (Ladak), he became the tree, fulfilling all wishes. He studied constantly and understood the meaning of the Paramita in three hundred sections. We pray for early meeting with this teacher of the Doctrine. With the good desires of the former life, he learnt that home is source of hundreds of voices and is like the walls of prison of disagree able thoughts. Mentally he became amenable to the Dharma.

6. The loving young heart, riding well the horse of wind, in the valley of Tibet covered with snow, ran as swiftly as electricity. He travelled whole of Tibet in a very short time. After this he travelled with his companions in all the directions and reached without difficulty in Bu-Tsang, Central Tibet. As soon as he visited Manjunath Lama Tsongkhapa, he was extremely pleased and felt as if he had seen the ever compassionate Bodhisattava Chhos-'phags. The teacher, the source of origin of perfection, like the

wish-fulfilling gem, who fulfills all the wishes of this and the next life, pleased him by granting his wishes. He had unsatiating desire for learning the vast amount of the literature. The Perfect One gave discourses on the sutra and mantra liberally like having poured the sand of gold into heaps.

7. He was adorned wonderfully in three varieties of grey robe. He having learnt the pure Law removed the cover of the false law from its root. He was not distracted from the teachings on the causes of the welfare of the others even for a moment. In this manner Jangsem became famous for being true to his words. Entering into the vehicle of *mantra* firmly he cleansed the dirt of fault with the power of self-initiation and became a great *vajradhara*. This is the description of the middle section. Then the king of Ladak, Dag-pa Bum De, decided to propitiate the Je Rinpochhe. The omniscient one of the Kali, degenerate age, the great Je Tsongkhapa Lozang Dagpa Pal Zangpo, sent an image of Tshe pag med, prepared with the blood of his own nose equal to the size of thumb, with Jangsem Sherab Zangpo.

8. With the message that either it should be handed over to one whose name is either Dagpa or lDe and he should propagate the doctrine specially and generally. Therefore Jangsem prayed for spreading and expansion of the Buddha's Doctrine, specially and generally, and the rare Doctrine of pair of *sutra* and *mantra* of Lozang Dagspa, in all the quarters.

9. The two saints Jangsem, master and pupil, reached in Mangyul, keeping in mind the Je Tshongkhapa's forecast that his Doctrine will flourish on the right side of river Sita (Sindhu). Nyima Dagpa was King of Nubra and the two saints went to him but he did not even cast his eyes on them and the two came back to Leh. The king Dagpa Bum De announced in the morning that today anybody, whosoever he may be, like saint, teacher, *beda, mon, mgar-ra*; strong or weak, may be allowed to come in without obstruction. At about the midday the two saints came in. The

king stood up and welcomed them. The two saints explained the objectives of the message of the great Je Tsongkhapa in detail. He offered the present of the blessed image of Amitayus and the king became extremely glad and arose with great reverence and honour for the Je Rinpochhe. He also paid respect and bowed before the two saints. Then the king, ministers and the subjects were bestowed blessings. Jangsem founded a monastery called Lha Khang Serpo (Yellow temple) in the village of sTag-mo, at the head of the valley of Thigse, the seat of *sthavir* Bhadra, as he was praying in the heart for development of the doctrine of the Je Lama (Tsongphapa) while earlier coming from Tibet. Jangsem sent an *upasak,* devotee, to sTagmo with a handful of hairs from his head saying that before reaching the Lhakhang Serpo he should go spreading these hairs taking the names of various kinds of trees on the way.

10. The *upasak* as he became absentminded forgot the instructions and when he reached before the monastery, he made effort to recollect. He instantly said *yar-gog, yar-gog* throwing away the hairs. At present there are *yar-pa* plants grown in abundance before the monastery. So it is heard. With the power of good omen the strength of the *sangha* grew to a great extent at that monastery and still there are seen always four or five monks doing the task of endowment incessantly. In this valley there are many carvings of self born castles on the face of the rock. It is named sTag mo (tigress) because the Lord is seen on the rock himself riding a tigress, so it became famed as sTag-mo. This place is blessed with many auspicious signs like the area of Yamuna river where *sthavira* Aryabhadhra stayed.

11. He bestowed many secret teachings and benediction of long life to the king, ministers and subjects of Ladak. King Dagspa Bum De, presented the areas of Lungsar Shes Rong in Rubsho, the areas around the Ra-bo Chhod-rten, Nag-tshur Tsha kha and the areas around the three streams of Kyang-chhu to Jangsem as

an endowment for the monastery. Areas around the Mani-chan gate at Shye, areas around Thigse, Chang-ga, Hemi, Mar-tse-lang, and the lower region of Kharu were also presented. The king said, "I have great faith in Lama Manjunath (Tsongkhapa). You accept these places as endowment. You may spread the teachings of the Yellow Hat in this valley, which will progress for long time". So he said. The tradition of sending of students from the side of Ladak to dBus-Tsang was started. Blessing the inanimate and the sentient beings of Ladak, they were driven towards the state of prosperity and happiness.

12. Master Paldan Sherab, Sherab Lodoe, Dung Do De Rinchhen, etc. many pupils of the Vehicle became carriers of the load of the Doctrine. Master Paldan Sherab founded the monastery of Thigse, named Tshul Khrim Namdag Ling. The number of monks in the *sangha* increased like water in the summer. It became the chief among the monasteries of Gelugs sect in mNgaris and the birthplace of many renowned personalities of the Yellow Cap. During the great congregations, Lama Jangsem gave discourses on the large and small redactions of Lam-rim, the teachings of three vows and many other holy subjects to the satisfaction of them all.

The fame of lama Jangsem spread far and wide in the land of mNgaris. The followers were bound under vows by his teachings on the three vows of the Law and many other subjects.

13. Mahasattva Vinayadhara Lodoe Bayepa, the direct pupil of Je Gedun Dubs, hearing the fame of lama Jangsem, came from Tibet through Tise, the king of the snowy mountains, and stayed in Mangyul in mNgaris sKor for six or seven years. He heard much discourses from Dharamraja Sherab Zangpo and he himself satisfied the congregation of monks of mNgaris with his own teachings. The teachers and pupils of Thigse entreated him to stay there. The *vinayadhara* replied, "leaving the monastery like Narthang, how can I stay here in this monastery," and did not

stay. While the *vinayadhara* was staying in mNgaris, Je Sherab Senge died on the 28th day of the 6th month of the wood-female-ox year (1445 CE).

This Je and Sherab Lodoe founded the monastery of dKyil in sPiti called Norbu dge-'phel and spread the good tradition of Ge-dan.

14. After reaching Nubra he laid foundation of the endowment property and offered three prayers at De Gon Gadan Tashi Chhos Ling. He visited Chags-ra-sa and the area on both the sides of the stream of Nubra. He left impressions of his feet in various villages. He founded monasteries in the lonely wild places and erected in them, as the main object of worship, statue of Je Tsongkhapa, so it is heard. Later on the king of Nubra, Nyima Dagspa also did according to the customs of the Law and invited the teachers. All the places of Nubra Na-brgya upto the face of the Khar-dong pass were presented to Jangsem, the owner of the monasteries of Gelug.

The king requested Lama Rinpochhe, "listen to me once. I request, lead me into the Doctrine in this and the next life. I offer all the estates of Nubra Na-rbgya at your service." So he said.

15. The teacher replied, "O king, according to your wishes, the subjects will soon enter completely into the pure land and the perfect practice, and the Doctrine of Yellow Cap will spread and develop. This is our humble prayer." So he said. He delivered the nectar of the Doctrine to the congregation of the awakened ones of the valley who were then led on the good path of the exalted birth and the state of bliss. It is said here.

Dagspa Bum De, the great Lord of Mangyul, hooked the subjects through the iron hook of his letters and held them under his crown. In the beautiful garden of happiness of the valley of sTagmo, with the objective of establishing the good tradition of Yellow Cap, he founded the monastery of Rab Ser and established the undiminishing tradition of the three worships. Tashi Shing, the place in sTag-mo, the ground where the Excellent Law has spread, is like the land of Yamuna where *sthavira* Bhadra had resided. The area belonging to the above and upto the Mani-go of Shye, were offered as the auspicious endowment.

16. The scales of laws of the kingdom which is identical with that of the Dharma, bringing prosperity to the beings, does not waver. Paldan Sherab by establishing the monastery of mKhar-dam of Thigse, removed the large thorns, the defects of the misfortunes. The virtuous saints of the monastery and the others spread prosperity in the red land (Ladak). The monasteries of Gelugs of this side spread the good tradition of the Yellow Cap. Like a father he protects the Dharma.

17. On going in the Nubra valley, the lonely place of the origin of purity, he got prepared there images of Jagannath. He showered the cool rain of the Excellent Doctrine on all the residents of that place. Producing the tree of the great height and emblem of goodness, he spread the Doctrine of the Excellent One. This is the composition of the middle section. From there he came towards Sham. The areas of the monastery of Lingshed and the areas from Wa-ka upto the royal temple were offered for the endowment. At Sod the Jobo, the ruler of the area, offered the monastery alongwith the village and the fields saying, "O Lama, I have great faith in you."

18. So he entreated for the favour. The Jo-bo, the noble, of Kartse from Karpo mKhar aroused faith for the Je. He learnt about the deeds of Je Tsongkhapa, the master and his pupils. He offered ownership of villages of Tshong-ra and Amdi, etc. "You are, Oh Lama! scholar and you love *siddhi*. Kindly lead us also." He suppressed the diseases, drought, war and conflict in all the sides of the country. "May the people live in happiness." So he said. Then he reached in Zanskar. King Rinchhen dPal lde son of

Khri Nam dPal lde and mother (queen) Zompa Gyalmo became very faithful to the Excellent Doctrine and the Doctrine of the Buddha, the congregation of the monks and the monasteries.

19. The two, the king and the queen, became patron of Jangsem Sher Zang and presented the three areas of Dakang, Karlang and Tshazar for the monastic endowment. Jangsem founded the Gonmo Chhe monastery on the hill of Tshazar and founded the congregation of the monks and the practice of the three basic worships.

The king and the queen said, we have accomplished the causes for the foundation of the Doctrine. "You have fulfilled a great task for the Doctrine by founding the monasteries and spreading the good practice of Yellow Cap. May we be able to see you in all our future births." So they prayed. While they were staying there, a Dakini said, "O! you the Excellent one, don't stay here. If you go towards Lung-Nag, it will be of great benefit for the beings. There are many self-born holy places on the mountains, and your own place is there and the followers also live there."

So he gained faith in these words and a child came and led him along the path to Lung-nag. As he saw the cave, he went to the place named Chhag-tshal-gang and thereupon the child disappeared. Sound of ringing of a bell was heard from the cave.

20. As he went up there, three sages welcomed him with great honour and took him inside the cave. They requested him with great honour and said, "It is good that you have come here, Oh! son of great lineage. The wishes of three of us have been fulfilled." They then presented a place for monastery and the house and the fields around the Yu-bar. "Staying here you will benefit a great number of followers of the Doctrine." So saying the three sages moved to other caves. Among them one went to a cave towards the east.

21. Another one went towards the south at the cave of Gitang-Jiwang, behind Dangze. The last one went towards the west at Thang zar. Here Jangsem founded the tradition of the three worships and that of the congregation of the monks.

In the cave there is the water of *siddhi* of Jangsem. About the hills on the right and left there are many self-born signs of wonderful objects. Jangsem stayed there for long time and meditated on the Lam-rim, etc. In the winter he made great labour on the meditation of the two sections of Lamrim. Tshang Gyalpo, king of Padum Castle presented the area of Mar-ling towards endowment of the Doctrine. From the benefits of this act may the beings in all their future births be led by Manjunath Lozang Dagspa, the teacher and his pupils to the birth of the human being. "May the voice become like that of the Tathagata 'the Lion'." Thus they prayed.

22. At Jampa Ling in Karchha he delivered much discourse on instructions of three worships, etc. to Doong Do De Rinchhen and the other faithful ones. There he began the works on Vinay and the three worships. Tshang Gyalpo, according to the purpose for which he had invited at sTod De Marpaling began the practice of three worships anew. The king of Tasta, Dechhog Kyab, presented the area from Gyi-Nyis Do-Thag to Thang-se-o below. Thereafter Jangsem and Tshang Gyalpo met together. They requested De Chhog Kyab-pa saying that you have told to the two of us for the appointment of a treasurer. So you kindly grant us a good piece of land, so they requested. He retaining for himself three fields and Lings-sa, the rest without leaving anything in the hills and valleys, presented to the king and the teacher.

23. The king made prayers. I have presented the endowments for the Doctrine, so that in all the lives to come, may we not be separated from the three Rare Ones and may we attain again the human lives. So it is.

Be-ta, the king of Ye-char, presented the area from Ye-char upto the Lower Castle. From Cha-ha the house and fields of the original habitat of Srong-bo pa, and the house and land of original place of Lozang-Tshering were presented. They presented the endowments for the Doctrine to Lama Jangsem and the congregation so that the wishes of all the beings could be fulfilled, their lives could become long and free of disease, and that he might lead them to the pure land. So it is said. The king of Kullu donated the areas of the monastery of Chhoe-ku tse, Lam-khram, Zholing, Demo of Gemur, the valley of Zhi, including the upper and Lower valleys, praying that, "Oh Lama! I have presented you these places as the endowments for the Doctrine. The beings may in all their future lives follow the practices of the Doctrine, learn the essence of the Doctrine, and follow the excellent and the good practices of the Yellow Cap."

24. This may flourish and stay for long time to come. So he prayed. Here only this much has been given, although it is told in more detail in the Records of donations of endowments in the monastery of Thigse and that of Phugthal.

In this manner the good tradition of Yellow Cap, the thought of the *vinay* and the three basic worships were established in all the directions. Dharamraj Manjunath, the Great Tshongkhapa, the other image of the Doctrine of the Buddha, revised well, the precious Doctrines of Sutra and Mantra which spread and developed well. Lastly the chaitya enshrining the relics of the sage who worked for the fulfillment of the welfare of others can be seen still in the centre of the cave of the Phugthal monastery. It is well known that on the auspicious days the strong wave of the fragrance of discipline arises from here. So it is said.

25. From the good sense of their voice, in the side of Sham, the kings and ministers have swarmed up like bees. Manjunath, the teacher and the pupils, enjoy the prosperity of nectar of the faith.

King of Zanskar, Rinchhen dPal and queen Zompa Gyalmo, the two, in the state of forgetfulness, obtained the nectar of the essential causes. The great monastery of Tsha-zar was founded and the good tradition of the essence of Manjushri was spread. There the vowful Dakini prompted him to come to Lung-nag. Three sages from the cave from where the sound of a bell was heard, received and honoured, and entreated him to work for the welfare of the Doctrine of the Buddha and the beings. There the water with eight branches and many other self-born good signs of worship exist. He remained there for long time. He strived alone in meditation.

26. The mountains are covered with snow. He remained in the profound meditation unwavered. Wise Rinchhen mDo sDe invited him to Jampaling. The ruler of Padum and Testa offered gifts. In this manner at that time they took back the places like Yee-char, from the owners of the lands, the king of Nyungti; made the Doctrine of the Je Lama immortal. The chaitya, enshrining the image of the one who has fulfilled the wishes, still lies in the middle of the cave.

The Biography of Guru Jangsem, sTod Jangsem Sherab Zangpo, socalled Precious Garland of Gold, was written, at the initiation of Ngagwang Jampa Tanzin, Shar-tul (incarnate of Sherab Zangpo), at the birthplace of the master at Thigse, by Kachhen Lochhen Zodpa, who holds the titles of Khanpo of Tashi Lhunpo and of Ngags Chhen (great *Mantrin*), after examining minutely the Kadam Chhosjung Sal-bai Melong, Vaidurya Serpo, the Gedan Chhosjung, the Chhosjung of Panchhen Sonam Dagspa, the records of endowments of the Thigse and Phugthal monasteries, etc. at the living room, called Pal-yon Kun-khyil, at Thigse monastery, in the year of fire dragon of the sixteenth cycle (corresponding to 1976 CE).

Note: - Existence of the biography of the teacher in Ladak was known since long as has been mentioned by Francke in his work (1924). The present manuscript reads that it was composed in 1976 but has missed reference to the original version.

D. Weights and measures

De and *khal* are common measuring standards in the region and around it but the measures vary somewhat from area to area.

20 *bre, de (patha* in Kullu) = 1 *khal (Lakh in* Kullu*)*
20 *khal* = 1 *khari (kha'r* in Kullu)

De is a measure of grains or flours of about a *kaccha ser*. Two *kaccha seers* make a *pacca seer*. Twenty handfuls make one *de, t*wo seers make one *batti*.

Lyall writes, 'The khal, of Spiti, is a measure based on the load of a sheep can carry, like the Lahauli, lakh, but it is smaller, ranging from 24 to 32 lbs; twenty *the* go to one khal. The two measures are really the same, the difference is only one of local names, and standard.' Some writers use *lakh* or *lac* for *khal*. The former term is used in Kullu. *De* is measured in volumes and the weight for a *De* varies from one kind of grain to that of the other according to its specific gravity. Trebeck gives eight *pakka seers* of Ne equal to one *khal*. Another source explains, "The grain collections consist essentially of barley. I may here explain that a *khal* which meant originally a sheep load, contains 20 *the* and that a *khal* of barley weighs 9 seers. The weight of a *khal* has been variously stated in the Kulu Gazetteer but I have verified the above by experiment and enquiry," (Settlement, 1891: para 25). Alexander Cunningham explains, 'The common *Khal,* whether by weight or measure, is the well-known quantity of sheep's load, *Luk-khal,* which is equal to eight battis, or one maund of sixteen Indian seers, or thirty-two pounds English.'

The term *khal* is sometimes translated as sheepskin, to mean that the measure of grain is equal to a sheep's skin full. It would be so in the language of Kullu but there the term used is *lakh* instead of *khal*.

Land is also measured by *khal* i.e. a piece of land which is equal to that requiring seed of one *khal.* A. Cunningham says, 'I should estimate the khal of land at about one-third of an English acre." The Settlement 1891 states that "It may be accepted that three khals of barley seed are sufficient for an acre of land as a rule." It may be added that in Lahul (sTod) the usual rate is one *khal* of Ne for a *bigha,* thereby five *khals* of seed of Ne may be required for an acre.

The difference in the data among the different authorities may be due to the fact that the utensil *bre* as is used in different places differs in size from place to place i.e. in Lahul, Kullu and Spiti, or elsewhere, and the standard is not the same everywhere. The *bre* of Lahul is said to be smaller than that of Kullu. Still this argument is not enough to answer satisfactorily the issue rising here as may be seen from the varying data adduced by different authorities. There may be difference in the size of the vessel within the area itself. There is a saying in Kullu: *ma'ng nhe' bi za'nha', pa'tha' bi a'pnha le' za'nha'*, which means that even if one goes to borrow, one takes one's own *pa'tha'* with him. This explains to what extent the variation in the size of the measuring vessels can be even within a small community.

The terms *khal* and *bre* are found used with the same notion in the seventh century CE Tibetan documents discovered from Tun Huang, Central Asia.

Bibliography

Archaeological Survey of India (ASI). *Indian Archaeology, A Review, 1999-2000.*

Aris, Michael. 1980. Bhutan: *The Early History of a Himalayan Kingdom,* Aris & Philips, Warminster.

Atkinson, E.T. 1882-1886. *The Himalayan Districts of the North-Western Provinces of India,* 3 Volumes, Allahabad, reprinted, 1973, Cosmo, Delhi.

Bajpai, S.C. 1987. *Lahaul-Spiti, A Forbidden Land in the Himalayas*, Indus, New Delhi.

Belleza, John Vincent. 2001. *Antiquities of Northern Tibet, Pre-Buddhist Archaeological Discoveries on the High Plateau, (Findings of the Changthang Expedition, 1999),* Adroit Publishers, Delhi.

Bruce, C.G. 1914. *Kulu and Lahoul,* Edward Arnold, London.

Chopra, Pran. 1964. *On an Indian Border*, Asian Publishing, Bombay.

Cunningham, Alexander. 1854. *Ladak, Physical, Statistical and Historical*, reprinted, 1970, Sagar, New Delhi.

Datta, C.L. 1973. *Ladakh and Western Himalayan Politics, 1819-1848,* Munshiram Manoharlal, New Delhi.

Egerton, P.H. 1864. *Journal of a Tour Through Spiti to the Frontier of Chinese Thibet,* Cundall, Downes, London.

Francke, A.H. 1907. *History of Ladak,* reprinted, 1977, Sterling, New Delhi.

Francke, A.H. 1926. *Antiquities of Indian Tibet*, Vols. I & II. reprinted, 1972, S. Chand & Co., New Delhi.

Gerard, Alexander. 1841. *Account of Koonawar in the Himalaya*, reprinted, 1993, Indus, New Delhi.

Gill, M.S. 2010. *Himalayan Wonderland, Travels in Lahaul and Spiti,* Penguin Books, New Delhi.

Grierson, G.A. 1908. *Linguistic Survey of India,* Vol. III, Tibeto-Burman Family, Part I, reprinted 1967, Motilal Banarsidas, Delhi.

Griffin, L.H. 1870. *The Rajas of the Punjab,* Punjab Printing Co., Lahore.

Gazetteer of the Kangra District, Parts II to IV, 1897. Reprinted, 1994, Indus, New Delhi.

Punjab District Gazetteers, Kangra District of 1917, Parts II to IV, Lahore, 1918.

Himachal Pradesh District Gazetteers, Lahaul & Spiti, 1975.

Hamid, Abdul. 2004. *Ancient Wisdom, (sgon dus kyi gtam dpe),* Author, Leh.

Handa, O.C. 1994. *Tabo Monastery and Buddhism in the Trans-Himalaya,* Indus, New Delhi.

Harcourt, A.F.P. 1872. *The Himalayan Districts of Kooloo, Lahoul and Spiti*, reprinted, 1972, Vivek, Delhi.

Hutchison, J. and J. Ph. Vogel. 1933. *History of the Panjab Hill States,* Vols. I & II, Lahore. Reprinted, 1982, Department of Language and Culture, Himachal Pradesh.

Ibbetson, Denzil. 1916. *Panjab Castes,* reprinted, 1993, Low Price Publications, Delhi.

Joshi, Lalmani. 1967. *Studies in the Buddhistic Culture of India*, Motilal Banarsidas, Delhi, 2nd edition, 1987.

Khosla, G.D. 1956. *Himalayan Circuit*, Macmillan & Co., London.

Klimburg-Salter, Deborah E. 2005. Tabo Monastery, Art and History, Vienna.

Massy, Charles Francis. 1890. *The Chiefs and Families of Note of the Punjab*. Allahabad.

Monier-Williams, Monier. 1899. *Sanskrit-English Dictionary*, reprinted, 1981, Munshiram Manoharlal, New Delhi.

Moorcroft, W. and G. Trebeck. 1841. *Travels in the Himalayan Provinces of Hindustan and the Panjab; Ladakh and Kashmir; etc.* reprinted, 1971, Cosmo, New Delhi.

Petech, L. 1939. *A study on the Chronicles of Ladakh (Indian Tibet)*, J.C. Sarkhel, Calcutta.

- do - 1977. *The Kingdom of Ladakh (c. 950 ṣ 1842 AD)*, Instituto Italiano, Roma.

Postel, M.; Neven, A.; Mankodi, K. 1985. *Antiquities of Himachal,* Franco Indian Pharmaceuticals, Bombay.

Rahul, Ram. 1973. *The Himalayan Borderland*, Delhi.

Randhawa, M.S. & Premnath. 1959. *Farmers of India: Punjab, HP and JK,* Vol. I, ICAR, New Delhi.

Rewaz-i-Am (Tribal Custom) of Kullu Sub-Division (which included then areas now known as Lahaul and Spiti district), from Settlement 1945-57, Controller of Punjab, Chandigarh, 1954.

Rose, H.A. 1883. *A Glossary of the Tribes and Castes of the Punjab and North-West Frontier Province,* Vol. I to III, reprinted, 1990, Language Department, Punjab, Patiala.

Sanan, Deepak and Dhanu Swadi. 1998. *Exploring Kinnaur and Spiti, in the Trans-Himalaya,* Indus, New Delhi.

Settlement Reports:

Barnes, George C. 1862. *Report on the Settlement in the District of Kangra* by George C. Barnes, Lahore.

Lyall, James B. 1875. *Final Report on the Revised Settlement of Kangra District.*

Diack, A.H. 1892. *Assessment Report on the Pargana of Spiti in the Kulu Tehsil,* (Settlement of 1887-92), (Not published).

Diack, A.H. 1898. Final Report on the Revised Settlement of the Kulu Sub-division of the Kangra District, Lahore.

Bachittar Singh. *Fourth Revised Settlement of the Kulu Sub Division of the Kangra District*, 1945-1952.

Sharma, Permanand: 1960. *Men and Mules on a Mission of Democracy*, Bombay, (not consulted).

Sherring, C.A. 1916. *Western Tibet and the Indian Borderland*, reprinted, 1974, Cosmo, Delhi.

Shuttleworth, H.Lee. 1929. *Lha Lung Temple, Spyi-ti*, Memoirs of the Archaeological Survey of India, No. 39.

Singh, Madanjeet. 1971. *Himalayan Art,* Macmillan, London.

Singh, Mian Goverdhan. 1983. *Art and Architecture of Himachal Pradesh,* B.R. Publishing Corporation, Delhi.

Sleen, W.G.N. Van Der. 1929. (Tr. By M.W. Hoper). *Four Month's Camping in the Himalayas,* Philip Allan & Co., London.

Snellgrove, D.L. 1957. *Buddhist Himalaya*, Philosophical Library, New York.

Snellgrove, David L. and Tadeusz Skorupski. 1980. *The Cultural Heritage of Ladakh, Vol. 2, Zanskar and the Cave Temples of Ladakh*, Vikas, New Delhi.

Steinbach, Lieut. Colonel, 1846. *The Panjaub, Being a Brief Account of the Sikhs,* Second Edition, Smith, Elder & Co., London.

Thomson, Thomas. 1852. *Western Himalaya and Tibet*, Reeve and Co., London.

Tobdan, 1984. *History and Religions of Lahul*, Books Today, New Delhi.

— —. 2000. *Kullu: A Study in History*, Book India, Delhi.

— —. 2011. *Exploring Malana, An Ancient Culture Hidden in the Himalayas,* Indus Publications, New Delhi.

Tropper, Kurt: 2008. *The Founding Inscription in the gSer Khang of Lalung (Spiti, Himachal Pradesh),* Library of Tibetan Works and Archives, Dharamsala.

Tucci, Guisseppe. 1932. *Rin-chen bzang-po (Indo Tibetica II)*, 1988, Aditya, New Delhi.

– –. 1933. *The Travels of Ippolito Desideri*, JRAS, 1933.

– –. 1935. *The Temples of Western Tibet and Their Artistic Symbolism, The Monasteries of Spiti and Kunawar (Indo-Tibetica III.1)*, Aditya, New Delhi, 1988.

– –. 1940. *Travels of Tibetan Pilgrims in the Swat Valley*, The Greater India Society, Calcutta.

– –. *Transhimalaya,* translated by James Hogarth, London.

– –. 1956. *Preliminary Report on Two scientific Expeditions in Nepal*, Is. M.E.O., Roma.

Vitali, Roberto.1996.*The Kingdoms of Gu.ge Pu.hrang, According to mNga'.ris rgyal.rabs* by Gu.ge mkhan.chen Ngag.dbang grags.pa, published by Tho.ling gtsug.lag.khang lo.gcig.stong 'khor.ba'i rjes.dran.mdzad sgo'i go.sgrig tshogs.chung, Dharamsala.

Vitali, Roberto. 2000. *A Short Guide to Key Gonpa*, Key Monastery, Key, Spiti, District Lahul & Spiti (H.P.).

Waddell, L. Austine. 1895. *Buddhism and Lamaism of Tibet,* London, reprinted, 1974, Heritage, New Delhi.

Wessels, S.J.C. 1974. *Early Jesuit Travellers in Central Asia*, The Hague.

Whistler, Hugh. 1924. *In the High Himalayas: Sport and Travel in the Rhotang and Baralacha, with Some Notes on the Natural History of That Area,* F.F. & G. Witherby, London.

Journals:

Cunningham, J.D. 1844. Notes on Moorcroft's Travels in Ladakh, and on Gerard's Account of Koonawur, including a general description of the latter district, *Journal of the Asiatic Soceity of Bengal,* No. 147, pp.172-222.

Cunningham, J.D. 1844. Notes on Moorcroft's Travels in Ladakh, and on Gerard's Account of Koonawur, including a general description of the latter district, *Journal of the Asiatic Society of Bengal,* No. 148, pp. 223-253.

Gerard, Alexander. 1842. Narrative of a Journey from Subathoo to Shipke, in Chinese Territory, in *JASB,* pp. 363-379.

Hay, Captain W.E. 1850. Report on the Valley of Spiti: and facts collected with a view to a future Revenue Settlement, in *Journal of the Asiatic Society,* No. VI, 1850, pp. 429-448.

Howell, G.C.L., I.C.S. 1918. Some Notes on Ancient Kulu Politics, in *Journal of the Panjab Historical Society,* Vol. VI, pp. 69-81, Lahore.

Hutchison, J. & J.Ph. Vogel. 1920. History of Spiti, *Journal of the Punjab Historical Society*, Vol. VIII, No. 2.

Petech, L. 1947. *The Tibetan-Ladakhi Moghul War of 1681-83*, The Indian Historical Quarterly, Vol. XXIII, No. 3, September 1947, pp. 169-199.

Roerich, Georges de: 1932. The Ceremony of Breaking the Stone, in *Journal of Urusvati, Himalayan Research Institute,* Vol. II, No. II, Roercich Museum Press, New York, pp. 25-51.

Theobald, W. 1862. Notes of a trip from Simla to the Spiti Valley and Choriri (Tshomoriri) Lake during the months of July, August and September, 1861, in *Journal of the Asiatic Society of Bengal,* Vol. XXXI, No. 4, pp. 479-527.

Tobdan. 1989. *Namthar Literature in Tibet and India*, in Journal of the Asiatic Society, XXXI, Nos. 3-4, Calcutta, 95-109.

Tobdan . 1992. Spiti - A Historical Survey, in *Himalaya Past and Present*, 1991-1992, Vol. II, Shri Almora Book Depot, Almora, pp. 303-318.

Tobdan. 2008. The Canda-Kinnara Jataka; and the Kinnara and the Canda Parvata, in *Expressions in Indian Art*, Vol 2, Agam Kala Prakashan, New Delhi, pp. 459-464.

Hindi - Books

Krishan Nath. 1998. *Spiti me Barish,* Vakdevi Pocket Books, Bikaner.

Pandey, L.P. 1981. *Prachin Himachal*, Indian Classics, New Delhi.

Prarthi, Lal Chand: 1971. *Kulut Desh Ki Kahani*, Nilkamal, Kullu.

Premi, Ek Itihas. 1942. *Shimla tatha Panjab ke deshi Naresh*, Rajkumar Yuvak Mandal, Banaras.

Sankrityayan, Rahul. 1948. *Tibbat me baudh dharma,* Kitab Mahal, Allahbad, reprinted, 1979.

- do - 1956(a). *Asia ke Durgam Khando me,* Allahabad.

- do - 1956 (b)- *Madhya Asia Ka Itihas,* Part I, Patna, 1956.

Sharma, Bansi Ram.1972. *Spiti ke Lokgeet*, Sheela Devi, Hamirpur, H.P.

Sharma, Banshi Ram. 1976. *Kinner Lok Sahitya*, Lalit Prakashan, Bilaspur.

Singh, Mian Goverdhan. 1996. *Himachal Pradesh ka Itahas*, Reliance Publicating House, New Delhi.

Hindi - Journals

Thakur, M.R. *Janjatiya Lok Natya evam Anusthan: Buchhen,* in Vipasha, January ș June, 1995, Language and Culture Department, Himachal Pradesh, Shimla.

Dorje, Chhering: *Spiti ș Bauddh evam Bauddh Vihar: ek rahasya*, in Somsi, Shimla, 2011.

Kunzom. Kullu. Year 1 to 4, 2005 to 2010.

Bhoti /Tibetan- Books

bK'a chhen bdsodpa.1976. bla ma byang-sems kyi rnam-thar rin-chhen sa-snying gi 'phreng-ba zhes bya-ba (Biography of Sherab Zangpo).

Travelogue and Biography of sTag Tshang Raspa:

a). *'ao-rgyan mkha'-'gro'i lam-yig thar-lam bgrod-pa'i them-skas.*

b). *aoo-di-yan-pa ngag-dbang rgya-mtsho'i ram-thar legs-bris baidurya dkar-po'i rgyud-mang.*

Gergan, Yoseb (Ed. By S.S. Gergan). 1976. Ladags rGyalrabs Chhimed gTer (History of Ladak), Sterling Publishers, New Delhi.

rje-btsun khyab-bdag chhen-po rang-rig ras-chhen gyi gsung-'gur dang zhal-gdams 'chhi-med bdud-rtsi-'I rlabs 'phreng.

dPal ldan bla-ma dam-pa 'khrul-zhig rin-po-chhe ngag-dbang tshering-gi rnam-thar, Vols. I & II (Travelogue of Lama Nawang Tshering), published by Topden Tshering, 1975, Delhi.

nGa-dbang gragspa, Guge mkhan-chhen. 1996. *mNgaris rgyal-rabs,* Organising Committee for the Commeration of 1000 years of Tholing Temple, Ngari Association, Dharamsala.

rGyal-ba rGod-tshang-pa'i rnam-thar, (Travelogue of rGod-tshangpa), published by Tobdan Tshering, 1974, Delhi.

Shastri, bLo-bzang. 2006. *Ri-bo gangs-chan-pa'i rtsom rig nang spi-ti dan ta-pho'i skor, (Spiti and Tapo in Tibetan Literature: A Preliminary note.)* (Manuscript).

Tashi Tshering. 2000. *sPyiti dkyil dgon norbu dge 'phel gyi byung-ba brjod pa'i rab-byed 'phags nor bdun ldan 'zhes bya-ba,* Kyi, Spiti.

rDorje tshe-bstan. 1977. *'Jig-rten mig-gyur lo-chhen rin-chhen bzang-po'i rnam-thar gsol-'debs,* dKyil Monastery, Spiti.

Index

❐ ❐ ❐

Plate-1. Lamas from Spiti (Courtesy Egerton)

Plate-2. A lama from Pin, donning long hair
(Courtesy Egerton)

Plate-3. A Buchhen farmer

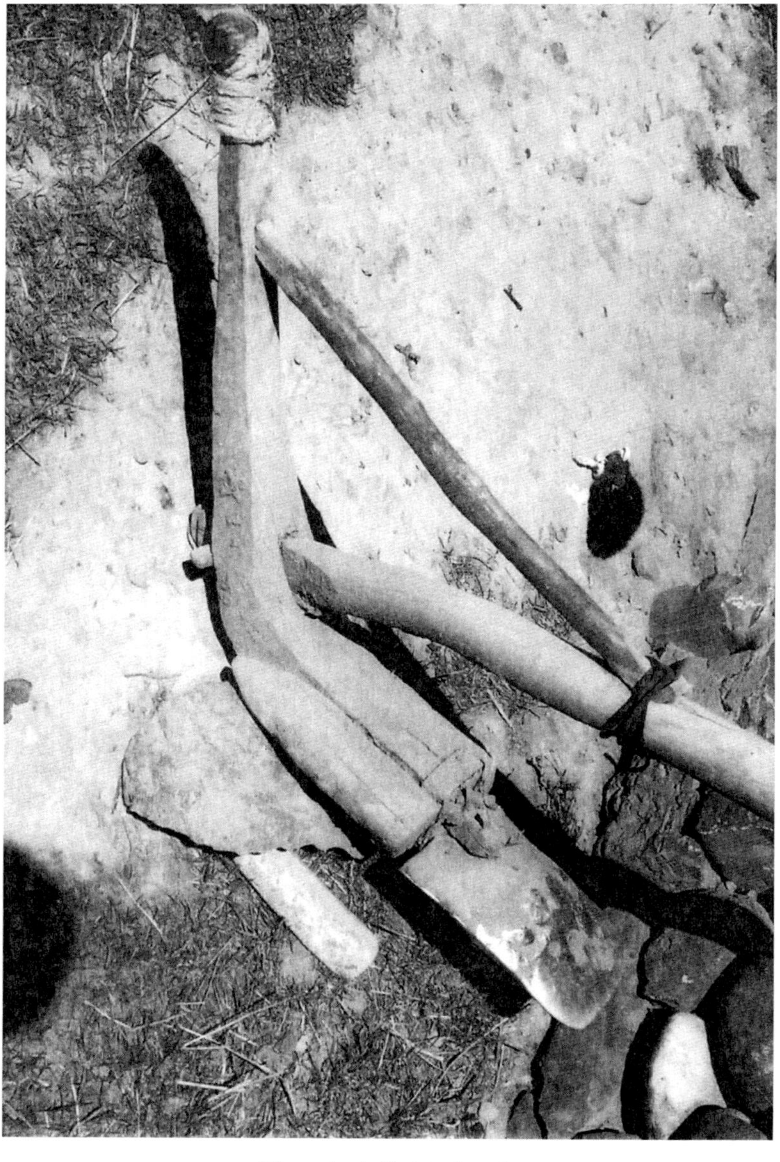

Plate-4. A Spiti plough

Plate-5. The Nono of Kyuling and his family
(Courtesy Egerton)

Plate-6. Inscription (Annexure 1-B)

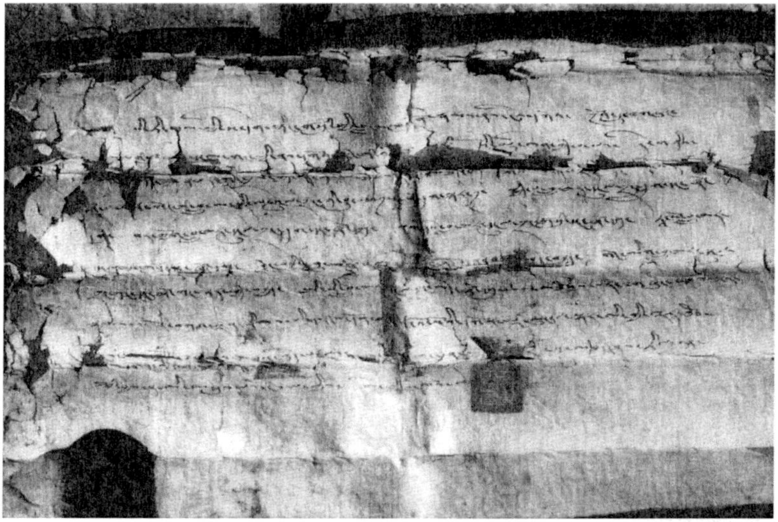

Plate-7. Inscription (Annexure 1-C)

Plate-8. Inscription (Annexure 1-D)

Plate-9. Lingza, shawl of Spiti woman

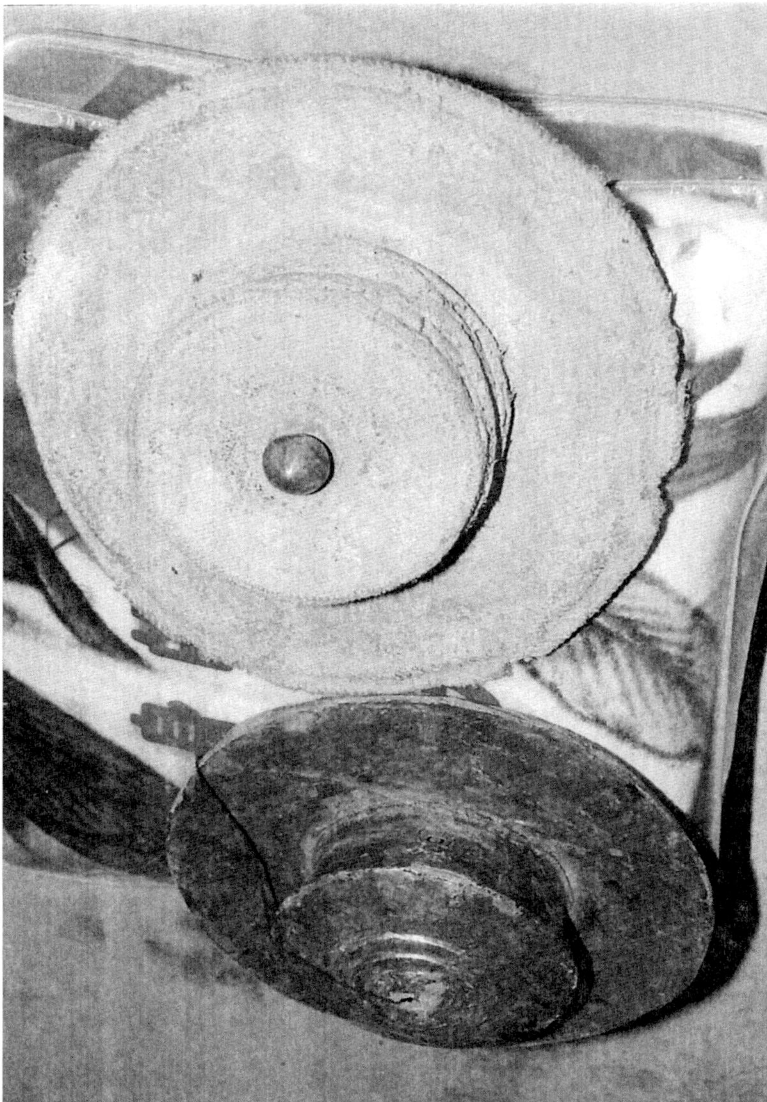

Plate-10. Old caps of the head lama of monastery